Uncertain Encounters

Uncertain Encounters

Indians and Whites at Peace and War in Southern Oregon
1820s to 1860s

Nathan Douthit

Oregon State University Press
Corvallis

Cover art: Detail from Fort Umpqua on the North Spit of the Umpqua River entrance. From *Frank Leslie's Illustrated Magazine* (April 24, 1858), Oregon Historical Society, OrHi 76449

The paper in this book meets the guidelines for permanence and durability of the Committee on Production Guidelines for Book Longevity of the Council on Library Resources and the minimum requirements of the American National Standard for Permanence of Paper for Printed Library Materials Z39.48-1984.

Library of Congress Cataloging-in-Publication Data
Douthit, Nathan.
Uncertain encounters : Indians and whites at peace and war in southern Oregon, 1820s-1860s / Nathan Douthit.
p. cm.
Includes bibliographical references (p.) and index.
ISBN 0-87071-549-6 (alk. paper)
1. Indians of North America—Oregon—History—19th century. 2. Frontier and pioneer life—Oregon—History—19th century. 3. Whites—Oregon—Relations with Indians. 4. Indians of North America—Wars—Oregon. 5. Indians of North America—Oregon—Sexual behavior. 6. Pioneers—Oregon—Sexual behavior. 7. Oregon—History—19th century. 8. Oregon—Race relations. I. Title.
E78.O6 D68 2002
979.5004'97—dc21
2002003646

Oregon State University Press
101 Waldo Hall
Corvallis OR 97331-6407
541-737-3166 • fax 541-737-3170
http://oregonstate.edu/dept/press

Contents

Acknowledgments

I want to acknowledge the people and institutions that contributed to the researching and writing of this book. I especially want to thank long-time friend Frank Walsh, historian of the Rogue River War (1855-56), whose willingness to share the results of his research and to read early drafts of material relating to the war has been invaluable. Lionel Youst's research on coastal Indians Annie Miner Peterson and Coquelle Thompson has stimulated my own writing about the immediate post-war period. Lionel, and his collaborator on the Coquelle Thompson study, William R. Seaburg, drew my attention to narrative accounts by Thompson and Hoxie Simmons that appear in condensed form in Chapter 7. For many years, archaeologist Reg Pullen has challenged my thinking about the archaeological record of Indian habitation in southern Oregon and, more recently, my thinking about Jedediah Smith's disastrous encounter with south-coast Indians. Other contemporary historians and anthropologists to whom I am especially indebted for their research are Stephen Dow Beckham, Jeff LaLande, Terence O'Donnell, E. A. Schwartz, Theodore Stern, Roberta Hall, Kay Atwood, and Dennis J. Gray. Along with nineteenth-century historians Frances Fuller Victor, A. G. Walling, and Orvil Dodge, these scholars have created a broad base of information and interpretations concerning Indian-white relations in southern Oregon.

My research would have been impossible without the help of local and regional research libraries. I have benefited from the resources of the University of California at Berkeley, University of Oregon, University of British Columbia, Oregon Historical Society, and Oregon State Library and Archives. Local library resources and staff of Southwestern Oregon Community College in Coos Bay, Coos Bay and North Bend public libraries, and Coos County Historical Society Museum in North Bend have made important contributions to my research on the history of southern Oregon for many years.

Some sections of this book first appeared in articles published in the *Oregon Historical Quarterly* ("The Hudson's Bay Company and the Indians of Southern Oregon," *OHQ* 93 (Spring 1992), 25-64; "Joseph Lane and the Rogue River Indians: Personal Relations Across A Cultural Divide," *OHQ* 95 (Winter 1994-95), 472-515; and "Between Indian and White Worlds on the Oregon-California Border, 1851-1857:

Benjamin Wright and Enos," *OHQ* 100 (Winter 1999), 402-33). The articles have been revised, adapted, and combined with research on other topics for this book. Editors Rick Harmon and Marianne Keddington-Lang, along with peer-review readers, made many excellent suggestions for revisions of the *OHQ* articles. Mary Elizabeth Braun, Acquisitions Editor for the Oregon State University Press, provided welcome encouragement during the critical review process for this book. Managing Editor Jo Alexander's questions and comments have led to many revisions and clarifications. And OSU Press editorial board members and peer-review readers offered numerous helpful recommendations for changes to early drafts of the book.

Finally, I want to thank friends who have offered me encouragement in various ways, and most especially, my wife Eva, for her much-needed critical support and affection.

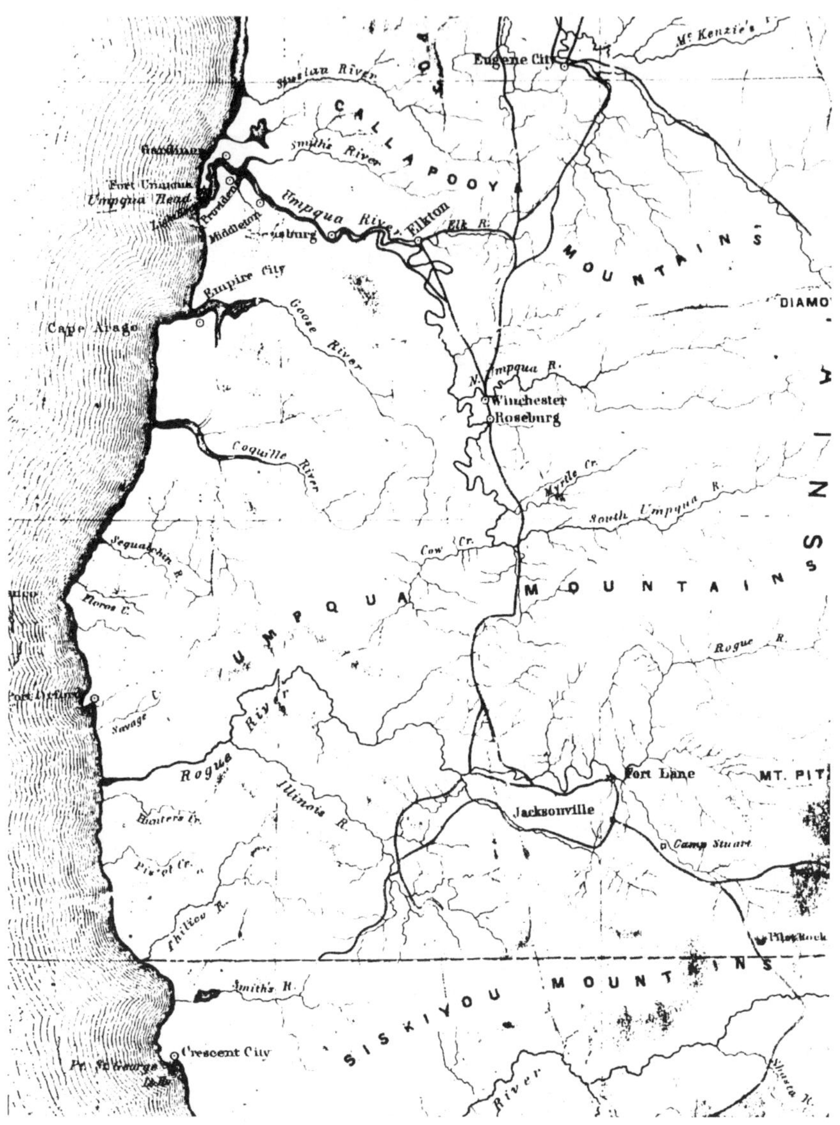

Detail of southern Oregon from "Map of the State of Oregon and Washington Territory compiled in The Bureau of Topographical Engineers ... 1859." (Courtesy of the Oregon State Library)

Introduction

THIS BOOK HAS EVOLVED through several stages. Over a decade ago, when I first began to research and write about Indian-white relations in southern Oregon, I was interested in reexamining the Hudson's Bay Company's relations with Indians of the region. The region's fur-trade era (1820s-1840s) had received only minimal attention from historians. Next, I turned my attention to the first negotiations with southern Oregon Indians by Oregon's first territorial governor, Joseph Lane. Lane's negotiation with Chief Joe (Apserkahar) established the first recorded interpersonal relationship between a white American and an Indian in the region. These two research explorations led chronologically to the culminating event of Indian-white relations in southern Oregon in the nineteenth century—the Rogue River War of 1855-56—one of the earliest and most destructive wars against Indians west of the Mississippi River. I focused on the lives of two men—one white and the other a mixed-blood—who crossed over Indian-white cultural boundaries and played key roles during the war. In this book, I have tried to place these earlier research inquiries, published as articles in the *Oregon Historical Quarterly*, in the context of Indian-white relations over the entire period of the 1820s-1860s. It is a period that stretches from the fur trade of the 1820s-1840s to Indian removal following the Rogue River War—the largest removal of Indians from their homeland since the "Trail of Tears" removal of the Southern Indians in the 1830s.

Earlier histories of Indian-white relations in southern Oregon have focused on well-documented incidents of violent conflict between the two groups. In my retelling of this story, I have tried to highlight moments of nonviolent interaction between Indians and whites, and their ambiguous and indeterminate aspects. Euro-Americans' pursuit of Manifest Destiny in the nineteenth century left no room for Indians to continue their way of life unchallenged. But despite the certain course of white American westward expansion and conquest of Indian lands and people, individual Indians and whites in specific local regions were often uncertain whether to relate to each other as friends or as enemies.

Twenty-five to thirty years of contact between Indians and whites led up to the Rogue River War of 1855-56. In retrospect, white victory in the war seemed inevitable. But only two years earlier, by which time whites outnumbered Indians on the upper Rogue River, whites feared an Indian uprising and were uncertain about their own survival. Indians were about equally divided between war and peace factions. With hindsight, we know the outcome of Indian-white encounters in southern Oregon, but at the time people could only guess at the future, and they lived each year with uncertainty about the next.

Despite the uncertain nature of Indian-white encounters in the years prior to the Rogue River War, these encounters led to the development of interpersonal as well as social, political, and economic ties between Indians and whites. I refer to these interrelationships as a "middle-ground." Richard White, in his book *The Middle Ground: Indians, Empires, and Republics in the Great Lakes Region, 1650-1815* (1991), makes use of the term in the different context of French, British, and Indian relations over an extended period of time.[1] The middle-ground in southern Oregon lacked the depth of cultural exchanges described by White. It was a middle-ground of short duration and limited scope, but it involved trade, sexual relations, diplomatic negotiations, and legal issues similar to those that existed on the seventeenth- and eighteenth-century colonial frontier described by White. However uncertain, middle-ground relationships in southern Oregon involved steps by Indians and whites toward limited accommodation and adaptation.[2]

In southern Oregon's fur-trade era (1820s-1840s), there was a limited middle ground of trade in furs. In the early settlement period (1850-53), the middle ground consisted primarily of relationships between Indian and white leaders arising out of peace negotiations. In the later period of settlement and the Rogue River War (1853-56), the middle ground expanded to include a wider range of Indian-white relations—economic exchanges, unions of Indian women and white men, employment of Indians by whites, land-use arrangements, and personal friendships. Middle-ground unions between Indian women and white men begun during or before the war extended into the removal and reservation era (1856-1860s), despite efforts of white officials to discourage them.

Cultural intermediaries made middle-ground relations possible. These people were white fur traders, Indian women who lived with white men, persons of mixed Indian-white parentage (then called "half-breeds," now *métis* or mixed-bloods), white men who lived among Indians, and Indian and white leaders who worked with their counterparts to keep the peace. In the case of the mixed-blood, Indian-literature scholar and novelist Louis Owens has argued that the concept of the cultural intermediary is "strangely mercantile and Eurocentric," with the mixed-blood "embodying contradictions" as much as or more than acting as a rational agent of exchange relationships.[3] This viewpoint takes into consideration the fact that, although cultural intermediaries moved across cultural borders and helped to create and sustain middle-ground relations, they also pursued their own self-interest, and they sometimes participated in intergroup violence. Because of the ambiguous loyalties of cultural intermediaries, Indians and whites often viewed them with suspicion and dislike.[4]

Some readers may question whether a collective middle ground could have existed in view of the frequent violent attacks by whites against Indians in southern Oregon. But as Richard White found to be the case with British "backcountry settlers," who more often than not hated Indians and did not hesitate to kill them, even the scalping of Indians by whites was a feature of the "new middle ground" of "common contact and common meaning."[5] Although the emphasis in this study is on nonviolent middle-ground links between Indians and whites, even violence involved the two groups in exchanges of what White refers to as "values and practices." Southern Oregon whites scalped Indians; Indians employed white military tactics in the later stages of the Rogue River War. Although it may seem to some readers that emphasis on middle-ground ties serves to deflect attention from white violence against Indians, my intention is to create a more complete picture of peaceful as well as violent Indian-white encounters, not to deny that white acts of genocide against Indians occurred.

A central argument of this study, however, is that development of a middle ground in Indian-white relations prevented the Rogue River War from becoming a war of extermination—in short, a genocidal war. The limited middle ground of the years 1850-55 collapsed with the onset of the Rogue River War, but key Indian agents, territorial leaders, military officers, and Indian chiefs remained committed to a peaceful resolution to the war. The war ended in Indian removal from southern Oregon, reflecting the objective of federal and territorial Indian policy, which was to separate whites and Indians. The removal of Indians from their homeland involved great suffering, and hundreds died shortly after reaching the Grand Ronde and Siletz reservations. But there is reason to believe that Indian mortality would have been even greater if Indians and whites had continued to live side by side after the Rogue River War.

The middle-ground relations of the early 1850s in southern Oregon existed alongside repeated acts of violence that created great uncertainty for both Indians and whites. But the process by which Indians and whites crossed over cultural boundaries to create middle-ground ties is a story of efforts at adaptation, accommodation, and peacemaking that should be overlaid on top of a better-known and well-documented story of frontier violence and acts of genocide.

THE GEOGRAPHICAL SETTING of this study, referred to in the title as southern Oregon, is more accurately southwestern Oregon, approximately the southwest quadrant of the state. However, all but a few pioneer settlements in Oregon Territory lay west of the Cascade Mountains so historians identified the region from the Umpqua River south to the Oregon-California border as southern Oregon.

Southern or southwestern Oregon is a geographical region bounded on the north by the Umpqua River system, which comes out of the Cascade Range of mountains that runs north and south and forms the eastern boundary of the region. The Siskiyou Mountains that run east and west form the southern boundary and separate northern California from southern Oregon. The California side of the Siskiyou Mountain range drains into the Klamath River, the Oregon side into the Rogue River. The mountains in this range are geologically a part of a larger Klamath Mountains complex that begins at the south end of the Coast Range and extends from Oregon into northern California. A coastal zone that stretches from the mouth of the Umpqua River to the California border forms the western boundary of the region.[6]

Southern Oregon is a mountainous region with scattered small and narrow valleys along its three major river systems: the Umpqua, Coquille, and, largest and longest, Rogue. Three smaller river systems—the Siuslaw River north of the Umpqua, Coos River south of the Umpqua, and Chetco River south of the Rogue River—also figure in the region's history. Indian and later white settlements were located primarily along the rivers and in the river valleys. The river systems also provided natural highways, although their mostly east-to-west direction made river travel possible only within the region. Whites extended their travel north and south by land with the help of horses, mules, and oxen. Indians, lacking animal means of transport before the arrival of the whites, probably confined their social and economic activities to the region, with trade beyond the region's boundaries occurring through individual and village trade intermediaries. If the geography of the region encouraged the Indian inhabitants to live within restricted territorial limits, so did the availability of varied plant, fish, and game food resources. Archaeologists believe that the region's first inhabitants (who, according to radiocarbon dating, had come to southern Oregon by at least eighty-five hundred years ago) were nomadic hunters and gatherers. But by fifteen hundred years before white contact and possibly earlier, semi-permanent villages had been established to take advantage of seasonal salmon and steelhead runs.[7]

Linguistic divisions reflect the successive migration to the region of native people speaking different languages followed by a more settled and insular way of life.[8] For example, from the Oregon coast eastward along the Rogue River, there were three major language groups. On the lower Rogue River lived Athapascan-speaking Tututni, Mikonotunne, and Shasta Costa. Upstream from Grave Creek lived various bands of Takelman-speaking Indians with pockets of Athapascan-speaking Galice Creek, Illinois River, and Applegate River Indians (with dialects varying from downstream Tututni) on either side of the Rogue River. Siskiyou Mountain Shastas, who lived on the east and south sides of the upper Rogue River Valley as well as in northern California, spoke a language grouped in the Hokan phylum. In the coastal zone, Indian bands from the mouth of the Coquille River north spoke Coosan- and Siuslawan-family languages (grouped in the Penutian phylum, as is Takelman); and from the upper Coquille River south, they spoke Athapascan languages (grouped in the Na-Dene phylum). In addition, there were local dialects within each linguistic family and language grouping. For example, on Coos Bay there were two Coosan language dialects—Hanis and Miluk—whose differences have been compared to those between northern-European Germanic languages.[9]

By the early 1850s, over a half-century after first contacts with Euro-Americans, southern Oregon Indians lived in villages that probably ranged in size from a few families of ten to twenty people to as many as one hundred twenty to one hundred fifty people, the size range reported in Indian agents' censuses in 1854-55. The Indian population of southern Oregon may have been larger before Euro-American epidemic diseases reached the Pacific Northwest in the late eighteenth century as a result of the Northwest coastal fur trade. But the impact on Willamette Valley and upper Umpqua River villages probably was far greater than on villages to the south and west of the upper Umpqua River, judging from white reports. My own estimate is that the Indian population of southern Oregon (approximately thirty-eight hundred by the early 1850s) had been about one-third larger at the time of first white contact; however, the size range of individual villages may have been about the same.[10] Archaeological evidence, in some cases dating back eight to nine thousand years ago, documents the location of villages and encampments in hundreds of locations throughout the region. But there is insufficient evidence to estimate aboriginal populations prior to the time of first white contact, especially in view of the fact that the earliest sites probably lie beneath ocean water. Sea level stabilized at its present level by four thousand years ago, after rising 300-400 feet following the last glacial melting.[11]

Villages were self-governing, although neighboring villages linked through kinship ties, language, and a common territory probably cooperated on many activities. To avoid marriages within families, marriages between members of neighboring villages were common, and these cemented relations between villages that had political significance in times of war. There was no overarching tribal governance of bands within the region. Each village had a headman or chief, who led because of his wealth and family status. Because some villages were substantially larger and wealthier than others, the leaders of those villages played a larger role in negotiating peace treaties with white Americans. [12]

The food resources of southern Oregon Indians varied from the coastal zone to inland valleys, but there were also common characteristics.[13] In general, food resources were close at hand and abundant, except during the winter months. With villages located next to rivers and streams or on coastal bays, salmon and steelhead runs provided a seasonal, annual food resource for most of the region. Edible plants—berries, nuts, plant roots—too, were seasonal, but predictable because of abundant rainfall; they were primary resources for Indians throughout the region, but inland valley Indians were especially dependent on acorns and camas bulbs as well as the seeds and nuts of various plants. Large game animals—deer, elk, and occasionally bear—generally supplemented fish and plant resources, but were primary food resources for Upland Takelma and Applegate River Indians. Small game (e.g., jackrabbits and squirrels) and birds (e.g., quail) were hunted and trapped; Rogue River Valley Indians speared beaver during the winter, when stored food supplies ran low. Inland valley Indians also gathered some insects (e.g., grasshoppers, caterpillars, yellow-jacket larvae, and snails) for food. Coastal Indians took advantage of a variety of marine food resources, including shellfish, smelt, beached whales, seals, sea lions, and eels, in addition to salmon and steelhead runs and edible plants. Although food resources were available close to coastal and inland valley villages, the variety of gathering and hunting activities required movement over large local areas, which led to the disruption of subsistence activities when white mining and settlement began.

In general, the archaeological evidence for long-range trade with people outside the region, whether with Indians or whites, is still scarce despite what is known from a number of scientifically conducted excavations in the last half of the twentieth century. The Indians of southern Oregon were part of a larger Pacific Northwest trading network, but probably on a much more limited scale than were Indians from the Columbia River on north and Klamath Indians, living east of the Cascade Range. Klamaths visited by Hudson's Bay Company's (HBC) Chief Trader Peter Skene Ogden in 1826-27 were reported to be familiar with trade and desirous of such trade items as rings, buttons, and knives. By contrast, Ogden's description of upper Rogue River Indians emphasized their limited technological means and wealth, as well as their lack of interest in trading. Archaeological sites have yielded only small quantities of such white trade goods as metal knives, glass, and beads. Some archaeologists believe that illegal looting of gravesites by whites may have distorted our picture of southern Oregon trade connections. But HBC reports indicate that southern Oregon Indians possessed few white trade items compared to the muskets, balls and shot, brass kettles, blankets, sailors' clothing, knives, beads, and other items that Lewis and Clark had reported seeing among the lower Columbia River Indians over twenty years earlier. However, by 1828 on Coos Bay, after HBC contact with coastal Indians over the previous two years, American fur trader and trapper Jedediah Smith reported that local Indians had at least one musket in addition to metal knives and tomahawks and items of white clothing.[14]

The Indians of southern Oregon shared cultural traits—shelter, clothing, food, and others—within coastal and inland-valley ecological zones. But despite these cultural similarities, warfare occurred between neighboring Indian groups. Typically there were tensions between Indian bands living upstream and downstream from each other on the rivers. On the coast, Umpquas raided the Coos, and vice versa. In the upper Rogue River Valley and Siskiyou Mountains area, along today's Oregon-California border, Klamaths fought Shastas, and Takelmas feared Klamath raids. Sometimes these raids were for the purpose of taking slaves. In addition to slave raiding, people could become slaves as a result of indebtedness (especially from gambling), punishment for a crime, being an orphan, and, if the girl of a poor family, being forced into marriage to a man of a wealthy family. Slave-holding was mentioned by HBC fur traders and explorers, and reported to later ethnographers. Anthropologist Philip Drucker, in writing about the Tolowa and their Oregon neighbors to the north, concluded that "slave-holding was practiced in a minor way," and that because it was primarily for "prestige," slaves were treated as "poor relatives" rather than as "economic assets." Although slaves probably were few in numbers, southern Oregon Indians apparently feared slave raids and, if poor, they feared becoming a slave.[15]

This natural and human setting influenced encounters between Euro-Americans and Indians from the late eighteenth century through the 1850s. Landforms and cultural differences made it difficult for Indians of the region to organize large-scale resistance to white migration through and settlement of the region. Their limited trade experience, related to geographical isolation, made it difficult to establish middle-ground fur-trade relationships. Food-resource gathering and hunting within local areas brought Indians into conflict with white miners and settlers. And once a general war started between Indians and whites—the Rogue River War of 1855-56—existing social and cultural divisions among Indian groups reinforced inevitable differences over whether to fight or to make peace.

The first contacts between Euro-Americans and the Indians of southern Oregon occurred in the coastal zone. There are no documented stops by Spanish explorers along the south coast of Oregon. But following on the voyage of Captain James Cook along the Northwest coast in 1776 and again in 1778, British and American merchants began a struggle for control of the coastal fur trade. Most of the trading occurred from the Columbia River north to present-day British Columbia, but a few ships stopped on the north coast of what is now Oregon in the late 1780s and early 1790s. British Captain George Vancouver anchored in the lee of Cape Blanco in 1792 and met local Indians who paddled out to his ship. Vancouver noted in his journal: "A pleasing and courteous deportment distinguished these people."[16] He also commented that the Indians eagerly bartered for "iron and beads." In the years that followed Vancouver's voyage of exploration, many ships of European and American fur-trading companies passed along the Northwest coast. Because most of these went unreported, there is no way to know how many contacts were made with Indians on Oregon's south coast.

The United States took a bold step in Pacific Northwest exploration when President Thomas Jefferson sent out the Lewis and Clark Expedition in 1804. The expedition reached the mouth of the Columbia River in 1805 after traveling along the Missouri River and then over the Rocky Mountains. Lewis and Clark spent the the winter of 1805-6 in Astoria, but did not explore the Oregon coast; they did hear of a "Cook-koo-oose Nation," a name referring to people who lived to the south.

American and British fur-trading companies probed the Oregon Country following Lewis and Clark's visit. In 1807-9 the Canadian-based North West Company's (NWC) explorer David Thompson established a NWC presence in the Pacific Northwest. John Jacob Astor's Pacific Fur Company (PFC) established a fur-trade outpost near the mouth of the Columbia River in 1811. The War of 1812 between the United States and England forced Astor's men to cut their losses and sell out to the NWC in 1813. Fort Astoria became Fort George, and the former Nor'Westers of the PFC rejoined their old company.[17]

At this point the fur trade in the Oregon Country seemed securely in British hands. But even British fur-trade officials realized that it was only a matter of time before Americans would return. In 1815, the NWC decided to send trapping parties south to California and east toward the Rockies, and established Fort Nez Percés (where the Walla Walla River joins the Columbia) as a new hub of operations.[18] The Astorians, a few years earlier, in the years 1811-13, had explored the Willamette Valley, perhaps going as far south as the Umpqua River. According to the account of the NWC's Alexander Ross, a brigade of about fifty-five men definitely reached the Umpqua River from Fort Nez Percés in 1818. A fight ensued between NWC Iroquois trappers and Kalapuya Indians, and it resulted in fourteen Indian deaths. This skirmish cost the company the good will of Willamette Valley Indians for a number of years, resulting in a reduction in the annual take of beaver pelts.[19]

In 1821 the NWC and HBC merged. Fur-trade operations in the Columbia District came under the overall command of Governor George Simpson, HBC head of North American operations, and, at district level, the leadership of Chief Factor Dr. John McLoughlin, who previously had worked for the NWC. At Simpson's direction, the Columbia District redoubled its efforts to expand operations to the south and east. The HBC built Fort Vancouver in 1825 and it became headquarters for the Pacific Northwest Columbia Department (composed of New Caledonia in northern British Columbia and the Columbia District in southern British Columbia and Washington-Oregon). This put the HBC's headquarters on a direct line with a route south to California through southern Oregon.[20] The insularity of Indian life in southern Oregon was about to end.

Chapter 1

Early Hudson's Bay Company Encounters, 1826-28

HISTORIANS usually have portrayed Hudson's Bay Company (HBC) operations in Oregon as being built upon a desire for trade in furs, avoidance of warfare, and tolerance of the Indians' way of life.[1] They have argued that conflict with southern Oregon Indians began with American migration through and settlement in the region in the 1840s. Although the HBC did maintain generally good relations with Indians north of and east along the Columbia River, the company's relations with the Indians of southern Oregon in fact were tense and uncertain. Early accounts indicate that HBC relations with Indians in southern Oregon and northern California were frequently hostile, and that HBC trappers regularly resorted to violence in retaliation for perceived injuries.[2] This made it difficult for the HBC to establish peaceful and cooperative relationships with Indians in southern Oregon as it did elsewhere.

In 1825 HBC's Governor Simpson gave orders for an expedition to proceed "up the Wilhamet River across a Mountainous country which we know little about to the Umpqua River."[3] Chief Factor McLoughlin wrote about the same time: "There is a River three days South of the Umpqua said to Extend a great way into the interior—and very rich in beaver. I have conversed with several Indians who saw it. The Natives of that place use Beaver Robes for coverings." To satisfy the curiosity of Simpson and McLoughlin, Chief Trader Peter Skene Ogden led a fur-trapping expedition southeast from Fort Vancouver into the upper Klamath Basin. The expedition was a continuation of Snake Country Brigade trapping and exploration begun by Donald Mackenzie in 1818. Although far from the Snake River, HBC leaders sought a "great river" outlet to the Pacific. After following the Klamath River downstream for a way, Ogden headed north across the Siskiyou summit between Mount Ashland and Pilot Rock, descending into the Bear Creek drainage of the Rogue River Valley on February 8, 1827. This marked

The "second" Fort Vancouver. Sketch by Henry J. Warre, 1845. (Oregon Historical Society, OrHi 803)

the beginning of recorded Indian-white encounters in the Rogue River country.[4] It also was the first of a succession of fur brigades the HBC sent into southern Oregon and northern California over the next decade and a half. Alexander Roderick McLeod led a brigade south from Fort Vancouver to Stockton in 1828-29; Michel Laframboise took the coast trail south to California in 1832; John Work, Laframboise, and Thomas McKay all led expeditions at different times in the 1830s and early 1840s. They traveled through the Rogue River Valley into California and then back to Fort Vancouver many times.[5]

Peter Skene Ogden's journal notes on the Indians of southern Oregon are the most detailed and important of the documents on early encounters between Indians and whites in the region. They provide a great deal of information about aspects of Indian culture and Indian attitudes toward white entry into their territory. In addition, Ogden's personal responses to the Indians and their behavior helps to explain why it was difficult for whites to respond positively toward southern Oregon Indians. Ogden's party came back to Fort Vancouver with impressions that shaped the reputation of southern Oregon Indians (exclusive of the Klamaths) as hostile toward whites.

The expedition spent almost two months (November 1826-January 1827) among the Klamath Indians, exploring the country, trapping, and trading.[6] Members of the expedition visited Klamath villages and Indians visited their camps without any difficulties. Ogden's reaction to the local Indians is captured in a journal entry he wrote five days after entering Klamath Country: "A number of Indians collected round the Camp and traded Roots and 1 Dog they appear well versed in trade but comported themselves peacibly and I am of opinion are good Indians but will not long remain so, two years intimacy with the Whites will make them like all other Indians villains."[7] Despite his favorable opinion of the Klamaths, Ogden's journal notes reflected his fatalistic belief that Indians in general degenerated through exposure to whites.

Winter snow and rain made life miserable for Ogden's party. Few beaver were taken, and there was so little wild game that Ogden had to continually trade with the Klamaths for dogs to eat. In mid-January Ogden confided in his journal that "a Porter in London is a King in comparison with me at the head of Freemen." However, "all this would be a trifle could I but find Beaver and not be obliged to return empty handed as from our present prospects we certainly shall." As the expedition descended the Klamath River, hunting and trapping improved slightly. On the advice of Indians that "on the other side of the [Siskiyou] Mountains we will find Beaver," the expedition left the Klamath River on February 6 and began to ascend Cottonwood Creek in the direction of the Siskiyou summit, trapping along the way. Ogden on February 7 wrote: "we have now 30 men in advance with Traps in three different partys so by this plan no Stream will escape observation."[8]

Ogden's company left the Klamath River in northern California, crossed over the Siskiyou summit between Mount Ashland and Pilot Rock, and descended to the Rogue River Valley. The expedition spent from February 8 to April 18 exploring southern Oregon and trapping beaver. Ogden's men explored upstream perhaps as far as present-day Trail and downstream to present-day Grants Pass. They also traveled northwest across the Grave Creek, Wolf Creek, and Cow Creek drainages, perhaps as far as the Middle Fork of the Coquille River in the vicinity of Camas Valley.

Ogden's exploring party, as well as HBC brigades working the route to California in the years that followed, typically included the Indian wives and children of trappers. The mixed inventory of Ogden's expedition consisted of 58 men, 268 horses, 352 traps, 61 guns, and an unknown number of Indian women and children. In a moment of happy reflection, Ogden wrote: "it is a pleasure to observe the Ladys of the Camp vieing with each other who will produce on their return to Fort Vancouver the cleanest and best dress'd Beaver."[9] Unfortunately Ogden does not tell us how many women and children were on this expedition. By comparison, the first Snake Country brigade of 1818 under Donald Mackenzie had consisted of 55 men, 195 horses, and 300 beaver traps. Alexander Ross's 1824 brigade had 54 men, 25 of whose wives accompanied the expedition together with 64 of their children, 231 horses, 206 traps, 62 guns, and 20 lodges. And John Work's brigade of 1830 consisted of 115 men, women, and children, 272 horses, 20 lodges, and 337 traps.[10]

Ogden's brigade was divided into three exploring and fur-trapping parties that went out from a central campsite, where there was always a contingent of men, Indian women, and children.[11] By helping to dress and care for the furs, the trappers' Indian wives helped add a few shillings to their husbands' salary (at the servant rate of £17-22 annually, compared to a chief trader's £300-500). Historian John A. Hussey has described work around camp: "In addition to preparing pelts, the women and their slaves had to make and break camp almost daily, gather firewood, cook, dry meat and fish, take care of the children, patch clothing, dry furs and equipment after rains, and, occasionally, fight Indians beside their men."[12]

At his first encampment on upper Bear Creek (near present-day Ashland), Ogden made initial contact with Rogue Valley Indians. On February 8 he noted in his journal that "an Indian came boldly to my Tent and presented me with two fresh Salmon also a Beaver Skin." This encounter showed a lack of fear, and the presentation of the beaver skin probably indicated knowledge of the fur-trading and -trapping objectives of the expedition. The presentation of salmon initiated a typical Indian gift-giving exchange. It was a friendly encounter and one that served Ogden's purpose of gaining knowledge about the beaver resources of the country. The Indian visitor told Ogden that "there were still a few Beaver remaining the natives having distroyed the greater part but in the Main Stream they were numerous." Although this information left in question the beaver-trapping potential of the region, it agreed with what McLoughlin had heard about the presence of beaver in the region and the Indians' extensive use of it.[13]

Ogden wrote in his journal on the second day: "upwards of twenty [Indians] assembled round our Camp as soon as we arrived." He described them as "bold and stout looking men" whose arrow quivers and caps were made of beaver skins, and who were also "well clad" in deer leather.

Ogden's observations for these first two days showed his concern about the shortage of deer for food and of beaver for trapping and trade. Ogden was also quite obviously concerned about whether the Indians were friendly or not. He noted that Indians in general "stand not in the least awe of Traders or Trappers indeed they entertain a most contemptible opinion of all Tradors they have seen." The reason, he believed, was the failure of whites to punish or make an "example" of the Indians who committed murders and thefts against whites.[14] Nevertheless, Ogden's general suspicion of and hostility toward Indians had thus far been contradicted by what he had to admit was friendly behavior. He had seen no evidence of the hostility toward whites among these "Sastise or [Castise)]" [Shasta Indians] of whom the ""Clammitts" [Klamath Indians] had warned him. Ogden suspected that the Klamaths "more from motives of jealousy than any other cause" wanted to keep him from making contact with Indians north of the Siskiyous.

In calling the first Indians he met on the northern slope of the Siskiyous "Sastise" [Shastas], Ogden correctly identified the use of territory by these Indians from the Rogue River south to the Siskiyous.[15] Although the main villages of the Shastas lay on the Klamath River side, several bands of Shastas inhabited the southern Oregon border. However, Ogden showed little or no awareness of other Indian bands in the Rogue River country. Ever mindful of his interests as a fur trader, he viewed possible rivalries and warfare among Klamath and Shasta Indians as their business. "They may distroy each other the more the better if they are fond of war let them enjoy it and we in the intervene will endeavor to wage war with their Beaver."[16]

Through a Klamath interpreter, Ogden was able to converse with several Shastas in the Klamath language at his campsite near present-day Talent on February 11. He was suspicious of the geographical information he received. The Shastas denied that the waters of the Rogue River drainage flowed into the Klamath River at some western point, but Ogden mistakenly assumed that they did.

From February 8 to 13, while in the Ashland-Talent area, the expedition had only one horse stolen and experienced only one threat of a night attack. The Shastas warned Ogden about the Takelma Indians who lived along the mainstream of the Rogue River from Table Rock to the vicinity of present-day Grants Pass. Ogden was pleased that the Indians were "so communicative ... and warning us to be on our guard when we reach the next Tribe with whom it appears they are at variance." But before the expedition left the Shastas' territory, several horses were injured by Indians. On the morning of February 14, before the party proceeded on down Bear Creek to the Rogue River, the "Horse Keeper" reported one horse killed and three wounded by arrows. Ogden was surprised by this turn of events, even though friendly Indians, including a chief who slept in Ogden's camp, had warned him. The chief explained that the horses had been attacked because "the Indians are displeased at seeing us daily destroy their Beaver and say they will in consequence starve."[17]

The destruction of valuable horses made Ogden furious, but he was helpless to retaliate. His trappers were scattered in all directions away from camp, leaving him only eight men. A few trappers who came back to base camp on February 14 also reported being attacked by a small group of Indians with bows and arrows. This pattern of attacks on the trappers continued after the party reached the Rogue River. On February 15, after establishing a campsite just a little west of Lower Table Rock, Ogden complained about the incessant rain that interfered with trapping and about the harassment of trappers in the field by "Natives most numerous bold and Insolant." Again, Ogden was forced to conclude: "they appear determined to oblige us to leave their Country."[18] It seems evident that the major concern of the Indians in the Bear Creek-Rogue River Valley was the trappers' reduction of an already depleted late-winter food supply. Ogden expressed surprise that, although there was an abundance of deer, the Indians he met appeared to be unskilled or unused to hunting them. Many Indian men, he noted, even lacked bows and arrows.

Approximately one week after Ogden's troubles with the Bear Creek-Rogue River Indians began, his relations with local Indians took an unexpected turn. On February 20, while he was still camped on the south bank of the Rogue River near Lower Table Rock, a delegation came to Ogden's camp. "Upwards of fifty Indians assembled near the camp," Ogden reported, "and sent two men in advance to inform us they wished to make peace with us."[19] Unfortunately, Ogden did not record what was discussed. One might assume that his earlier journal notes reflected most of the Indians' concerns. Ogden distributed "two Dozen Buttons" as a token of good will. The Indians, however, did not reciprocate. Ogden thought it was because they were too impoverished, but perhaps they had other reasons.

Over the next two months of his stay in southern Oregon, Ogden traveled from the Rogue River to the Middle Fork of the Coquille River. In response to the party's only recorded approach to an Indian village, the inhabitants fled in fear. On March 1, Ogden returned to a spot below Lower Table Rock from an upstream exploration and wrote that on the opposite side of the river he "saw a large Villiage containing six large Houses sufficiently so to contain upwards of 100 Indians."[20] This was probably the largest of the upper Rogue River Indian villages, one called Dilomi.[21] On seeing Ogden's party, the Indians immediately fled their village and retreated to the safety of nearby hills, "with their Children and property no doubt from fear and to secret themselves." Only two men and a woman remained behind in the village to receive Ogden's men.

In the days that followed, as the expedition made its way downstream to the vicinity of present-day Grants Pass and then northwest, Ogden had difficulty making contact with Indians. On March 18, on Cow Creek, a local Indian guide ran off. An old Indian man who was detained that same day, after being fed and given some beads, explained that "he had received tidings of our coming and with no other intention but to seize them as Slaves."[22] Ogden accepted this explanation and blamed the Klamath for having circulated the rumor.

Ogden's journal notes refer to the impoverished condition of Indians he met in southern Oregon: "The natives in this quarter are in a starving state not from the want of Deer as the Country abounds with them but laziness and want of ingenuity in discovering ways of killing them ... [T]heir sole support all over this Country appears to be the Camass Root which appears also to be most abundant but of any other kind very scarce." Ogden's other journal entries indicate that beaver rather than deer was the major meat supplement to the local Indian diet. Culturally preferred food resources provided a precarious existence by late winter and early spring. A great amount of effort was expended to provide a minimal diet of roots. Ogden also observed a number of new graves that he believed to be a sign that Indians were starving to death.[23]

Historian E. A. Schwartz disagrees with this interpretation of Ogden's journal notes about the use of beaver for food. He suggests that signs of Indians killing beavers (with spears, arrows, wooden traps, snares, and fire) show that they were in fact involved in trapping and trading pelts with Indians to the north, who perhaps acted as intermediaries with the HBC. Rather than telling Ogden that they were starving, the Indians were actually trying to tell him that he was starving them, in Schwartz's words, of "their stock in trade." Schwartz also suggests that Indian hostility may have been due to earlier ravages of smallpox.[24]

Fur traders often referred to "starving" Indians, in order to explain why Indians were not using their time to trap beaver, or why they were begging for goods.[25] But the situation Ogden described was closer to a literal definition of near-starvation.[26] He was no doubt aware that Indians in other parts of the HBC's empire used beaver as a food resource. Clerk John McDonnell on Fraser's Lake (in New Caledonia) wrote in 1823: "It is well known that Carrier(s) [Indians] kill Beaver, as much, at least, on account of the meat as for the skin."[27] Arthur J. Ray has written that "The Western Carrier ... [of Central British Columbia] were very fond of beaver meat, which was an important item on feast menus, particularly at very important funeral feasts."[28] Archaeologist and historian Jeff LaLande also has noted that the Klamaths and Shastas used beaver as a food resource.[29]

If the Rogue River Indians wanted to trade beaver pelts, why not trade directly with the HBC's Snake Country brigade or later Southern Party? Apparently, they had few to trade. Brief references in Ogden's notes indicate that although trade took place between Indians of southern Oregon and other tribes, it occurred rather infrequently. There is little documentary evidence to show what kind of trading relations existed between upper Rogue River Indians and their neighbors.[30]

Ogden's encounter with the Indians of southern Oregon was disappointing to him. Although his trappers managed to take beaver, the rainy weather and the effect on the beaver of Indian hunting methods, which Ogden claimed made the beaver "very wild," hurt trapping. Ogden also was unable to establish fur-trade relations with southern Oregon Indians, perhaps because of their limited trade experience. This may have been due to the geographical remoteness of the Rogue River Valley, as well as to hostile relations between Rogue River Indians and their neighbors.[31] These adverse conditions made the southern Oregon region undesirable as a major focus of HBC fur-trapping operations. However, due to its location, the region from this time forward would be a corridor of passage between Oregon and California.

The other major reason why Ogden did not establish fur-trade relations had to do with his mission: his was a fur-trapping, not a fur-trading, expedition. The HBC strategy was to delay American advances by trapping out the beaver west of the Rockies, thereby discouraging American fur companies from further westward penetration. This led the HBC to adopt a different attitude toward the Indians south of the Columbia River than they had adopted previously to those north of it. Instead of treating them as partners in the fur trade, the HBC now took whatever beaver pelts it wanted by force of men, arms, and its own fur-trapping activity. It traded for furs with Indians in Oregon, Idaho, and California when it could, but on a small scale compared with the fur trapping done by its hired men or freemen. The HBC chose a site across the Umpqua River from present-day Elkton as its trade and communication outpost for its Southern Brigade (called the Southern Party), not in the Rogue River Valley. In 1832 Jean Baptiste Gagnier met the Southern Party on the Umpqua with supplies, and, by 1836, Fort Umpqua began to serve as an HBC trading post for the southern Oregon region.[32] Its primary purpose was to service HBC fur trapping in northern California.

Despite Ogden's disappointment with the Indians he met in southern Oregon, his journal notes do not support a view of them as warlike "rogues" or "rascals," characterizations that soon took hold among whites. The Indians of the region were not noticeably involved in conflict with each other; and Ogden's party suffered only minor attacks on its horses and threats to its men. The Indians lacked firearms, and they even appeared to be poorly equipped with bows and arrows. Indian responses to Ogden's expedition indicated fear, some hostility, and a general sense of uncertainty about how to deal with these new white strangers.

PETER SKENE OGDEN opened contact with the Indians of southern Oregon along the eventual main route of white travel and later settlement in the region. But a few months prior to Ogden's visit, another HBC explorer and fur-brigade leader, Alexander Roderick McLeod, had made contact with Indians in the coastal zone of southern Oregon between the Umpqua River and Rogue River.[33] McLeod's descriptions of Indians on the southern Oregon coast were the first recorded by Euro-American explorers since the brief coastal stop by British sea captain, explorer, and cartographer George Vancouver in 1792.

On September 15, 1826, four days after Peter Skene Ogden left Fort Vancouver on his second Snake Country exploration, McLeod departed for the Umpqua River country with a group he described as "ten men and an Indian." But his party also included Indian women and children, families of HBC hunters and trappers. Accompanying this initial party was the British botanist David Douglas and HBC interpreter Michel Laframboise, who, a few years later, would lead fur-trapping expeditions through southern Oregon into California.[34]

The coast and Snake Country brigades amounted to about half of the total complement of men at Fort Vancouver. Dr. McLoughlin wrote at the end of the winter of 1826-27 that he had ninety-four men in his department, of whom thirty worked on the Snake Country brigade, twenty at Fort Vancouver, and sixteen on the coast trade, in addition to other assignments.[35]

Over the next month, additions were made to McLeod's party, although his journal entries make it difficult to know exactly how many. On October 6, the party was increased in number by the addition of Jean Baptiste McKay and two Iroquois Indians.[36] David Douglas's journal entry for November 2 mentions that "thirteen of our hunters arrived," but he also indicates that McLeod and five men had still not returned to camp.[37] By this time the party probably numbered eighteen hunters and trappers, McLeod, Douglas, Laframboise, McKay, two Iroquois, and several families of women and children. McLeod's assignment was the same as Ogden's, to explore the river system that was believed to drain from the Great Basin interior and that was bound to be "very rich in beaver."[38]

McLeod's descriptions of Indian life and responses to whites, as well as the conduct of his party during their travels through the country between the Umpqua River and Rogue River in the period from October 16, 1826 to February 21, 1827, can be compared with Ogden's account of simultaneous encounters with Indians between the Bear Creek-Rogue River Valley and upper Middle Fork of the Coquille River. Between them, McLeod and Ogden made contacts with most of the Indian cultural groups living in southern Oregon.

On October 16, McLeod's party set up camp about thirty-six miles from the ocean, near present-day Elkton. It made contact with Umpqua

River Indians the following day: "An Umpqua Indian came to us, and we availed ourselves of the moment to apprize his countrymen thro' him, the object of our mission so as to avoid giving any groundless alarm." A few days later the party reached the end of the open bench country along the Umpqua River in the vicinity of present-day Wells Creek and Scottsburg. The Indians were friendly and McLeod successfully negotiated for the use of canoes. The "principal Chief," whose village was located somewhere upstream from present-day Elkton, arrived with a party of "followers" and together with the local chief agreed to accompany McLeod's party downstream to the ocean.[39]

McLeod traveled in a canoe with "five men and two Indians … accompanied by the old Chief and suite in another craft." The group arrived near the mouth of the Umpqua River on October 23. McLeod bartered with local Indians for salmon. The next day, after reaching the ocean, the party "landed at a Village of two houses, where we were very hospitably treated and breakfasted on sturgeon and salmon, after satisfying our host with a few trinkets." The party proceeded on south along the beach toward Coos Bay, later in the day reaching Ten Mile Creek where Indians who lived nearby were fishing for salmon. McLeod wrote that the Indians "came to us with extreme caution [and] apparent dismay, which soon was dispelled when notified of our friendly intentions." McLeod conjectured that they were the first whites the Indians had ever seen.

McLeod's party reached Coos Bay on October 25. "Trinkets" were exchanged for "salmon trout" from local Indians. McLeod had trouble finding anyone among the Coos Indians to serve as "linguist" or interpreter to accompany his party to the "next river," now Coquille River. But he finally managed to get two Indians to agree. After spending the night among the sand dunes on the North Spit of Coos Bay, he "hired a sizeable canoe" to take his party to the head of South Slough, from which the party proceeded on by land to the coast and then down the beach to the Coquille River.

The party's arrival at the mouth of the Coquille River at first alarmed the Indians living there. But, within a short while, they got over their fear and agreed to notify Indians living upstream of the party's approach. On October 27, McLeod's party proceeded upstream. McLeod noted that although the Indians possessed beaver, "they were not very eager to open a trafic with use." However, he did manage to trade for "3 Sea Otters, 27 large and small beavers and 3 common Otters."

Three days later, McLeod returned to the sea. He traded for thirteen beavers, but when he asked about Indians to the south, the Coquille gave him little information, professing "themselves ignorant, [stating] ... that they never Venture in that direction beyond another small river [Sixes River?] about thirty miles from hence, where a few of their friends reside." However, the Indians told McLeod of an "old man" who did occasionally visit a large river to the south. But there was no time left on this trip. By November 1, McLeod had returned to Coos Bay, where he briefly traded for ten more beavers. Two days later he reached the Umpqua River encampment near present-day Scottsburg, where Laframboise had remained with the women and children.

McLeod did not mention any trouble with Indians on this first exploration of the coast, but British botanist David Douglas did. He noted complaints by Laframboise and McKay, who said that "the [nearby] tribes ... are so hostile, that one of the party has been killed, and an Indian woman, wife of one of our hunters, with five children, carried off; what became of them we have never been able to learn." McLeod, on his return to the Umpqua encampment, made preparations to send the furs that had been trapped and received in trade back to Fort Vancouver with Douglas and two of his men. McLeod and the rest of his party, however, returned to the coast on November 9. The expedition found beaver trapping to be poor in the Coos Bay country, and Coos Bay Indians brought in only a few beaver skins for trade.

On November 25, McLeod again reached the Coquille River. Two days later he wrote: "the Indians grumble at our presumption in trapping without paying them tribute." After investigation, he learned that these complaints originated with two Umpquas accompanying the expedition. McLeod dismissed the complaints: "appearances denote no cause of danger, as those stories came thro' a channel not much to be relied on." However, he did admit to a "little uneasiness, for it is evident those Indians ... endeavor to excell one another in fictions most likely with an intent to dissuade us from prosecuting our Journey to the Southward."

Due to heavy rain, it was difficult to trap beaver in the rising streams. McLeod proceeded up the south fork of the Coquille River and talked to Indians along the way. It became increasingly evident that Indians in the region rarely hunted beaver. "These people seemingly never molest those animals [beaver]," he wrote, being dependent "solely on the produce of the waters for subsistence, with roots that grow spontaneously in the vicinity." He noted that "the same observation is applicable to the natives on the great river [Rogue River], who never trouble themselves about furs, and have little or no intercourse with strangers."

On December 14, McLeod left the Coquille River region and returned briefly to the Umpqua River. But by the end of December he was back at the forks of the Coquille River on his way to the coast and the Rogue River. This third leg of the 1826-27 expedition brought McLeod to the "Toototonez" or Rogue River on January 11 without hostile incident. Indians in several villages along the coast fled, but Indians on the Rogue River soon overcame their fear after "trinkets" were distributed. Here, too, McLeod discovered that "these people like the rest of their brethren dont trouble themselves about beaver." He found no evidence of beaver skins among the Indians, but they did report that beaver was "plentiful" upriver. They also told McLeod that they were ignorant of methods for hunting beaver and had no market for them.

On January 14, while encamped at the mouth of the Rogue River, McLeod's party discovered that a small hatchet was missing. Convinced that it had been stolen, McLeod detained a half-dozen Indians and sent a message to the nearby village urging that the hatchet be returned. Three chiefs and sixty of their people showed up and protested that the thief was several days away. But in a gesture of accommodation, "they offered us a hostage and gave us up the services of an Indian of their tribe till our return when they would recover the stolen article and restore it." McLeod observed that "to have passed it [the hatchet theft] over in silence might not only leave a bad impression but actuate them to further aggression."

With both Indians and whites agreed on this course of action, McLeod's party departed, retracing its course back up the coast. But on January 25, after it reached the Coquille River again, the Indian hostage escaped, ending any hope of recovering the hatchet. Running low on provisions, McLeod's party went back over snow-covered coastal mountains to Camas Valley and then to the Umpqua River, reaching the "old establishment on the Umpqua" on February 6.

From there McLeod proceeded to the encampment near Scottsburg, where he received confirmation of earlier news that one of his trappers, who had returned by way of the "river Cahouse" [Coos Bay], had been killed. His name was Ignace and he was an Iroquois freeman trapper, survived by a wife and at least one child. McLeod wrote that Ignace was "killed by natives of river Cahouse in retaliation for an Indian of that tribe who was shot by the accidental going off of a gun, lying in the bow of a canoe." Ignace's three companions had run off, leaving the impression that the firing of the gun had been intentional. McLeod warned the Umpqua Indians that "we would not suffer the case to pass unnoticed," and they seemed eager to join the whites in getting satisfaction. But McLeod was due back at Fort Vancouver, and the matter of settling accounts seems to have been dropped.

On first reading, McLeod's journal indicates that his exploration of the lower Umpqua River and coastal zone of southern Oregon was almost free of hostile encounters. He managed to trade for and trap a number of furs ("215 large Beavers 64 small" as well as 31 otters) on his first swing down the coast. Indians guided him and provided information on geography and the location of beaver. His journal reflects a determined effort not to alarm the Indians his party met along the way. When local Indians fled, he sent members of his party out to try to persuade them of the party's peaceful intentions. He distributed "trinkets" as gifts, and he urged Indians to bring in furs to trade. He traded for salmon and camas roots to supplement his party's diet of deer and elk. And he shared the game his hunters killed with local Indians.

There were, however, five major exceptions to this picture of friendly relations with the various Indian cultural groups of the coastal zone. The first was the loss of a trapper, an Indian woman, and five children in the vicinity of the Umpqua River reported by Douglas. Secondly, Laframboise complained of Indian harassment of the main camp near Scottsburg. A third exception was the theft of a hatchet and subsequent negotiations on the Rogue River. A fourth was the accidental killing of a Coos Bay Indian and retaliatory killing of the Iroquois freeman, Ignace. Lastly, complaints were circulated against McLeod's party for not making payment for the beavers it trapped. While these negative responses to the expedition have to be viewed in the larger context of what seem to have been friendly relations, one is left with evidence of an undercurrent of resentment and several substantial unresolved grievances.

By contrast with interior Indians of the Bear Creek-Rogue River Valley region, coastal Indians apparently made little or no use of beaver for food. Therefore, fur trapping by McLeod's men did not pose the same threat to their economy. However, Indian complaints that the party was trapping without paying tribute was a serious grievance, which McLeod tended to dismiss, thereby reflecting insensitivity to coastal Indians' concepts of property rights and exchange relationships. Although Indian concepts of land ownership varied widely throughout the Pacific Northwest, the coastal Indians of southern Oregon had clearly defined village and individual territorial boundaries.[40]

It is surprising that McLeod took lightly the matter of paying "tribute," in view of his fur-trade experience. Studies of the fur trade have placed emphasis on the concept of "symbolic capital," that is, gifts or exchanges that helped "to maintain honor, prestige, or simply to achieve recognition for acting in an officially approved manner." Typically, Native people were accustomed to exchanging material goods for a variety of political and social, as well as economic, reasons.[41]

Although Indians reacted with less hostility to McLeod's party than to Ogden's, the fact remains that McLeod's party suffered greater injury. It also left behind unresolved disagreements with Indians on the Rogue River and at Coos Bay. Despite the assistance the expedition received in locating beaver sites along the Coquille River, its trapping there probably caused resentment. McLeod's fur-trade and -trapping visit also may have reignited rivalries between coastal Indian groups. Umpqua Indians encouraged him to join them in fighting Indians on Coos Bay. An Umpqua chief traveling with McLeod's party tried to abduct a young boy from the Coquilles. McLeod returned the boy to his parents and reprimanded the chief, but he worried about how the Coquilles would react.

McLeod was more successful than Ogden in establishing a foundation for continuing fur-trade relations with southern Oregon Indians. When the HBC established Fort Umpqua in 1836 to service the fur brigade that operated in northern California, Umpqua River and coastal Indians traded furs there in what were probably small quantities. Fur returns at Fort Umpqua were good for about five years, but they came mainly from northern California.[42] HBC leaders did not view the coastal zone north and south of the Umpqua River mouth, or the interior Rogue River Valley, as regions of major fur-trapping or fur-trade potential. But although McLeod left coastal Indians interested in the possibility of future fur-trade exchanges, he also left them unprepared for and possibly resentful toward the next white visitors.

A YEAR AFTER MCLEOD'S VISIT to the coastal region, another fur-trapping party made its way along the Oregon south coast and tested how well McLeod had established a middle-ground of Indian-white relations. On August 10, 1828, McLoughlin wrote to Governor Simpson that "an American of the name of Black reached this place [two days earlier] ... the only survivor of a Party of Nineteen (19) Americans, the remainder having been massacred by the Natives of the Umpqua River."[43]

This was the first that the HBC had heard of the American fur-trade exploring expedition led by Jedediah Strong Smith, which had come north from the Sacramento or Bonaventura Valley of Alta California to the Oregon coast. Smith was a fur-trade partner of David E. Jackson and William L. Sublette, the three of whom had bought out William Henry Ashley's Missouri Fur Company in 1826. Smith had been hired by Ashley in 1822 as a young man of twenty-three years and quickly rose to be one of Ashley's most trusted fur-trade employees. He developed a reputation for uncommon bravery in fighting Indians, religious sobriety, and a love of exploration. In the spring of 1824, Smith led a party over South Pass in the Rocky Mountains to the Snake River country of southern Idaho. There he met Alexander Ross's Snake Country Brigade and accompanied it back to the HBC's Flathead House in northwestern Montana in the fall. This was the HBC's first warning of the impending American challenge to its monopoly of the fur trade west of the Rocky Mountains. In early August 1826, Smith led an exploring party of eighteen men through the Great Basin country and into California. After delays caused by trouble with Mexican authorities in California, he left his party behind and returned to his company's rendezvous in Cache Valley, near Salt Lake. From there he led a second expedition to California in the summer of 1827. It unexpectedly continued on to Oregon later that year.[44]

Smith's second expedition of 1827-28 to California, and then to Oregon, had a troubled beginning. His party included eighteen men and at least two Indian women. While crossing the Colorado River, it was attacked by Mojave Indians. Ten of his men were killed, and the two Indian women were taken captive. Smith placed the blame on the

Mexican authorities in California. In a later report on his journey he stated that "the Governor [of California] had instructed the Muchaba [Mojave] Indians not to let any more Americans pass through the country on any conditions whatever."[45] Smith may or may not have been right to blame the Mexican governor, but in any case he had been on good terms with the Mojave Indians the previous year.

After rejoining the eleven men he had left behind earlier that spring, Smith spent several months of difficult negotiations with California authorities. Then, on December 30, 1827, he headed north with twenty-one men, two of whom soon deserted. Before starting for Oregon, Smith purchased about two hundred fifty horses to add to an existing herd of sixty-five, over three hundred horses in all. He planned to sell them at the next year's rendezvous. Initially the expedition followed a branch of the San Joaquin River, then picked up the Sacramento River, and in mid-April turned northwest to the headwaters of the Trinity River to avoid what looked like more difficult mountain country in southern Oregon. Smith and his second-in-command, Harrison Rogers, kept journals of the expedition's day-to-day progress. Their Oregon destination was the HBC's Fort Vancouver on the Columbia River.[46]

It took the expedition until June 8 before it finally reached the California coast by following the Trinity River to its junction with the Klamath River, and then the Klamath River to its mouth. From there the party headed north, and reached Oregon on June 23.[47] While still in California, the Smith expedition experienced both hostile and peaceful encounters with Indian tribes; these encounters are a necessary context for considering the expedition's experience with Indians along the coast of southern Oregon because of the possibility that word of the encounters may have preceded the expedition.

While Smith's party was crossing over the mountains west of present-day Red Bluff to the headwaters of the Trinity River, hostile Indians shot arrows at their horses and refused to respond to Smith's efforts to get them to stop. In return, he ordered his men to fire their rifles at them. After one incident in which nine horses and two mules were injured, Smith wrote that the Indians "in all probability paid for the damage they had done me by the sacrafice of two or three of their lives." The next day Indians continued to follow the party, yelling from nearby hills. Smith made signs to show that he wanted to talk. When these efforts failed, he and his men fired at them again, as he wrote, "to intimidate them and prevent them from doing me further injury."[48]

As the expedition neared the confluence of the Trinity and Klamath rivers, it entered Hupa Indian country. The Hupas were peaceful; they visited the expedition's camp and traded skins, eels, and roots for awls and beads without incident. But as the men struck out to the west into the territory of the Chilula Indians, they ran into trouble. Some Chilulas shot arrows at their horses and in retaliation Smith's party killed at least one of them. As the expedition left the Trinity and continued along the Klamath River into Yurok Indian country, Rogers noted that "they appear friendly and say nothing about the Ind. that Mr. [Thomas] Virgin killed."[49]

The Yuroks helped the expedition cross the Klamath River and guided it a short distance downstream. The party camped near another Yurok village close to the river mouth and people of the village came to trade fish for beads. But one expedition member, Peter Ransa, made several of them angry. Rogers believed that Ransa tried to take their fish without paying for them, and that when they threatened him, he fired his rifle to drive them off.[50]

A few days later, after camp visits by the Yuroks, the expedition discovered that an axe and drawing knife were missing. In retaliation, Smith took an Indian hostage and forced him to accompany the expedition as it proceeded northward. When, after two hours, none of the hostage's friends came after him to give back the knife, Smith turned the Indian loose.[51] It is possible that news of these hostile incidents preceded the expedition as it traveled up the northern coast of California and into Oregon. Fear generated by this news may account for empty villages the expedition found later in Oregon. Governor George Simpson of the Hudson's Bay Company in fact believed this to be the case.[52]

However, the expedition encountered no difficulty with the Tolowa Indians in the vicinity of present-day Crescent City. On June 18, Rogers wrote: "A number of Inds. visited our camp with clams, fish, strawberrys, and some dressed skins for sale, also commerss [camas] roots, ready prepared for eating; they appear friendly but inclined to steal without watching." Two days later at Smith River, "About 20 Inds. came to camp in their canoes, and brought lamprey eels for sale; the men bought a number from them for beeds." At Winchuck River, on June 23, Indians also came into their camp to trade strawberries and camas for beads.[53]

At the Chetco River, the behavior of the Indians abruptly changed. Perhaps the expedition came too close to an Indian village. Rogers wrote on June 24: "Enc[amped]. close by some Ind. lodges; they all had fled and left them; no visits from them as yet at this camp." The next day Smith found that two of his horses had been "wounded with arrows" and that another was missing. That evening, June 25, on arriving at Thomas Creek, the expedition again camped near an Indian village, and again the inhabitants fled. In the morning, Smith's men found that three horses had been badly wounded with arrows.[54] The expedition reached Rogue River on June 27, and again Indians living in several villages near the mouth of the river fled. Rogers commented: "All the Inds. for several days past runs off and do not come to us any more." At the Rogue River the expedition committed its first overt act of aggression against Indians on the southern Oregon coast. Rogers wrote in his journal: "we tore down one lodge to get the puncheons to make rafts, as timber was scarce along the beach."[55]

The next encounter with coastal Indians was on July 3, when the expedition reached the Coquille River. Smith, on horseback at the head of his party, rode up on some Indians in a canoe with the intention of seizing the canoe to cross the river. The Indians tried to deny its use by starting to break it up. According to Rogers Smith "screamed at them, and they fled, and left it, which saved us a great deal of hard labour making rafts."[56]

The next contact with coastal Indians came two days later, when the expedition was just south of Coos Bay. On July 5, at Shore Acres on Cape Arago, Rogers wrote that two Indians who spoke Chinook jargon came into their camp and told them they were close to the Willamette Valley. A day later, at Sunset Bay, Rogers wrote: "About 100 Inds. in camp, with fish and mussels for sale; Capt. Smith bought a sea otter skin from the chief; one of them have a fuzill [musket], all have knives and tommahawks. One a blanket cappon, and a number have pieces of cloth."[57]

According to a story told among the Coquilles in later years, the lower river Nasomah, after the canoe incident, sent messages of warning to Indians on Coos Bay. There, as George B. Wasson, Jr. tells the story, "a respected Miluk headman … responded with great military pomp and diplomacy, taking 300 armed men dressed in their finest skins and feathers out onto the coastal headlands near Cape Arago and ceremoniously welcoming the astonished whites."[58]

Two days later, on July 8, the expedition reached Coos Bay, at present-day Charleston, where there was a large Miluk Coos Indian village. The reception of the expedition was friendly and trading took place, but a hostile incident also occurred. Rogers wrote in his journal: "They commenced trading shell and scale fish, rasberrys, strawberrys, and 2 other kinds of bury that I am unacquainted with, also some fur skins. In the evening, we found they had been shooting arrows into 8 of our horses and mules; 3 mules and one horse died shortly after they were shot. The Inds. all left camp, but the 2 that acts as interpreters; they tell us that one Ind. got mad on account of a trade he made and killed the mules and horses."[59] This Indian's father was Coos and his mother a lower Umpqua Indian, or Kalawatset, which meant that he "belonged" to the lower Umpqua band and the Coos Indians could disclaim responsibility for his actions.[60]

The next day the expedition crossed over to the east side of lower Coos Bay and spent the night with Indians there. Rogers commented that "we bought a number of beaver, land, and sea otter skins from them in the course of the day." Again the expedition traded for fish and berries. The next morning the party crossed to the north spit of Coos Bay. Although there were no hostile incidents, Rogers commented that "Capt. Smith ... was some what of opinion the Inds. had a mind to attact him from their behavior."[61] But no hostile incident occurred.

The expedition arrived at the mouth of the Umpqua River on July 11. Rogers wrote in his journal: "Today we enc. where there was some Inds. living; a number of them speak Chinook; 70 or 80 in camp; they bring us fish and berris and appear friendly; we buy those articles from them at a pretty dear rate. Those Inds. call themselves the Omp quch." The expedition made camp on the south bank and spent the night peacefully, then crossed over the next day to the north side of Winchester Bay. Some of the Kalawatset Indians from the south bank village accompanied them. One of them, Rogers wrote, "stole an ax and we were obliged to seize him for the purpose of tying him before we could scare him to make him give it up." Captain Smith "put a cord round his neck, and the rest of us stood with guns ready in case they made any resistance, there was about 50 Inds. present but did not pretend to resist tying the other." The action resulted in recovery of the axe, and the rest of the day passed peacefully enough in trade for "land and sea otter and beaver fur."

On July 13 the expedition left camp near present-day Gardiner and continued on around the east side of the bay about four miles until it reached the mouth of the Smith River where camp was made that evening. In what was to be the last entry in his journal, Harrison Rogers wrote: "50 or 60 Inds in camp again to-day (we traded 15 or 20 beaver skins from them, some elk meat and tallow, also some lamprey eels). The traveling quite mirery in places; we got a number of our pack horses mired, and had to bridge several places. A considerable thunder shower this morning, and rain at intervals through the day. Those Inds. tell us after we get to the river 15 or 20 miles we will have good travelling to the Wel Hammett or Multinomah, where the Callipoo Inds. live."

The morning of July 14, Smith left camp with two other men to look for a route east to the Willamette Valley. He warned Harrison Rogers not to let the Kalawatsets, with whom they had been trading, into camp. Rogers, however, apparently disregarded the warning. Unknown to the men of the expedition, the Kalawatsets had been on the verge of attacking them since the previous day, when one of their people had been seized and bound for having stolen an axe. Sometime later in the morning, when the men of the expedition were cleaning their rifles, the Kalawatsets attacked them with knives and axes. One man, Arthur Black, fled into the woods and eventually made his way up the coast until he met up with Tillamook Indians who guided him to Fort Vancouver. Several other expedition members apparently also ran away from the camp, because only eleven skeletons were found by the HBC's Alexander McLeod three months later. But they were never heard from again.[62]

Jedediah Smith and two other men—John Turner and Richard Leland—had gone upriver. After turning downstream toward camp, they were fired on by Kalawatsets from the riverbank. Smith escaped their fire and reached the opposite side of the river. He climbed a hill to see the camp. It looked deserted. Smith decided that nothing could be done for the rest of his men, and he and his two companions headed north. Like Arthur Black, they eventually reached the Tillamook Indians and were shown the way to Fort Vancouver, where they arrived on August 10, two days later than Black and nearly a month after the Umpqua massacre.

Chief Factor John McLoughlin immediately wrote to Governor Simpson expressing his shock and grave concern. Fifteen lives lost to Indians out of a party of nineteen was no small matter. Moreover, Smith had lost 228 horses and mules, 780 beavers, 50-60 large otters, and several hundred pounds of beads, tobacco, and other trade goods. The economic loss alone would have impressed a fur-trade businessman like McLoughlin. But his concern reached beyond the human and financial loss to the implications for HBC control over the Oregon Country. If the Kalawatsets could attack one group of whites with impunity, they or other Indians could attack again. Immediately after Black's arrival, McLoughlin sent "Indian runners with tobacco to the Willamette chiefs to tell them to send their people in search of Smith and his two men, and if they found them to bring them to the fort and I would pay them, and telling them if any Indians hurt these men we would punish them."[63] The arrival of Smith, Turner, and Leland two days after Arthur Black made a rescue mission unnecessary.

The Smith expedition massacre came to McLoughlin's attention only a little more than six months after he had received news that Alexander Mackenzie and four other HBC men had been killed by Clallam Indians on Puget Sound. McLoughlin wrote to Governor Simpson that "from every information I have been able to collect, [the Clallam Indians] committed this crime without having had the least difference with our people & murdered them merely for the sake of their apparel & Arms." Moreover, the Clallams had challenged the HBC to do something about it. In McLoughlin's opinion, and that of "every one acquainted with the character of the Indians of the North west Coast ... they can only be restrained from Committing acts of atrocity & violence by the dread of retaliation."[64] As recently as June, McLoughlin had sent Alexander McLeod, four clerks, fifty-nine servants and freemen, and a cannon-armed schooner on a punitive expedition against the Clallams, resulting in the killing of twenty-one Indians and the burning of an Indian village and forty-six canoes. McLoughlin admitted to Governor Simpson that the actions taken were "a subject on which perhaps there may be a diversity of opinions."[65]

McLoughlin again turned to Alexander McLeod to handle a difficult situation.[66] McLeod had been preparing for a fur-trapping expedition to northern California, and McLoughlin now ordered him to help recover Smith's property and gave him authority to act as he saw fit to punish the Kalawatsets.[67] McLeod's party eventually numbered nearly forty-four men, including Smith and his three men.

As McLeod's party moved down the Willamette Valley, it received word that the Umpqua Indians were ready to engage in fighting. They had evidently become emboldened by the example of the Kalawatsets. "Pillage is their object unmindful of the Consequences," McLeod believed.[68] But as his party advanced it grew in size and fire power. On

October 2, McLeod wrote that "D'Epatis & Gervais with their followers, are now attached to our Party, forming in all twenty Men, nearly as many Slaves, besides Mr. S. [Jedediah Smith] & his three Men, which in the Eyes of the Natives, makes a forcible impression if we can judge from the alarm a few Indians s[e]en in course of the day, got." By the time the party reached the Umpqua River at "the site of the Old Establishment" opposite Hubbard Creek, the rumors of opposition by Umpquas had dissolved.

On October 11, McLeod met with one of the Umpqua chiefs and a dozen of his men. This chief had visited the Kalawatsets and reported to McLeod on the reasons for the attack on Smith's expedition. He mentioned the incident of the missing axe that resulted in an Indian having been taken hostage. The hostage had been a man of some "Rank" who tried to get his people to retaliate, but "he was overruled." Another reason for the attack, not previously reported to McLoughlin, was that on the morning of the massacre another "Individual higher in Rank and possessing greater influence" than the first had mounted one of the expedition's horses to take a ride and he had been forced to dismount. Horses were a novelty to the Kalawatsets. This Indian together with the one who had been taken hostage the day before decided to retaliate. The Umpquas also reported that Smith's men had stated that "they were a different people from us [the HBC] and would soon monopolize the trade, and turn us out of the country." In answer to these charges, Smith readily admitted tying up an Indian until the missing axe was recovered, but he denied using undue force. He blamed talk of opposition to the HBC on "a Slave boy [Marion] attached to his Party, a Native of the Willamette" who could "converse freely." It was evidently Arthur Black who had made the Indian Chief get off the horse, but he claimed that he had not spoken in "an angry tone neither did he present his gun," although he admitted having had it in his hand.

One final charge that went unmentioned by McLeod in his journal, but that showed up in later statements by Governor Simpson and McLoughlin, was that one of Smith's men had tried to force an Indian woman into his tent. Harrison Rogers was blamed for this act in Governor Simpson's report of March 1, 1829 to the Governor and Committee of the HBC. The Kalawatsets claimed that "they had not formed any plan of destruction, until … 'Rogers' a Clerk, in Smith's absence, attempted to force a Woman into his tent, whose Brother was knocked down by Rogers while endeavoring to protect her."[69] In later years McLoughlin made the charge more general. In his autobiography he wrote that "to gratify their passion for women," Smith's men against orders allowed the Kalawatsets into their camp.[70] While there is no way to confirm or refute the charge, it seems curious that McLeod did not mention it in his journal when he was getting first hand reports from the Umpqua Indians. He had no reason to suppress this particular information.

We can only speculate as to the Kalawatsets' view of the Smith expedition prior to these events. They may have heard enough about the white strangers before they arrived to put them under suspicion. The fact that the Smith party moved up the coast without taking the time to overcome Indian fears and meet with Indians contrasted sharply with the behavior of McLeod's party the previous year. The Kalawatsets claimed in justification of their action that Smith's party had been "destroying all the Natives that came within their reach." But that claim is unsupported by the evidence of Smith's and Rogers' journals. The fact that Smith's party received a friendly reception on Coos Bay suggests that the expedition's trouble with the Kalawatsets stemmed from the nature of their local encounter.

When Smith had an "Indian of Rank" taken hostage and tied up, he raised the level of suspicion and anger, but not enough for an attack. The Kalawatsets had to weigh the possibilities of getting satisfaction for injured pride and seizing the Smith party's possessions against the Americans' superior weapons and the possibility of retaliation by the HBC. But by the morning of July 14, the Kalawatsets thought they knew that Smith's party of white men were enemies of the HBC. All that was needed was an emotional spark to turn Kalawatset resentment into an attack. That spark was either the incident involving the chief being forced to dismount from a horse, or the alleged act or acts of rape, or both.

The Kalawatsets immediately gave much of Smith's property away, apparently to improve relations with neighboring villages, and to demonstrate their victory over whites and their newly acquired wealth. McLeod reported that Smith's possessions were widely and generously distributed to two villages on the lower Umpqua River (probably near Scottsburg), one on Tahkenitch Creek (north of the Umpqua River mouth), one on Ten Mile Creek (south of the Umpqua River mouth), and one on the Siuslaw River. Most of the furs were recovered from one of the Umpqua River villages, but each of the other villages seem to have received a somewhat equal distribution of weapons, cooking kettles, beads, and miscellaneous items. A large number of horses were apparently killed for food, while others were distributed inland along the Umpqua River and north along the coast to the Tillamook Indians. McLeod, however, was remarkably successful in recovering many of the Smith expedition's possessions without resorting to violence against the Kalawatsets or other Indians. Altogether some seven to eight hundred beaver and otter skins and about forty horses were recovered in addition to several rifles, cooking pots, traps, clothes, beads, and, most important of all for historians, the journals of Jedediah Smith and Harrison Rogers.

The moral of the Smith expedition's disaster was not lost on the HBC. It never sent brigades out with less than thirty to forty men, and it always exercised due caution. The Smith expedition massacre also ended any possibility of American fur trappers encroaching on the HBC's domain south of the Columbia River.

Although HBC leaders believed that Smith's party brought disaster upon itself, the Kalawatsets' action may have resulted from ambivalence toward the HBC. McLeod's trips through the lower Umpqua area only established the beginnings of a fur-trade relationship. The Kalawatsets' effort to enlist the upper Umpqua Indians in warfare against McLeod highlights the uncertain nature of the new relationship between HBC and coastal Indians. Trouble with the Indians on the Umpqua River did not end in 1828. Chief Factor James Douglas ten years later referred to them in a letter to the Governor, Deputy Governor, and Committee of the HBC, as "the fiercest, most intractable and vindictive of all the lower Columbia tribes."[71]

The Umpqua massacre of the Jedediah Smith expedition became one of the stories of Indian "savagery" most often told by early Oregon pioneers. Survivors of the massacre—Arthur Black, John Turner, and Richard Leland—continued to live in the Oregon Country and kept the story alive. It helped shape hostile attitudes toward southern Oregon Indians and interfered with creation of a middle-ground of accommodation. Coastal Indians told their own story of the Jedediah Smith Expedition, and for those who survived into the late twentieth century, it stood as an example of justifiable Indian resistance to white violation of Indian customs and territorial rights.[72]

Chapter 2

Along the Southern Route, 1829-49

IN THE TWENTY years following the fur-trade and fur-trapping probes of southern Oregon by Ogden, McLeod, and Smith, the region provided a major corridor of travel for the HBC and Americans, linking Oregon, California, and eastern trail approaches across the northern Great Basin (of present-day Utah and Nevada). The Indians of southern Oregon, who had been relatively isolated from contact with Indians outside the region and with whites, now watched white strangers pass through their homeland each year. At first, the strangers were HBC fur-party members; after them came American explorers, and, briefly on the Umpqua River, two American missionaries. By the late 1840s, wagon trains of white settlers began to pass through southern Oregon on their way to the Willamette Valley. The nature of contacts over these twenty years helped shape middle-ground relations that followed in the early 1850s. The HBC and Americans blamed each other for their troubles with the Indian "rogues" of southern Oregon. But violent conflict between whites and Indians was limited, and Indian groups showed restraint in their efforts to encourage whites to pass quickly through their territories.

Alexander McLeod's expedition to the lower Umpqua in September 1828 to recover Jedediah Smith's horses, furs, and other possessions was supposed to be the start of the "first authorized HBC expedition to Alta California." Instead, McLeod's party returned to Fort Vancouver from the Umpqua River. Angered at what he considered to be McLeod's malingering, McLoughlin sent him out again in January. McLeod reached the Rogue River in February and the Sacramento Valley in April, wintered over in the Shasta Valley and did not return to Fort Vancouver until July 1830.[1]

On this 1829-30 trip, McLeod had a brief encounter with Rogue River Indians..In a letter to McLoughlin he reported that when he reached "a River which I supposed to be a fork of the Clametti River," the Indians carried away traps as fast as McLeod's trappers could set them. As a result, he said, they "had to resort to arms" to drive the Indians away. After leaving the Rogue River and entering northern California, McLeod reported that his men killed seven or eight Pit River Indians and an additional seventeen to twenty members of other groups along the way from Mt. Shasta south to the Sacramento Valley. On the return trip, the expedition had another encounter with Rogue River Indians. According to McLoughlin, they were "very impudent and troublesome ... [going] so far as to take the people's kettles from the fire and help themselves to the contents." McLoughlin blamed McLeod for being too kind and preventing his men from punishing them, and as a consequence he wrote, they "have been troublesome to the Whites ever since."[2]

John Work took over the Snake River Brigade from Peter Skene Ogden in 1830, and returning from California in September 1833, the brigade came under Indian attack. Work wrote that "Indians descended from the Mountain in the night and shot with their arrows several of our horses ... Thus these savages without any provocation kill our horses & would doubtless treat ourselves in the same manner were it not [for] fear." Work's party consisted of twenty-eight white men and seventy-two Indians and mixed-bloods (twenty-two women, forty-four children, and six men), a total of one hundred, when he left California for Oregon. His journal entry for September 16 refers to a "River Coquin" ("coquin" being the French word for rogue or rascal). This is the first reference in the HBC's published records to a "River Coquin," Rogue, or "Rogue's" river.[3]

After McLeod, Michel Laframboise led the HBC's Southern Party to California for the next ten years (except for 1841-42). Laframboise had come to Oregon in 1811 on John Jacob Astor's ship *Tonquin* at age seventeen. In 1813 he joined the North West Company, and later became part of the reorganized HBC. He accompanied Alexander McLeod on his expeditions to the coastal region in 1826-28, serving as interpreter. Before leaving for California in 1832, Laframboise was sent to the coast to punish the Tillamook Indians for killing two HBC trappers. His party took the lives of six Indians in retaliation. Under Laframboise, when the Southern Party came under Indian attack, it did not hesitate to take Indian lives.[4] In the spring of 1834, Laframboise's party skirmished with Indians on the south side of the "Umpqua Mountain" (probably on the north side of the Rogue River). John Work, who was at the Umpqua River, received news by Indian messenger that Laframboise and his party had been killed. In fact, eleven of the Indians who had attacked the Southern Party, but none of its members, had been killed. Such false or exaggerated reports no doubt contributed to uncertainty in Indian-HBC relations.

Near present-day Scottsburg, John Work visited with "Joe the master of the only house that is here." Joe was one of several Indians on the Umpqua River employed by the HBC. From other Indians, Work learned that Joe was much feared: "He is said to have killed 4 Indians during the winter & is represented as a very bad character & a great hand for taking other people's wives." Although Joe had furs to trade that he had acquired from coastal Indians, Work, by trading with the Indians, learned that they only wanted green beads and had little interest in trade goods other than ammunition "except at very low prices."[5]

Laframboise's skirmishing with Indians and Joe's relations with the Indians on the lower Umpqua River show that by 1834 HBC relations with Indians in southern Oregon were less than satisfactory. Fur trade with Umpqua River Indians no doubt helped to moderate tension in that river valley, but south of the Umpqua Mountains sporadic Indian attacks on white parties seem to have become common.[6]

In 1834, Americans became a larger part of the story of Indian-white relations in southern Oregon. In a letter of November 18, 1834, McLoughlin reported the arrival at Fort Vancouver a month earlier of the Methodist missionaries Jason and Daniel Lee, entrepreneur Nathaniel Wyeth, mountain man Ewing Young, and the promoter of American settlement of Oregon, Hall J. Kelley. McLoughlin wrote that Jason and Daniel Lee had gone to the Willamette Valley to settle and "to devote their attention to the instruction of the natives and expect to be joined by some more of their country men next year." Wyeth told McLoughlin of his plans "to salt salmon for the Boston market ... to equip some American trappers in the mountain and to farm in the Willamette." Kelley planned "to form a colonization society among his Countrymen to settle in the Willamette." Young arrived accused by the Governor of upper California of having stolen several hundred horses "belonging to various Mexican citizens."[7]

Ewing Young and Hall J. Kelley had met in California that summer. Kelley persuaded Young to guide him to Oregon. On August 8, the

Lower Umpqua River Indian plank house. From Frank Leslie's Illustrated Magazine *(April 24, 1858). (Oregon Historical Society, OrHi 6450)*

two set out from Monterey with five other men and forty to fifty horses; the party grew to sixteen men and nearly one hundred fifty to two hundred horses. The nine latecomers to the party were what Kelley later called "marauders" and horse thieves. Even Young admitted that they probably added fifty-six stolen horses to the party's herd. In the San Joaquin Valley, these men stopped at an Indian village, raped the women, and stole possessions. The next day they shot an Indian. A few days later, along the Sacramento River, they killed seven more Indians in retaliation for an equal number of horses having been killed by unknown Indians. According to Kelley, Ewing Young approved of these acts of violence on the grounds that "we must protect ourselves while in the wilderness among hostile Indians."[8]

These incidents in California serve as a background for what happened when the party reached the Rogue River. By then several members were suffering from malaria, so the party camped on an island to rest. While they were there, two Indians visited them. Fearing that the Indians would carry word of the party's sick members back to their village, and that this might make them vulnerable to attack, expedition members killed the Indians as they left the camp. S. A. Clarke, who in 1905 was the first to tell of the incident in print, said it was the cause of Rogue River Indians later killing "traveling white men, who they supposed were affiliated to those ruffians who so ruthlessly slew their brothers." When viewed in the light of Work's report on Laframboise's skirmish a few months earlier with Indians south of the "Umpqua Mountain," it seems more likely that by this time all whites, whether HBC or American, were viewed with distrust.[9]

Rogue River Indians took revenge on another party of Americans who came through the Rogue River Valley the next summer, a party of eight men, including John Turner, a survivor of the Smith expedition massacre, and two young Englishmen, William J. Bailey and George Gay. Indians, who had been allowed to enter their encampment, killed four men in the party. Ornithologist John Kirk Townsend, who was at Fort Vancouver when the survivors arrived (July 18-20, 1835), wrote that the Indians who attacked the party are "called by the inhabitants of this country, the 'rascally Indians,' from their uniformly evil disposition, and hostility to white people." Townsend's reference to "rascally Indians" supports John Work's journal reference in 1833 to "River Coquin."[10]

Through the late 1830s, the HBC's Southern Party under Laframboise passed through southern Oregon on the way to California without suffering injury from Indian attacks. McLoughlin bragged in an October 31, 1837, letter to company headquarters: "We stand high in the opinion of the Canadian Trappers, and Freemen in the Willamette, as a proof, we have made Six hunts in the vicinity of the Settlement of California, and have not lost a man."[11] A year later, Chief Factor James Douglas reported that along the route of the Southern Party "the Natives ... were uniformly peaceable," and that "the warlike Chief of the powerful Sasty [Shasta] Tribe, evinced his desire of peace, by sending an escort of his people, to protect the Party while travelling through his Country."[12] However, Douglas's remarks, while emphasizing the chief's desire for peace, also referred to "numberless causes of mutual exasperation." Douglas also reported trouble the HBC had experienced the previous year with Umpqua Indians, who had threatened to destroy the HBC's newly built Fort Umpqua (located across the river from present-day Elkton). Douglas explained: "The sole cause ... was the prevalence among the tribe ... of an unknown and fatal disease attended by alarming mortality which they charitably ascribed to our ill offices." A year later, according to Douglas, the "former friendly understanding appears to be quite restored [as of 1838]." [13] Although Indian hostility may not have been as overt, it seems likely that Indians remained fearful of white diseases.

If relations between HBC parties and the Indians of southern Oregon had reached a temporary "friendly understanding" by 1838, the same cannot be said of relations between Americans and the Indians of the region. In 1837, a representative of the United States government, Lieutenant William A. Slacum, arrived in the Willamette Valley. He was informed by American settlers of the need for cattle and offered passage to California on his ship *Loriot* to a group of Americans representing a newly organized Willamette Cattle Company. This group, soon to become cattle drovers, sailed with Slacum to San Francisco and Monterey. The group included Ewing Young and Webley Hauxhurst of Young's 1834 party and three survivors of the 1835 attack: Englishmen George Gay and William J. Bailey, and the American, Turner.[14] On returning to Oregon, the cattle drovers shot and killed a man and a boy, the first Indians they met after crossing the Rogue River. How many other Indians the party killed, we do not know. Indians retaliated and wounded George Gay. Two hundred out of 630 cattle were lost on the drive, but it was considered a success, and three years later the HBC brought four thousand sheep and two thousand cattle from California to Oregon over the same route using Scotch sheepherders and company fur trappers as cattle drivers.[15] These cattle and sheep drives constituted a new threat to the Indians of southern Oregon, and further established southern Oregon as a transportation route between the Willamette Valley and California.

By the late 1830s, white attitudes toward the Indians of southern Oregon had become stereotypical; Indian reactions to the whites were more courageous and probing. What is striking about the limited descriptions of these encounters with southern Oregon Indians by Americans in 1834, 1835, and 1837 is that Indians persisted in approaching and entering white camps. There is no evidence to indicate that whites approached any Indian villages in the same manner. In fact, except for Ogden's brief reference to an Indian village, none of the surviving journals of this period even describe what an Indian village and its dwellings looked like. The Indians who entered the Turner party camp in 1835 were probably hostile, but we know from journal descriptions that the Indians who entered Young's camp in 1834 and 1837 were friendly. Neither whites nor Indians could be certain of what might happen when they met.

In 1840-41, two new kinds of American intruders passed through southern Oregon and made contact with local Indians. One party consisted of three American Methodist missionaries; another, larger, party was an official United States government exploring expedition. These missionaries and naval officers-explorers began a process of information gathering by Americans that was continued by later military officers, Indian agents, and late nineteenth- century anthropologists. But even these first low-impact, noncommercial amateur American ethnographers left the region frustrated by their experience and apparently left local Indians no less hostile.

A group of Methodist missionaries and their children arrived at Fort Vancouver on June 1, 1840, after about an eight-month journey by ship from New York. Gustavas Hines was among the passengers on the ship *Lausanne* commanded by Captain Josiah Spaulding (who became a harsh critic of Chief Factor McLoughlin's Indian policy). He and the other thirty-six adults on board the ship were reinforcements for missionary work in Oregon, recruited by Jason Lee. Hines expected to be assigned as a missionary to the Umpqua Indians. By June 16, he and the other *Lausanne* party members arrived at the Oregon mission in the Willamette Valley.[16]

Two months later, on August 18, Hines, Lee, Elijah White, and an Indian guide set out for Fort Umpqua, arriving there on August 22. White returned to the Willamette Valley, but Hines and Lee proceeded on down the Umpqua River to its mouth. Hines wrote about the experience in his book *Wild Life in Oregon* (1881).[17] Jean Baptiste Gagnier, who had selected the site for Fort Umpqua on the south bank of the Umpqua River, was still in charge when Hines and Lee arrived.[18] For a few years, Fort Umpqua was a highly successful fur-trade outpost. In 1840, when Hines and Lee arrived, the HBC Southern Party's return in furs reached a peak of 1,592 beavers, then declined to about half that number (765) by 1843, when the last Southern Party went through southern Oregon.[19]

Fort Umpqua consisted of three buildings: a house for Gagnier and his family, another one for HBC employees, and a storehouse. A twelve-foot-high palisade surrounded the fort, and at two opposite corners of the square, blockhouses had been built to defend against Indian attack.[20] The fortifications were necessary, as Hines pointed out in his report, because "not long since the place was attacked by a band of savages, outnumbering ten times the inmates of the fort." No one had died in the skirmish, but several Indians had been wounded. The Indians had finally called off the attack.[21] On a small farm of fifty acres surrounding the fort, Gagnier and the other HBC "servants" raised wheat, corn, potatoes, and garden vegetables, as well as livestock, at one time numbering forty-six horses, sixty-four head of cattle, and forty-five hogs, making the fur-trade outpost self-sufficient.

Fort Umpqua HBC employees made contact with Indians downstream at or near Scottsburg. Indians brought their pelts there, or to Fort Umpqua. Coos Indian Lottie Evanoff told anthropologist John Harrington in 1940 that her father Chief Doloose or "Jackson" had walked from Allegany to Scottsburg with beaver pelts as a young man. "With the pay for the hides he bought some clothes. He said those were the first clothes he ever put on. Jean Baptiste Gagnier of the Hudson's Bay Company was buying the furs."[22] There was a special relationship between Gagnier and Lower Umpqua Indians because his wife belonged to a local village. Lionel Youst in his book *She's Tricky Like Coyote* (1997), about Coos Annie Miner Peterson, writes that a relative of Gagnier's wife (whose name is unrecorded) had a stepfather who set traps. "The hides would be packed and carried away .... Some of our relatives would sometimes bring in a canoe a great quantity of hides .... Everybody wanted hides."[23]

When Hines and Lee told Gagnier of their plans to travel to the mouth of the Umpqua River, Gagnier initially warned them about the local Indians, saying "there would be great danger in our going among them alone, and, indeed, he appeared to stand in the utmost fear of them."[24] Fortunately for the two missionaries, the brother of Gagnier's Indian wife arrived from downstream with a party of Indians. The missionaries asked if Gagnier's wife, who was "a relative of the principal chiefs of the [Kalawatset] tribe," would accompany them to the mouth of the Umpqua River. Gagnier gave his consent, apparently assured that his wife and her brother's presence would ensure the missionaries' safety.

As the party proceeded down the Umpqua River, Indian men and women from one of the villages joined them. The Indian women shared their broiled salmon. At the mouth of the Umpqua River, Hines found "three small villages," one on the south side and two on the north side of the river. He estimated the population to be about two hundred, but observed that a third of the people were "absent in the mountains, for the purpose of gathering berries." Shortly after their arrival, the missionaries were surrounded by a formal gathering of three chiefs and fifty-five other people, who sat in "a semicircle in front of the tent." Lee addressed them, informing them of the reasons for the visit and asking if "they approved of our visit, and whether they desired to be instructed." Each of the chiefs gave a speech, which Hines summarized and condensed, as follows:

> *Great chief! We are very much pleased with our lands. We love this world. We wish to live a great while. We very much desire to become old men before we die. It is true, we have killed many people, but we have never killed any but bad people. Many lies have been told about us. We have been called a bad people, and we are glad that you have come to see us for yourselves. We have seen some white people before, but they came to get our beaver. None ever came before to instruct us. We are glad to see you; we want to learn; we wish to throw away our bad things, and become good.*

Hines was impressed by what the chiefs said, but equally surprised, and perhaps a little scared, by the way they said it: "They spoke very loud, and their gestures were remarkably violent. Sometimes they would rise upon tiptoe, with both hands stretched high above their heads, and then throw themselves forward until their faces almost touched the ground." When the chiefs finished speaking, Hines sang a hymn, and then the two missionaries prayed and preached to the gathering, "as well as we could in the jargon of the country." At the conclusion of the meeting, the chiefs expressed their good pleasure and left. That night they returned, and the hymns, prayers, and preaching were repeated. Again the Indians left. Lee "slept soundly," but Hines kept peering nervously out of his tent.

Gagnier's wife, her brother, and another Indian kept a fire burning all night. The next morning, before departing, Lee and Hines visited the lodges of the Indians. They were given gifts of a beaver skin and a woman's cedar-bark dress, which they reciprocated with gifts of their own. They left promising to send someone to live and teach among the Kalawatsets the next summer.

When Hines's party returned to Fort Umpqua, Gagnier informed them that they would have been robbed and possibly killed if his wife and her brother had not been with them. One of the lower Umpqua chiefs had been at the fort when Lee and Hines arrived and had been frightened by Lee's "fowling piece" and "patent shot pouch." He had hurried downstream and "reported many evil things about us, intending thereby to instigate the Indians to prevent our going among them." The shot pouch had been described as a medicine bag that when opened would kill all the Indians. Gagnier's wife told Lee and Hines that they had been in great danger during the night. By keeping an all-night vigil, she and her brother had prevented the Indians from attacking. Somewhat skeptical, Hines remarked in his account that he and Lee had not felt "particularly exposed," especially not with their "Heavenly Father" watching out for them. But, as if to allow for the possible truth of what Gagnier and his wife told him, Hines related to his readers the story of the Smith expedition massacre as told to him "by the gentlemen of the Hudson's Bay Company."

On their way back to the Willamette Valley, Hines and Lee stopped to visit an upper Umpqua Indian village. As they arrived, the village chief had just finished shooting and killing his wife with his musket, because he believed that she was guilty of infidelity. The chief greeted the two white men and invited them to stay overnight, while trying to explain his action. Meanwhile, behind the chief, on the opposite bank of the river where the village was located, Indian women of the village were "scratching and biting one another, and tearing each other's hair, and squalling most frightfully," probably in mourning. Hines and Lee were so horrified that they decided to leave immediately. Their Umpqua Indian guide, however, insisted that they had to stay, "saying that it would be using his people very ill, and that the chief would be very angry with us, if we did not stop and sleep with them one night." After agreeing to pay their guide an "extra shirt" to get him to break protocol and leave with them, the two missionaries fled in terror through the night, half-expecting pursuit by the wife-killer chief.

Safely back at the mission station in the Willamette Valley, Hines summed up his Umpqua Valley experience. He observed that there were about 375 "souls" living on the Umpqua River organized into two "clans" (Umpquas upstream and Kalawatsets downstream), speaking "two distinct languages." "Disease and their family wars" had reduced the upstream Umpquas to "less than seventy-five souls." Hines questioned whether it was worth establishing a mission among them. The Indians had been receptive, but he observed that they "seem to think that the greatest benefit it would confer on them, would be to enable them to sell their beaver and deer-skins for a higher price." "Temporal good," he pragmatically observed, "is the sole object they would have in view." A mission to these Indians would be very costly because of the "inaccessible" country. He concluded that "the doom of extinction is suspended over [t]his wretched race," and that ended any possibility that the Umpqua Valley Indians would ever get their own missionaries and mission station.

Hines's experience shows that it was difficult even for an educated and humane white observer of southern-Oregon Indian culture to view it favorably. At the same time, the Kalawatsets must have viewed the visit of Hines and Lee as another example of a broken promise by white people. They had provided hospitality and gifts to the visiting white religious men and teachers. Hines and Lee had promised to send a teacher to them the next summer. But as a result of the decision not to establish a mission station among the Umpquas, no teacher was sent to the Kalawatsets; and there was no improvement in their trade with white people as a result. Hines and Lee's brief visit to the Indians of the Umpqua Valley illustrates how the best of intentions for peaceful intercourse could lead to greater misunderstanding for Indians and whites.

A YEAR LATER, beginning on September 7, 1841, a party of men set out from the Willamette Valley for California under the command of Lieutenant George Foster Emmons of the U.S. Navy.[25] With him were four other naval officers, five natural scientists, six trappers, a guide, and several families of settlers including women and children, a total of thirty-six persons and seventy-six animals.[26] The naval officers and scientists were members of the U.S. Exploring Expedition of 1838-42, commanded by Lieutenant Charles Wilkes. Congress had authorized the expedition in 1836 for the purpose of making a survey of Pacific Islands and exploring the Pacific Northwest coast. The expedition reached the Pacific Northwest in the summer of 1841. The Emmons party was one of several that Lt. Wilkes sent out to explore Washington and Oregon; after traveling from Oregon to California, they were to rendezvous with the ship *Vincennes* in San Francisco.[27]

When the party reached Fort Umpqua on September 17, Jean Baptiste Gagnier greeted it as he had the American missionaries a year earlier. He tried to dissuade Lt. Emmons from continuing on southward, as he had tried to warn Hines and Lee against going to the mouth of the Umpqua River. Midshipman George M. Colvocoresses wrote in his journal: "He [Gagnier] stated that he had long before heard of the intended journey, through the Indians, and that the news had passed on to all the tribes, who were collecting in large numbers, to oppose our passage."[28] Gagnier told them of recent Indian attacks and attempts to burn down the fort. He blamed the general state of hostility toward whites on a recent outbreak of smallpox,[29] which the Indians, he said, blamed on the HBC parties under Michel Laframboise and Thomas McKay. Lt. Emmons later recalled that the Indians also claimed that "ague and fever" (most likely malaria) had been unknown to them prior to 1830.[30]

These references to outbreaks of disease among the Indians of southern Oregon point to a more widespread impact of epidemic diseases. Robert Boyd has described a succession of epidemics that devastated Northwest Coast Indians beginning with the first white contacts in the 1770s and continuing until the early 1860s.[31] There were smallpox outbreaks in the 1770s, and in 1801-2, 1824-25, 1836-37, 1852-53, and 1862; venereal diseases and tuberculosis throughout the period; "fever and ague," 1830-35; localized epidemics of meningitis, smallpox, influenza, mumps, and dysentery, 1835-47; and a measles epidemic, 1847-48.

Malaria had arrived in 1830, either by ship from malarial areas or by land with trappers and traders. The HBC's Dr. John McLoughlin wrote that three-fourths of the Indians near Fort Vancouver had been "carried off" by the "Intermittent Fever."[32] Whites, as well as Indians, came down with malaria, but Indians mostly were the ones who died. In some nearby villages, everyone died. In 1832, a third fever season arrived. British botanist David Douglas wrote that nearly everyone at Fort Vancouver came down with fever. HBC brigade trappers took the malaria with them through southern Oregon and on into California. As a consequence of their exposure to white contact, the Willamette Valley Kalapuya population went from 7,785 to 8,780 people (Boyd's estimate) in the 1820s to five to six hundred people by 1841.[33] The hostile reaction of the Umpquas indicates that they also had suffered from the epidemic, although the number of their deaths is unknown. The reappearance of smallpox in the late 1830s, which spread from Alaska to California and then to southern Oregon, at least on the Rogue

River and Umpqua River, most likely was the outbreak that had led to attacks on Fort Umpqua and attempts to burn it down.

In 1854, sub-Indian agent Josiah L. Parrish took a census of Oregon south coast Indians (those living from the Coquille River to Chetco River, and up the Rogue River to its meeting with the Illinois River). He wrote: "They show evident marks of smallpox having been among them about thirty years ago; also the measles, about eighteen years since, both of which were very destructive to them from their mode of treatment [sweating and cold water plunges] … so that many of their once populous villages are now left without a representative."[34] Thirty years before was 1824, and eighteen years earlier was 1836; Boyd's findings suggest that the order should be reversed, measles first and then smallpox.

Lt. Emmons regarded the suffering caused by disease, especially the recent smallpox outbreak, as the major cause of Indian hostility toward his party's "passing through" southern Oregon in 1841. Gagnier was so frightened that he had not left Fort Umpqua for "many days," and he had been on the verge of notifying McLoughlin when the Emmons party arrived.[35] Two former employees of the HBC, who had been living with the Indians, had been killed. The Rogue River Indians had sent word that they were waiting for the Emmons party, and the Umpquas had even prepared to ambush the party at a customary Umpqua River crossing.These preparations by some Indians of southern Oregon to oppose the southward advance of the Emmons party represented a serious deterioration in Indian-white relations. As Lt. Charles Wilkes later noted in his report on the U.S. Exploring Expedition, because the Indians relied on Fort Umpqua for trade goods (ammunition, blankets, tobacco, and other items), they normally were peaceful: "The self-interest of the Indians is … the true safeguard of the white traders."[36] Apparently the recent smallpox epidemic had raised Indian fears of whites to the breaking point, only a year after the visit of the Hines-Lee missionary party.

The fur trappers in Emmons's party were reluctant to move on until the HBC's Southern Party under Laframboise arrived with reinforcements. However, on September 19, Lt. Emmons with full company left Fort Umpqua without the Southern Party. On September 22, the exploring party started up over the Umpqua Mountains. On the south side it passed through burned-over forest. Lt. Wilkes speculated in his expedition report that "the fire had evidently been lighted by the Indians for the purpose of causing the trees to fall across the path; they had also tied some of the branches together and interlocked others."[37] Wilkes showed no awareness of the Indian practice of setting fires to renew forage for deer and elk, which is a more likely explanation for the fires.

One of the scientists in the party, Titian Ramsay Peale II, who was also a painter and the son of famous artist Charles Willson Peale of Philadelphia, discovered that he had lost several items crossing the Umpqua Mountains. When he turned back on the trail, he met several Indians along the way. They were friendly and helped him hunt for his lost possessions. Peale wrote in his diary:

> *These Indians are known by the name of "Rascals," and were the first of the tribe we saw; they have always been considered hostile to the whites, and justly entitled,—though but little intercourse has taken place. They were armed with bows and arrows, (with flint points) with which they kill Elk and Deer, etc which abound in the mountains, but their principal food, to judge the signs must be berries and roots,—they appear to be scattered in small family parties over the country and have no houses, tents or permanent residence, their only shelter being made of grass thatched over hoopes about four feet high and only capable of holding 4-5 persons sitting—or prostrate.*[38]

Despite their guide's characterization of the Rogue River Indians as "the most rascally set in all Oregon," and the earlier warnings of Gagnier, the Indians that the party met along the trail seemed outwardly friendly and quite willing to come into the Americans' camps. The only act of hostility by Rogue River Indians occurred just after the party crossed the Rogue River on September 25. One of the party's hunters, an Indian named Inass or Ignace, reported being attacked by about twenty Indians, but apparently without injury to him. On September 26, the party set out along the south bank of the Rogue River. Indians were seen "spearing salmon from their canoes." Colvocoresses described the canoes as "very rude, and dug out square at the extremes." Peale wrote that they "saw a few Indians behind trees near our path, who finding themselves discovered, came out professing friendship; we saw others and in one place about 50 were together on the bank of the stream up which our path led." That evening two Indians came into their camp. One was dressed in a kind of armored jacket made of "sticks as large as a man's thumb, woven together so closely as to resist the force of arrows." Later, Indians built a fire on the other side of the river and danced and yelled into the night.[39]

On September 27, the party prepared to go past a rocky point along the river (on the south bank across from the west end of present-day Gold Hill), where a "high perpindicular bank confined the path to very narrow limits." The party was armed and ready, and the Indians made no threats of an attack. But after the party had passed the rocky point, they came out of the forest and taunted them in a way that angered the Indian wives of the party's hunters. Lt. Wilkes noted that they "had prepared themselves for an attack, apparently with as much unconcern as their husbands. Michel LaFramboise with his party had been twice assaulted in this place."

Lt. Emmons was impressed by the Indian women's familiarity with firearms. He noted that the women as well as their husbands were armed, and "whenever we came to a bad place, where it was suspected Indians might be lying in wait for us, they took the precaution to examine their flint and priming." On another occasion one of these Indian women also helped the expedition with her knowledge of the country. Emmons related how, when "about half way in our journey … in a mountainous portion of the country, where there was not the least sign of a path or trail to guide us," the men of the party were uncertain which way to go. "Not agreeing, it was finally left to an Indian woman who was the wife of one of the trappers," Emmons wrote. She pointed to a stone that she had left in a tree on an earlier Hudson's Bay Company trip.[40]

A few miles beyond the potential ambush site, the party moved away from the river and crossed over a low rise of hills (no doubt following closely the route of present-day Interstate-5). Beyond lay a valley area on either side of Bear Creek between the Rogue River and the Siskiyou Mountains. Three Indians on horseback fled when the Emmons party approached. The valley was burned over. Peale noticed a number of snares set for deer and rabbits inside hedges of "thorny brush." At the southern end of the valley, the party came upon an Indian woman, "who was so busy setting fire to the prairie & mountain ravines that she seemed to disregard us." She was dressed in a "mantle [cape] of antelope or deer skin, and cup shaped cap, made of rushes," Peale wrote.

"She had a large funnel shaped basket, which they all carry to collect roots and seeds in."[41]

The Emmons party continued to be on the alert for an Indian attack until it crossed over the Siskiyou Mountains and finally reached the Shasta Valley. But the attack never came. In the light of Gagnier's predictions at Fort Umpqua, it is surprising that Emmons' party passed through the Rogue River country without being attacked. It is also surprising that no one in the party killed any Indians. The party made numerous contacts with Indians: men hunting; women collecting roots and setting fires; men fishing for salmon from canoes; and men visiting in camp. All communication with expedition members indicated a desire for peaceful intercourse. At night, however, Indians chanting around a fire across the river and signs of nighttime surveillance made the party apprehensive. During the day the fact that Indians shouted taunts and followed the party in large groups across the river raised fears of a possible attack.

The knowledge that earlier white parties—Turner's party in 1835, Laframboise's party on two occasions—passing through the region had been attacked heightened fear of the Rogue River Indians. Lt. Emmons expressed the prevailing attitude of suspicion when he described Indian declarations of friendship as an element of their "usual mode of attacking parties of whites, in which they have several times been successful … by first straying in and about their camp in large numbers, unarmed, but pretending friendship, and watching for the first favorable opportunity to seize upon and massacre the whole."

And yet the presence of Indian women along the trail seems to suggest that the Rogue River Indians generally were not on a war alert. It is unlikely that the Indians spearing salmon from their canoes were decoys; they rather appear to have been going about the normal fishing activity of September. It is easy to assume from reading Lt. Wilkes's report and the journals of expedition members that the Emmons party was in imminent danger. But it is more likely that the Indian activities that made the expedition fearful were meant as harassment, designed primarily to discourage it from lingering in the Rogue River country and to speed it on its way.

The Americans who visited southern Oregon in 1840-41 had an opportunity to make a new approach to the Indians of southern Oregon. The Hines-Lee and Emmons parties both brought back new information about Indians of the region. But the Methodist missionaries decided they could not afford to put it to work in the development of a new cultural exchange relationship. The Emmons party had a chance to establish initial peaceful contacts on behalf of the American government, as Lewis and Clark did with many Indian groups on their route of exploration not quite forty years earlier. Instead, the party accepted stereotypical views of Rogue River Indians held by HBC fur trappers, and American frontiersmen like Young and Turner. Newly opened windows of opportunity abruptly closed, leaving white relations with the Indians as uncertain as before.

In 1842 Indian-white relations in southern Oregon came under scrutiny in the distant capitol of the United States, as a result of growing enthusiasm for the acquisition of Oregon. U.S. Senator Lewis Fields Linn of Missouri, who introduced a bill to establish an Oregon Territory in 1838 for the first time, tried again in 1841 and 1842.[42] Between 1838 and 1842, supporters of territorial status circulated considerable information about the Oregon Country, much of it, as historian Frances Fuller Victor later wrote, in "a tone of accusation and enmity toward the British fur company."[43] Debate on Sen. Linn's Oregon bill finally began in December 1842, and ended in February 1843; twenty-seven out of fifty senators took part in the debate, indicating lively interest. The bill passed in the Senate, but failed in the House of Representatives. The enmity of Americans toward the HBC focused on the company's occupation of territory that most people insisted belonged by right to the United States. HBC treatment of Indians received attention insofar as it related to Indian interaction with Americans.[44] Some documents supporting the bill were highly critical of HBC activities in Oregon and California, especially excerpts from the journal of Josiah Spaulding, who had been captain of the ship *Lausanne* that brought Methodist missionaries to Oregon in June 1840.[45]

American officer Lt. William A. Slacum had earlier criticized HBC treatment of Indians and charged that the company instigated attacks on whites.[46] McLoughlin responded with denials.[47] A similar critique of HBC treatment of Indians surfaced in a letter from the Reverend Herbert Beaver to the Aborigine's Protection Society of London in

1842.[48] Rev. Beaver served at Fort Vancouver in the period 1836-38, and he made several references in his letter to trappers killing Indians. Captain Spaulding's indictment of the HBC was much longer and more detailed than Slacum's or Beaver's. He praised McLoughlin for being a "gentleman of pleasing address" and "unbounded hospitality," but then went on to excoriate the HBC for its monopolistic control of the Oregon Country's resources and its treatment of the Indians, describing HBC treatment of the Indians south of the Columbia in the harshest terms:

> *They annually send a large party through the acknowledged territory of the United States, to California, to trap beaver and kill sea otter; while in passing through the country, they commit every depredation upon the poor defenceless and peaceful Indians living within the defined and acknowledged jurisdiction of the United States, actually murdering hundreds of them every year; for, in passing through the country of the two tribes, extending from the Umbiquas [Umpquas], in about 44 [degrees] north, to the Chester [Shasta] or Spanish Valley, in 42 [degrees] 50 [minutes], they make it a point of instantly, and without the slightest provocation, to shoot down every Indian they see.*[49]

Spaulding singled out Southern Party leader "Le Fremboiz" [Laframboise] as being "notorious for murdering the Indians above referred to." He continued: "Besides the murders and depredations alluded to, I was informed, upon the best authority, that there is among them [HBC personnel] a leader by the name of John McKey [McKay], and one by the name of Tumen [Turner?], who are distinguished for their cruelties, barbarities, and murders among the Indians, as also are the notorious McCloud [McLeod] and Ewing Young; and these outrages are rendered more criminal and cruel from the fact that these two tribes of Indians are very friendly, and performed many kind offices for the whites."

Despite its inaccuracies and exaggerations, Spaulding's account was taken seriously. He met with U.S. President John Tyler, Secretary of State Daniel Webster, and Sen. Linn. As a result of discussions with these national leaders, Dr. Elijah White received appointment as a sub-

Indian agent for Oregon, four years before the United States and Great Britain agreed by treaty that the Oregon Country should be American and six years before Oregon became a territory.[50]

By 1843 McLoughlin came into possession of the extracts from Spaulding's journal that appeared in the records of the U.S. Congress and wrote a detailed rebuttal to the Governor, Deputy Governor, and Committee of the HBC in London. In it he recounted major episodes of Indian-white conflict as he remembered them.[51] He recalled that in 1820 Thomas McKay explored south of the Willamette Valley and fought with Indians, but he did not recall the number of Indians killed. He mentioned the Jedediah Smith expedition, although he mistakenly cited 1829 instead of 1828 as the year of Smith's arrival at the Umpqua River. He described what happened to Smith's party and the aid given to him following the massacre. He noted that Alexander McLeod made his first trip to California and returned "without having had any quarrel with the Indians, except at Rogue's River," where Indians had helped themselves to food out of the McLeod party's kettles. McLeod's men wanted "to punish them for their impudence," but McLeod prevented them from doing so. McLoughlin blamed McLeod's "humanity and forbearance" for future trouble with the Rogues. He noted the attack by Rogue River Indians on the Turner party of 1835 (which McLoughlin mistakenly dated to 1832), and the killing of two Indians by Ewing Young's party. Finally, McLoughlin mentioned an unverified incident that occurred two years later in which "16 white men from the Wallamette Settlement accompanied by a number of Indian followers, in travelling towards California, were way-laid and attacked in a difficult mountain pass."

Except for incidents involving the Thomas McKay party in 1820 and McLeod's party in 1830, McLoughlin described incidents that did not involve the HBC. His rebuttal placed the responsibility for serious confrontations and loss of life on American parties traveling through southern Oregon. McLoughlin defended Laframboise, declaring that when "he did fight, it was because, he was obligated to do so in self defence, and in punishing the wrong others had suffered." McLeod, according to McLoughlin, had been involved in only one punitive expedition, against the Clallam Indians on Hoods Canal.[52] McLoughlin even defended the American, Ewing Young: "I never heard of his having acted, so as to deserve the character, Captain Spaulding, gives him."[53] In rebutting the speech made by Sen. Linn in January 1843,

McLoughlin argued that the HBC had been of enormous benefit to the Americans seeking to settle in the Oregon Country, especially in relation to the Indians:

> *Having by our system of management, and protracted intercourse, subdued the ferocity of the Indian tribes, converted their former hostility against the whites into feelings of respect and attachment, introduced order, and a respect for property, and moral obligation which did not before exist among them, in short we have the merit of having reclaimed them from a state of barbarism to comparative civilization, and of having established our amicable relations with them, on so firm a basis, that the British or American Government have only to send an Officer with a Commission in his pocket, to have their authority acknowledged and maintained.*[54]

McLoughlin acknowledged that these conditions existed where the HBC had established its forts and drawn the Indians into the fur trade. But this had not occurred south of the Umpqua and only minimally to the west along the Umpqua River and Oregon south coast. Therefore, although his claim to having benefited the Oregon Country had a certain general validity north of the Columbia River and east to the Rocky Mountains, it had scant justification in southern Oregon.

Although McLoughlin successfully rebutted the wilder charges of Spaulding and Linn, his defense of McLeod, Laframboise, and the Southern Party that made regular passage through southern Oregon to California in the years 1832-43 left some unanswered questions. How often had the Southern Party resorted to punitive actions? How many Indian lives had been taken in southern Oregon and northern California? From HBC reports, we can estimate the approximate number of Indians killed by HBC personnel. McLoughlin took note of McKay's probable killing of an unknown number of Umpqua Indians in 1820. On his 1829-30 expedition to California, McLeod mentioned a "resort to arms" by his men to protect their traps from the Rogue River Indians, but he made no report of Indians killed. Once in California, however, he reported seven or eight Pitt River Indians killed and another seventeen to twenty Indians killed.[55] In 1832, a punitive expedition against the "Killamook [Tillamook] Indians" led by Laframboise took six Indian lives.[56] In 1834, John Work intercepted a report from Laframboise concerning the killing of eleven Indians south of the Umpqua Mountains.[57] In 1837, while passing through the Sacramento Valley, the American, Philip L. Edwards, heard stories from Indians that HBC trappers had been killing Indians.[58] These scattered reports (not including ambiguous ones) add up to about forty-five Indians actually reported killed by HBC personnel in Oregon and California (seventeen in Oregon and twenty-eight in California).[59]

In view of the frustrations in trapping that Ogden's and McLeod's journals reveal, it is probably reasonable to assume that additional Indians were killed in individual encounters between fur trappers and Indians. The total number killed is probably much fewer than Spaulding's charge that hundreds of Indians were being killed by the HBC Southern party "each year." But enough Indians lost their lives in skirmishes with HBC brigade personnel, in addition to probably even more deaths from epidemic diseases, to create hostility toward the HBC among the Indians of southern Oregon and northern California. By comparison, reported killings of Indians in southern Oregon by the American parties of Young and Turner in the 1830s numbered about twelve. In the period 1826-43, Oregon Indians south of the Columbia River were reported to have taken the lives of six HBC personnel and nineteen Americans (fifteen of whom were members of the Jedediah Smith expedition).

THE CONSEQUENCES of HBC failure to establish "amicable relations" with the Indians of southern Oregon became increasingly apparent as more and more Americans migrated to Oregon. McLoughlin's spirited rebuttal of charges that HBC fur brigades indiscriminately murdered Indians south of the Columbia closed a chapter in white relations with the Indians of southern Oregon. The last of the Southern Party fur-trapping expeditions to California left and returned in 1843. From then on, the Indians of southern Oregon would have to deal mostly with American pioneers and the mixed nationalities of gold miners.

Young Lansford W. Hastings, who, along with Dr. Elijah White, led the first major emigrant party to Oregon in 1842, described what Oregon looked like a year later. The initial center of American settlement was a Methodist mission station located about fifty miles upriver from the falls of the Willamette River. Here Jason Lee presided over a community consisting of about fourteen detached buildings and several large farms, each consisting of several hundred acres under cultivation. At the time, thirty or forty Indian children attended the mission school. About a hundred families were settled on non-mission lands nearby. Hastings estimated that the combined Willamette Valley population of Americans, Canadians, and mixed-bloods or *métis* was about four thousand. At the falls of the Willamette River, the town of Oregon City had grown to "fifty three buildings ... among which, were four stores, four mills, two of which were flouring mills, one public-house, one black smith's shop and various other mechanic's shops." Most of the houses in Oregon city were "with a few exceptions, framed and well-finished." In the surrounding countryside most of the buildings were of log construction. Everywhere, Hastings saw signs of growth and progress stimulated by the arrival of new emigrants over the Oregon Trail. Within seven years the white population in the Willamette Valley would expand to about ten thousand, and new emigrants would be redirected to outlying valleys like those in southern Oregon.[60]

From 1843 until 1846, several parties passed between the expanding Oregon settlements and California. In May 1843, Hastings left Oregon for California with an emigrant party of fifty-three persons that included twenty-five armed men. When the party reached the Rogue River, it was assisted in crossing by Indians who, as Hastings noted, "proffered their aid, which we were under the necessity of accepting." Hastings ordered twelve men to go to the south bank to receive the baggage, while the others remained with women and children. Meanwhile, Indians in "great numbers ... thronged around" the party, "frequently rushing upon us, in such a manner, that it became necessary for us to draw our forces out, in battle array, against them ... discharging a gun or two occasionally, in the open air, in order to deter them from any further hostile movements."[61] This caused them to fall back, but then they crowded around again. Hastings viewed this as a tactic to "produce general confusion and disorder," during which time items could be stolen or the party overpowered and killed. No harm, however, came of these mob scenes, and the party passed on.

Several days later Hastings' party met "cattle drovers and emigrants" heading north from California to Oregon. Joel P. Walker, who with his family had accompanied the Emmons exploring party to California in 1841, led this party. He was returning to Oregon with a herd of twelve hundred cattle, two hundred horses, and six hundred sheep. As a result of unfavorable reports about California from Walker's men, about a third of the California-bound Hastings party emigrants turned back to Oregon.[62]

Two years later, in 1845, the ex-mountain man James Clyman led a party of thirty-five men, a woman, and three children through southern Oregon without incident. However, Clyman's party heeded Walker: "Be careful to never Let any Indians come amongst you" and "Keep careful watch both day and night." When they reached the "Clamet or Rogues River," Indians came to their camp but they were kept out. Clyman wrote in his journal: "nothing short of a cocked rifle would prevent them" [from coming into camp]. But, he noted, "we succeeded to keep them back without violence and they sung their war songs in hearing of our camp all night." Clyman commented on the limited food resources available to Indians of the Rogue River Valley: "no game," "but few roots," and acorns plentiful in some years but not in others.[63]

The Walker, Hastings, and Clyman parties seem to have had no significant impact on the Indians of southern Oregon. But in 1846 a party of fifteen men captained by Jesse Applegate passed through the Rogue River Valley in search of a southern alternative to the Snake River-Columbia River route for new settlers entering Oregon.[64] Their route went southeast from the Rogue River Valley over the Cascades, south of Klamath Lake, and into the Humboldt River country of northern Nevada. This became known by the names Southern Route, Scott-Applegate Road, and Applegate Trail. The Applegate Trail opened the Rogue River Valley and the rest of southern Oregon to a small but steady stream of American settlers in the late 1840s and early 1850s. After 1846, the Indians of southern Oregon had to contend with an ever-increasing number of white settlers looking for a shortcut to the Willamette Valley.

The Applegate party experienced what had become almost a routine or standard reception from the Rogue River Indians. Lindsay Applegate, recalling this trip in 1877, wrote: "As we advanced towards the river [Rogue River; approaching from the north], the Indians in large numbers occupied the river bank near where the trail crossed." The party, however, took special precautions to be on guard, and the Indians watched the river crossing from concealment without attacking. "After crossing," Lindsay Applegate said, "we turned up the river, and the Indians in large numbers came out of the thickets on the opposite side and tried in every way to provoke us."[65] Some Indians were on foot, some were mounted on horses, and they followed the party along the river. Later that evening, the Applegate party saw signal fires on the mountains to the east. In his later reminiscence, Applegate recalled that a large party of about eighty French Canadians and Indians that had preceded the Applegate party on the trail had come under attack and had horses stolen. Charles E. Pickett, an American who rode with the Canadians, told a different story only a year after the incident. He recalled that the Canadians had burned an Indian village and shot at Indians. Pickett claimed that he had "strongly censured" those who took this action.[66] In any case, Lindsay Applegate attributed his party's minor trouble with Rogue River Indians to a "proper degree of caution" and "proper care."[67] The Applegate party of fifteen men was one of the smaller parties to pass through the Rogue River Valley. But Lindsay Applegate's description of his party's reception seems identical to earlier descriptions by HBC fur-brigade leaders and by members of the Emmons party.

When white parties reached the Rogue River, Indians turned out in large numbers (groups approaching one hundred or more). From what we know of village sizes and locations along the Rogue River, this probably means that Indians from several villages showed up. Their first objective was to demonstrate their presence; the second to enter white encampments. Where it proved impossible to get close to the white parties, they followed at a distance. Their demonstrations from the north shore of the Rogue River—yelling, perhaps obscene gestures, and the like—impressed white parties as expressions of hostility. Signal fires and "war dances" in the night were similarly threatening. Occasionally, horses were stolen, but only rarely did white travelers report an open attack. Notably, except in the case of the HBC's Southern Party in the late 1830s, there was apparently no effort on either side to talk or negotiate.

Whites feared being attacked and killed, but as Lindsay Applegate wisely observed, this need not, and in most cases did not, happen. Lt. Emmons's and James Clyman's observations that white safety depended upon the Indians' lack of firearms was only partially correct; it did not protect the Turner party. The actual probability of attack was relatively small if white parties kept Indians out of their camps, maintained a ready guard, and traveled in companies with at least fifteen to twenty men.

The 1846 emigration on the Southern Route through the Rogue River Valley in early October 1846 was made up of ninety to a hundred wagons and four hundred fifty to five hundred persons. The first 1846 emigrants reached the Rogue River Valley on about October 11; the slower emigrants arrived about a week later. It took the lead emigrants from October 12 to 16 to pass through the Rogue River Valley from present-day Ashland to Grants Pass. The emigrants crossed the Rogue River approximately four and a half miles downstream from or west of Grants Pass (near the mouth of Vannoy Creek). This was the site of the later Perkins, Long, and, finally, Vannoy ferry.[68]

One can only imagine what impression this made on the Indians of the Rogue River Valley, because there are no documented Indian accounts. Several effects are evident from the white emigrant journals. The cattle posed a new threat to Indian food resources. The emigrants found good grass for their cattle; and because the trail through the valley followed along Emigrant Creek and Bear Creek, this 1846 emigration must have begun the process of disturbing camas-root gathering areas in the wet lowlands of the valley. Indians observed and followed the emigrants through the valley, but at a distance. Emigrant J. Quinn Thornton referred in his diary to "a great many hostile savages." Virgil K. Pringle in his diary wrote: "Plenty of Indians about, but none come near." He noted that they lost some cattle to the Indians; another family had twenty-five sheep stolen, but otherwise the 1846 passage through the Rogue River Valley occurred without any incidents of violence.[69]

The 1846 emigrants on the Southern Route experienced their greatest trouble before reaching the Rogue River Valley, while crossing the territory of the Modoc Indians along the present-day Oregon-California border at the north end of Tule Lake. The Modocs took ten cattle from one emigrant party, and killed one man who had become separated from the rest of his group. The whites killed two Indians in recovering the cattle. Pioneer Tolbert Carter, years later, recalled that he and a group of nine other white men came upon "five Indian houses," which they destroyed: "Everything ... was destroyed—pots, kettles, mats, baskets .... Some baskets which we destroyed were full of some kind of seeds ... we spilled the seed and destroyed the baskets." For emigrants to Oregon over the Southern Route, this was only the beginning of hostile encounters with the Modocs of northern California.[70]

The worst stretch of the Southern Route or Applegate Trail for the 1846 emigrants came after leaving the Rogue River Valley and just before reaching the Willamette Valley.The lead party in 1846 took from October 25 to 29 to get through a stretch between Canyon Creek Pass and Canyonville that became known simply as the Canyon, a distance of sixteen miles. Nature rather than Indians challenged the emigrants' endurance. Tabitha Brown recalled in 1854 that "of hundreds of wagons [that went through the Canyon] but one came through without breaking." Other accounts testify to the suffering described by Tabitha Brown: "Some people were in Canyon two and three weeks before they could get through; some died without any warning from fatigue and starvation; others ate the flesh of the cattle that were lying dead by the wayside."[71]

After getting through the Canyon, John Newton was killed and his possessions taken by several Umpqua Indians. Tabitha Brown mentioned another man who was killed by Indians on the Applegate "cutoff," but she does not indicate where he was killed. Virgil Pringle's experience with the Umpquas, however, was notably friendly. He wrote in his diary that after crossing the North Fork of the Umpqua River near present-day Winchester his party met some Indians and from them got "six venison hams, a great relief to our minds." A few days later he got "3 deer and a salmon from the Indians." He does not tell what he gave or was asked to give in exchange. Thomas Holt, who went out to bring food and help the emigrants struggling toward the Willamette Valley from the Canyon, bargained hard with Indians on the North Umpqua for their help in river crossing.[72]

The Southern Route or "cutoff" received a great deal of attention as the 1846 emigrants straggled into the Willamette Valley. Many of them narrowly escaped starvation because of relief parties that went out to meet them. Newspapers compared the Southern Route with the Barlow Road around the south side of Mount Hood, and called attention to the possibilities of settlement in the Rogue and Umpqua River valleys. In 1847 Levi Scott led a party of twenty to thirty men east over the Southern Route to guide emigrants to the Willamette Valley. Four wagon trains and a total of seventy-two wagons probably followed the Southern Route to the Willamette Valley that year.[73]

In 1848 a party of twenty-three men led by Isaac Pettijohn went east over the Southern Route, but, by late July, news of the discovery of gold in California prompted a rush of Oregon men south. Peter

Burnett left for California in September along with about one hundred fifty men and forty-six wagons; another group of twenty-five men and twenty wagons from north of the Columbia River followed. The only westward-bound group of emigrants, under Peter Lassen's lead, turned south into California from Goose Lake. In 1849, the Applegate Trail, from the Humboldt River to Goose Lake, was heavily used, but then gold seekers cut south into California. That year thirty men, intending to supply a party of mounted riflemen headed for Oregon, went south on the Applegate Trail into northwestern Nevada with fourteen wagons and sixty beef cattle. But there is no record of emigrants using the Southern Route to come to Oregon in either 1849 or 1850.[74]

This chronology indicates that in 1846 and 1847, the years of heaviest emigration on the Southern Route, about eight to nine hundred persons (a conservative estimate of five persons per wagon) and one hundred sixty to one hundred seventy wagons with the oxen to pull them, as well as additional cattle, passed through southern Oregon. It is difficult to estimate the number of oxen and cattle in each wagon train. But typically each wagon was pulled by two yoke of oxen or four oxen altogether (four mules might also be used, but oxen were more common). However, families would normally have one or more extra yoke of oxen. Virgil Pringle, who followed the Southern Route, bought "two teams [two yoke of oxen?] and 5 head of loose stock." On reaching Tule Lake, Pringle counted fifty wagons in his wagon train. Modoc Indians drove off some of the cattle in the wagon train, and Pringle and others spent the day rounding them up again. All but ten head of cattle were recovered.[75]

From Pringle's remarks about the incident, one can infer that a loss of ten head of cattle was slight. This suggests that the number of oxen and cattle must have numbered an average of six to eight per family, a total of three to four hundred cattle in Pringle's wagon train. Horses and mules would be in addition to this figure. If this estimate of oxen and cattle per wagon is applied to the total number of wagons for the years 1846 and 1847, then, as a conservative estimate, probably thirteen to fourteen hundred oxen and cattle passed through the Rogue River Valley in those years. In 1848, an estimated sixty-six wagons went through southern Oregon. At eight oxen or mules per wagon, this would total more than five hundred animals. In 1849 another fourteen wagons, or one hundred twelve oxen and mules, and an additional sixty head of cattle came over the Applegate Trail. This amounts to a total of about two thousand oxen, mules, and cattle. Probably another one to two hundred horses (belonging to approximately eighty to one hundred mounted horsemen) passed through southern Oregon along the Applegate Trail and the Oregon-California Trail in the years 1846 through 1849. Although few contacts with Indians were recorded, the large number of white people and animals must have greatly deepened a sense of uncertainty about the future among Indians of the region.

Despite the uncertainty of encounters between whites and Indians in the 1830s-1840s, the surprising fact is that violence was intermittent and limited in scale. No incident of contact led to an explosive act of retaliation on the scale of the Smith expedition massacre of 1828. At the same time, no close personal relationships were established between whites and Indians to create a middle-ground of continuing relations. Indians seemed interested in speeding whites on their way, and whites were happy to get through the region without being attacked. The only missionary effort to make contact with southern Oregon Indians, on the Umpqua River, ended in a quick retreat. But the pioneering of a southern route for white settlers through the region, together with the spread of the 1849 gold rush in northern California to the Rogue River Valley, soon encouraged some settlers to stop there rather than continue on to the Willamette Valley. The need to protect gold miners and settlers from Indian attacks led in the early 1850s to the first middle-ground relations since the establishment of fur-trade ties between the HBC and coastal Indians.

Chapter 3

First Negotiations and Peacemaking, 1850-52

AS EMIGRATION increased over the Southern Route, chances for contacts between Indians and whites, and for misunderstandings and violence, multiplied. The HBC no longer sent fur brigades into southern Oregon, the Oregon Provisional Government lacked any regular military or police forces, and the U.S. government still had not posted any troops to the region. In August 1846, the editor of the *Oregon Spectator*, Henry A. G. Lee, wrote that "difficulties between the whites and natives are constantly increasing and gradually assuming a more serious aspect."[1] However, these very difficulties, because they involved increased contacts between the two groups, also provided an opportunity for the development of middle-ground relationships between Indians and whites. This chapter highlights this development through the interpersonal ties of several Indian chiefs with white leaders and pioneers. But before a middle ground could emerge in southern Oregon, Oregon's new white settlers had to pass through a major crisis in Indian-white relations to the east.

The *Oregon Spectator*, then the only newspaper in Oregon, contained frequent, short editorial notes and letters to the editor about Indian difficulties. When viewed collectively, they provide a clue to the attitudes of the growing white population of Oregon. In June-July 1846, trouble between settlers and Molalla Indians resulted in formation of a white volunteer militia company, one of many to be formed in the next decade. In early August an Indian was killed and several wounded by settlers in the upper Willamette Valley and lower Columbia areas because Indians were killing settlers' cattle. An incident that resulted in loss of an Indian's life for "the loss of a Spanish cow," editor Lee believed, was excessive compensation. Lee conjured up for his readers a "horrid picture … of human butchery and bloodshed, to which a system of unscrupulous retaliation and revenge is rapidly tending." Although Lee's editorial indicated the seriousness of recent violent incidents, it also presented a pro-Indian point of view that encouraged middle-ground accommodation.[2]

News that the U. S. government planned to terminate its agreement with Great Britain on joint occupancy of Oregon drew attention to the issue of Indian title to the land. Governor George Abernethy pleaded with the Oregon Provisional Government legislature for help in protecting Indian villages from being overrun by unscrupulous settlers. "Cannot some way be devised, by which their villages can be surveyed, and stakes set, inside of which boundary the white man may not be permitted to enter and build?" he asked.[3]

When emigrants, who had come over the Southern Route, arrived in the Willamette Valley in fall of 1846, they reported on difficulties of the route itself, but they also mentioned several incidents of Indian hostility.[4] In early 1847, an anonymous correspondent to the *Oregon Spectator* warned against travel on the Southern Route, because "Indians along the route not being dependent upon any trading establishment, have nothing to restrain them from the exercise of their natural disposition to plunder."[5] Another writer, Charles E. Pickett, told those who passed through the Rogue River-Siskiyou Mountain region to "use your pleasure in spilling blood ." He advised that "were I traveling with you, from this [the Siskiyou Mountains] on to your first sight of the Sacramento valley, my only communication with these treacherous, cowardly and untameable rascals, would be through my rifle."[6] Shortly after this, Pickett was appointed by President James K. Polk to be Indian agent for Oregon, However, another writer who sympathized with the Indians for religious reasons, countered that these "poor people, howbeit low in the scale of humanity" deserved protection, and urged the legislature to pass laws specifically for their defense.[7]

How many Oregon settlers believed, as this latter writer did, in philanthropy for the Indians? In fact, among the educated and religious white pioneers, quite a few did, judging from journals, letters, government documents, and newspaper correspondence. In the 1840s, the United States as a whole showed interest in various movements of reform, involving such issues as temperance, women's rights, and abolition. Concern for the plight of Indians, as historian Francis Paul Prucha has pointed out, was a natural extension of these Protestant evangelical and reform interests. Reform-minded Christians believed in the possibility of civilizing and making Christians out of Indians.[8] And those who did not believe in philanthropy for the Indians at least realized that treating them fairly would pose the least danger to themselves. Frances Fuller Victor, pioneer historian of the Indian wars in the Oregon Country, noted that Oregon pioneers understood that the Indians would seek revenge "upon any person of the white race" when whites killed Indians.[9]

In 1847 the temporary appointment of Pickett as an Indian agent for Oregon brought the question of tough versus humane Indian policy to the forefront of public debate. Pickett was forced to give up his appointment in the face of opposition from Oregon pioneers who wanted peace not war with Indians. The Oregon Provisional Government legislature turned over responsibility for Indian affairs to Governor George Abernethy, and he in turn to Henry A. G. Lee.[10]

But Indian affairs, especially regarding land issues, required federal action. In late 1847, Peter H. Burnett, George L. Curry, and L. A. Rice petitioned the U. S. Congress to extend U. S. government jurisdiction over Oregon.[11] The petition referred most directly to the Indians of the Willamette Valley, where white settlers were concentrated and the Indian population had been reduced to a small remnant, but it addressed the major concern of all Indians: they expected compensation for lands they gave up. Their rapidly declining numbers from diseases transmitted by white people made them fearful that they would never receive compensation. The petitioners seemed impressed by Indian restraint. They had "sympathy" for a "doomed race of men," but only for men at peace, not war. Uppermost in their minds was the possibility of a general war between Indians and whites.

The major crisis in Indian-white relations that white settlers had feared came on November 29, 1847, when Cayuse Indians (in what became eastern Washington) sought revenge for many deaths their people had recently suffered from an epidemic of measles brought by white emigrants passing through on the Oregon Trail. The Cayuse attacked the Waiilatpu mission station (near present-day Walla Walla) run by Marcus and Narcissa Whitman, killing the Whitmans and eleven other men and boys. Women and girls at the station were taken prisoner; they were later released after the HBC's Peter Skene Ogden negotiated a ransom payment. Although the location of this event was hundreds of miles from the Willamette Valley and southern Oregon, it struck fear into the hearts of white pioneers near and far.

Oregon's Provisional Government legislature immediately authorized Governor Abernethy to raise a "company of riflemen, not to exceed fifty men" to protect a mission station at The Dalles, and a regiment of up to five hundred riflemen to retaliate against the Cayuse.[12] It "empowered" Jesse Applegate, A. L. Lovejoy, and George L. Curry to negotiate a loan with the HBC to pay the cost of preparing for war against the Cayuse. In addition to raising a volunteer military expedition to deal with the Indian threat east of the Cascades, the legislature also authorized the governor to appoint a delegation consisting of Joel Palmer, Robert Newell, and Henry A. G. Lee to negotiate with the hostile Indians. It also prohibited sale of firearms and ammunition to Indians. (This act was modified in 1849 because, according to historian Frances Fuller Victor, it was seen "as unjust to a people which lived by the chase, and whose sustenance was being cut off by the spoilations of the superior race."[13] Scarcity of game made it difficult for the Indians in the Willamette Valley to survive without firearms for hunting.) These military, diplomatic, and trade initiatives demonstrated the Oregon legislature's fear that Indians of the Oregon Country might follow up the massacre at Waiilatpu with a general uprising against whites on both sides of the Cascades.

These various actions had no direct effect on the Indians of southern Oregon, but they created a new climate of concern about Indians among whites, and they gave pioneer leaders experience in dealing with Indians that would influence later relations with those in southern Oregon. The muster rolls for the Cayuse War show that approximately 1,122 men served in some capacity as members of the volunteer companies organized in 1847 and 1848.[14] The mobilization of such a large force served as an introduction to organized warfare against Indians, and it made mobilization against southern Oregon Indians easier a few years later.

The immediate object of the military expedition and peace negotiations was to gain custody of the Cayuse responsible for the deaths at the Waiilatpu mission; but the volunteer militia forces met with little success. Shortage of funds made it difficult to put and keep volunteers in the field, despite a wave of new volunteers in the spring of 1848, and by July 5 the first regiment of Oregon riflemen had been discharged. Joseph Lane, the newly appointed governor for the Oregon Territory, who reached Oregon in March 1849, negotiated with Indian tribes east of the Cascades to get their assistance in capturing the murderers of the Whitmans. In the spring of the next year, five Cayuse, under pressure from their own people, voluntarily turned themselves over to military authorities, claiming to be the parties responsible for the 1847 massacre.[15]

These five Cayuse were brought to trial in Oregon City in May 1850, two hundred miles from the scene of the Waiilatpu massacre. The trial was important both as the first formal trial in the Oregon Territory, and as the first formal trial of Indians. It opened with a full panoply of court officials—a clerk and his deputy, three defense lawyers, a United States prosecuting attorney, two interpreters (of English, Cayuse, and Chinook Jargon), and Judge Orville C. Pratt. Judge Pratt had read and practiced law in New York and Illinois, and he had an appointment as territorial judge from President Polk. After the five accused Indians pleaded not guilty, a jury of twelve white men was finally selected, but only after defense lawyers excluded twenty others. The defense argued that no one could prove that the defendants were the killers of the Whitman mission victims, that the testimony of witnesses was confusing, and that the deaths of their women and children from disease had provoked Cayuse warriors to their rash action. The jury was not convinced by these arguments and it found the Indians guilty; they were hung, as other Indians accused of killing whites were in following years.[16]

THE GENERAL HEIGHTENING of tension between Indians and whites in the Oregon Country because of the Whitman massacre coincided with the discovery of gold in California, which increased traffic through southern Oregon. After two years of heavy emigration to the Willamette Valley over the Southern Route, hundreds of Oregon men passed through southern Oregon in the fall of 1848 on their way to the gold fields in California. Peter Burnett, who started for the gold fields in September 1848, later estimated that "at least two thirds of the male population of Oregon, capable of bearing arms, started for California in the summer and fall of 1848."[17] Burnett traveled in a company of one hundred fifty men and fifty wagons and ox-teams. He made no mention of contact with Indians while passing through southern Oregon.

In the spring of 1850, Indians attacked some white miners on their way back to the Willamette Valley from California. The attack occurred at a place called Rock Point on the south side of the Rogue River and opposite the west end of present-day Gold Hill. While the miners defended themselves, the Indians drove off their gold-dust-laden pack animals. The returning miners, stripped of their wealth, sought the help of Joseph Lane. Lane, who had resigned as governor of the Oregon Territory, organized a party of twelve to fifteen whites, and an equal number of Klickitat Indians, to try to recover the miners' gold before going on to the California gold fields. This led to the first peace negotiations with southern Oregon Indians and to the beginning of a brief but significant period of middle-ground relationships between Indians and whites in southern Oregon.[18]

When Lane and his party reached the Rogue River, he told the first Indians he met that he wanted to talk with their chief. Two days later about a hundred Indians, led by Takelma chief Apserkahar, came to meet with him. As Lane later told the story, the Indians formed a semicircle on one side, and Lane and his men positioned themselves opposite them. Just as the two groups had taken their places in the circle, Lane recalled that "a party of about seventy five warriors came marching down on our side of the River all armed with bows and arrows except some twenty who carried guns in their hands."[19] Despite the tense moment, Lane persuaded them to put down their weapons and join the other Indians. Then Lane spoke and promised that Indian rights would be protected "as long as they would keep good faith, that our people must pass and repass through their country in peace and safety." Chief Apserkahar spoke next. Whatever he said, it caused his men to jump up as though they were about to attack Lane's party. Klickitat Indian chief Quatley, who was an enemy of the Rogue River Indians, immediately seized Apserkahar and held a knife to his throat. Lane, with revolver in hand, stepped forward to the line of Indian warriors and ordered them to sit down again. The meeting ended shortly after, but Apserkahar was taken prisoner. With this tense breakdown of negotiations, a special interpersonal relationship between Lane and Chief Apserkahar had its beginning.

Apserkahar was held prisoner for two days, and finally agreed to sign a peace treaty, his first experience with the white man's insistence on written documents. During these two days, the chief developed a genuine affection for Lane. When Apserkahar's first wife asked to see her husband, Lane invited her into camp and responded positively to her "conjugal affection." He also came to appreciate her influence: "She was a squaw of more than ordinary inteligence and exercised considerable influence among her people." The chief asked to adopt Lane's name, and Lane agreed that he could use his first name. From then on Chief Apserkahar became known to whites as Chief Jo (Lane's spelling) or Joe (the spelling most commonly used by historians). He also asked Lane to give names to his first wife and his two children, so Lane renamed his wife Sally and his children Ben and Mary. In return for these name gifts, the chief gave Lane a young Modoc slave boy. Named John by Lane, he became his personal servant and later saved Lane's life during an Indian raid in the California gold fields.[20]

Joseph Lane's negotiation of a peace treaty with Chief Joe and his development of a personal relationship with the chief and his family in June 1850 was a unique event in the history of relations between Indians and whites in southern Oregon.[21] It was the first of many interpersonal relationships that would develop between Indians and whites over the next several years, creating a middle-ground between Indian and white worlds. Lane's relations with Chief Joe and his family provide us with a glimpse into the personal life of a southern Oregon Indian family.

What made this relationship possible? Joseph Lane's background and reputation give us part of the answer. Lane (1801-81) was an enormously popular man in his lifetime. Born in North Carolina, he moved westward to Kentucky with his family as a young boy. At twenty-one he settled in Indiana, and there he served for many years in the Indiana legislature and as an officer in the state militia. This was the beginning of a career that made him a western man of military and political qualities in the heroic vein of Andrew Jackson. He established a military reputation as a bold, fighting general in the Mexican-American War. This led to his appointment as Oregon's first territorial governor and his election in the 1850s as Oregon's territorial delegate to Congress. Biographer James E. Hendrickson has summarized Lane's personal qualities as those of "a man of humble origins and simple ways, a man whose folksy mannerisms and bluff good cheer made him popular in Congress and the departments."[22]

When the Democratic party split over the issue of slavery expansion in 1860, the National (or Southern) Democrats nominated Lane as the vice-presidential running mate of presidential nominee John C. Breckinridge. Southerners would not have nominated him if he had not shared their paternalistic ideology toward slaves and Indians. Paternalism toward Indians was equally characteristic of northern Indian reformers who advocated a reservation policy. In dealing with

Joseph Lane. (Oregon Historical Society, OrHi 1703)

Chief Joe and his family, Lane acted as a father figure, a role that fit his personality and the prevailing white ideology of Indian-white relations.[23]

The Takelma chief was an equal player in this relationship by asking for the gift of Lane's name. The adoption of a new name is a well-documented event in the history of acculturation. Non-English immigrants to this country adopted new names to make their identities easier to grasp. African slaves received new names from their U.S. masters in the early years of slavery; and later, when slaves were encouraged to become Christians, native-born slaves were given biblical names. The renaming of Indians by whites also was a common phenomenon in the history of Indian-white relations. Historian James Axtell has pointed out that Indians saw an advantage in taking an English name. Most importantly, it could improve trade opportunities with whites, even if, as Axtell comments, "around their own fires they were still known by their Indian names."

Early anthropologists gathered little information about naming among the Rogue River Takelmas. More is known about naming customs among neighboring Klamaths and Shastas, which perhaps is suggestive of Takelma customs. Among the Klamaths, there was no difficulty adding an anglicized name to existing Indian names. Anthropologist-historian Theodore Stern explains that "it had been native practice to use age terms for the very young … and to employ relationship terms when addressing kinsmen and occasional names in referring to others." A person might, in fact, have several "occasional names." Among Shastas, personal names usually had reference to a characteristic of the child or of a relative for whom the child was named. Although more distant from the Takelma than either the Klamath or Shasta people, Clackamas Indians, according to anthropologist Melville Jacobs, regarded the names of powerful tribal leaders as possessing special power. In discussing the Clackamas myth, "Fire and His Son's Son," Jacobs remarks that "a certain kind of spirit-power connects with the pronunciation of a name of a very wealthy and supernaturally powerful man." Jacobs also reminds us that Clackamas Indians believed that people and spirit-powers existed in cooperative relationships with each other. From this perspective, it is probable that Chief Joe viewed Joseph Lane's name as possessing special power deriving from Lane's personal courage and status as a white leader.[24]

Lane's account of his naming of the Takelma chief and his family shows no evidence that he understood the significance of names and naming among Northwest Indians. His story of the incident fits a white paternalistic view of Indian-white relations. But the reality of this event for the chief was surely different. It established a personal tie between Lane and himself, his family, and his people. It may have been seen as an act of reciprocation for the treaty agreement he made with Lane. In receiving Lane's name, he gained access, in a magical or spiritual sense, to Lane's personal power. This would be of tangible value to him in his relations with whites as well as his own people. Lane understood that he and other whites would benefit from this personal bond between himself and Chief Joe and his family; but he probably did not understand the exchange value of his name as a source of spiritual and therefore political power.

Lane's naming of Chief Joe and his family gave the peace treaty of 1850 with the Rogue River Indians a personal foundation. But how binding could one expect such a treaty to be? Would the personal tie between the two men be strong enough to create a larger middle-ground for Indians and whites generally?

Historian James P. Ronda calls attention to a difference between Indian and white points of view about making peace. He notes that Lewis and Clark failed to understand plains Indian politics: "In a world where 'peace' meant 'truce' and where warriors fought one day and traded the next, Lewis and Clark were simply unable and sometimes unwilling to face the facts of native life."[25] Lane had intervened in a dispute between Rogue River Indians and a group of white miners passing through their country. According to Takelma customs, the resolution of disputes occurred through negotiations that led to the payment of compensation for injuries. While Lane personalized his relationship to Chief Joe, he treated his negotiations with him as a process leading to permanent resolution of differences between Rogue River Indians and whites passing through their territory. It is unlikely that the chief and his people regarded the negotiations in such terms. Their willingness to keep the peace would only last until the next individual act of injury against them. In this sense, it seems likely that they regarded the peace agreement with Lane as a truce rather than a permanent peace. But even if Chief Joe and his people had interpreted the peace agreement with Lane as something more than a truce, how capable was he of controlling the Indians inhabiting the Rogue River Valley? Lane assumed that Chief Joe could speak for the Rogue River Valley Indians, but what was their relationship to him and his to them?

By the summer of 1850, when Lane met with Chief Joe, whites recognized four major divisions among the Indians of southern Oregon and northern California: Umpquas, Klamaths, Rogues, and Shastas. Alonzo A. Skinner was the first person to take out a donation land claim in the Rogue River Valley (near present-day Central Point), and the first to become a local Indian agent. In September 1851, he distributed "presents" to the "Umpqua band of the Rogue's River Indians," the "Shasta band of Rogue's River Indians," and the main group of Rogue River Indians or Takelmas under chiefs Joe and Sam (Toquahear, also called Kokohawah). Skinner mentioned different bands of Indians living on Grave Creek, on the main stem of the Rogue River, and at the foot of the Siskiyou Mountains. He identified at least two separate bands of Shastas. He also reported a favorable impression of the two Takelma chiefs and their willingness to keep their people at peace: "I have no doubt they will use all their influence to keep their people quiet." Chief Joe was known as a peace chief and Chief Sam as a war chief, although both had led attacks on whites.[26]

Chiefs Joe and Sam headed a village at the Big Bar of the Rogue River near Lower Table Rock. An 1854 census listed eight different bands in the Rogue River Valley district (which included the Applegate and Illinois river valleys), as well as the area on the north side of the Rogue River extending into the Umpqua Mountains (i.e. Jump-Off-Joe and Grave Creek drainages). Treaties made with Indian bands in the Rogue River Valley and adjacent areas (i.e. Siskiyou Mountains, Applegate Valley, Illinois Valley, and Cow Creek) in 1853 and 1854 indicate that there were approximately fourteen bands of Indians in the region, exclusive of lower Rogue River Indians (below Grave Creek). In 1852, Indian Agent Skinner estimated that there were 1,154 Indians living in southern Oregon west of the Coast Range. In 1855, then-Indian Agent George H. Ambrose counted 836 Indians living in the upper Rogue River area, but only after several hundred Indians had died from disease and warfare.[27]

These approximately fourteen bands constituted the Rogue River Indians for whom Lane assumed that Chief Joe spoke in making peace in 1850. However, each of these bands was autonomous. Joe and Sam were principal chiefs of Takelmas on the Rogue River between the mouth of the Applegate River and Table Rock. George Gibbs, a young Harvard Law School graduate who traveled with the Indian agent for northern California along the Klamath River in 1851, commented that "Joe, the head chief of the Rogue's river Indians … claims the Shaste tribes as properly his subjects, although they yield him no allegiance.""[28]

The attitude of Rogue River Indians was tested in January 1851, when a party of about twenty-seven men traveling from Portland to mining areas in northern California passed through southern Oregon. James A. Cardwell led this company and later described his experience with the Indians. Cardwell knew Chinook Jargon and used it to communicate with Indians he met along the way. Before the party left the Willamette Valley, it received warnings about "the treacherous disposition of the Rogue River indians." Umpquas gave the company its first trouble by shooting arrows at its horses and by stealing one of them. A few days later, the company met Indians on Grave Creek, who led them on to the Applegate River's junction with the Rogue River. Indians living in a village at the rivers' junction fled into the woods when the white party appeared, but Cardwell and the other men in his party calmed them by giving presents to their chief. "Every man of us gave … a small present of some kind some gave … tobacco some gave up their pipes while some others gave handkerchief pocket knife all made a present of some thing," Cardwell recounted later.[29]

The next day several villagers acted as guides, taking Cardwell's party up the Applegate River Valley. The following morning, however, the guides disappeared. A little later in the day, Indians appeared on surrounding hills, yelling, and rolling stones downhill, perhaps trying to scare the Cardwell party's horses. Afraid of an attack, the company hurried back to the Rogue River with Indians in pursuit, and stopped a few miles west of present-day Grants Pass at the ferry operated by a white man named Perkins and later by Vannoy. Cardwell explained that Perkins "had an arrangement with old indian Jo the head chief of the rogue river tribes."[30] When the pursuing Indians showed up at the ferry, Cardwell recalled that Chief Joe, who probably had heard of the trouble, spoke to them. According to Cardwell, he then promised him "safe passage through the country." The Cardwell party continued without incident through the Rogue River Valley and over the Siskiyou Mountains to Yreka, arriving there on March 12, 1851. Cardwell's account shows that Joseph Lane and Chief Joe's peacemaking effort had been successful, at least for the time being, and that a tentative middle-ground had been established.

ACROSS THE SISKIYOU Mountains in northern California, Indian-white relations were headed in a different direction. Along the Klamath River and in Shasta Valley, the arrival of gold miners in the spring of 1850 caused immediate hostilities with Shasta Indians. According to Elijah Steele, miners found the Indians to be "troublesome—both in stealing stock in the daytime, and attacking camp by night." Two white packers were killed on the Klamath River in August 1850. Initially, injuries to Indians may have been limited, but that situation soon changed.[31]

Many Shastas lived in the vicinity of Yreka Flats, where the mining town of Shasta Butte City sprang up. According to Elijah Steele, who arrived at the northern California mining camps on Scotts River in February 1851 with Lane, white miners were received in "a very friendly manner" at first. Lane mediated between whites and Indians, as he had in southern Oregon. He made as good an impression on Shasta Chief Tolo as he had on Chief Joe. Major hostilities between Indians and whites in the Yreka Flats area were temporarily held in check.[32]

But the population of white miners along the Klamath River continued to grow. By the fall of 1851, George Gibbs wrote to his mother from Scott Valley near Mt. Shasta: "Three thousand men are now at work upon the mountains round."[33] When Gibbs reached the Shasta Valley with U. S. Indian Agent Col. Redick M'Kee in October, he discovered that whites and Indians were on the verge of war. People had been killed on both sides, and Indian villages had been burned. Gibbs noted that Indian families were destitute, and that white miners, fearful of working in groups of only two or three in scattered locations, were talking about waging "a war of extermination against the Indians on the upper Klamath and its tributaries generally."[34]

In the spring and summer of 1851, the Rogue River Valley was still being used as a route of passage between the Willamette Valley and gold-mining areas along the Klamath River, but there were few miners or settlers in the Rogue River Valley itself. Alonzo A. Skinner had filed the first donation land claim in the valley in June 1851, and the first mining claim was filed in December of that year.[35]

Indian attacks on white miners in the Rogue River Valley in May and early June led to a request for help from U.S. Army regulars under the command of Major Philip Kearney. Maj. Kearney, commander of the First Dragoons, U. S. Army, headed a party of surveyors looking for an alternate route through the Umpqua Canyon to the Rogue River.[36] With a force of sixty-seven men guided through the Umpqua Mountains by Levi Scott and Jesse Applegate, Maj. Kearney fought with Rogue River Indians on June 17. He later reported, probably with exaggeration, that he had encountered an Indian force of two hundred fifty to three hundred warriors in this first Indian-white battle in the region. He estimated that fifteen Indians were killed; his forces suffered two men wounded and one killed (Brevet Capt. James Stuart, who lost his life in a cavalry charge).

After the initial engagement, Maj. Kearney took steps to recruit a volunteer company of miners. By June 22 this volunteer force numbered about one hundred men. Joseph Lane hastened south to join them. The next two days, according to Maj. Kearney's report, "were spent in breaking up Indian ranches and in destroying such war parties as we could meet." This was followed by three more days "making a circuit around the stronghold near Table Rock." This search for Indians resulted in the capture of about thirty women and children, including the "family of the Head Chief" (probably of Chief Joe or Sam). In this second round of fighting, Maj. Kearney reported “a number of wounded, but none seriously.” Lane later recalled that the Indians suffered heavy casualties (fifty killed and many wounded). Joseph Lane personally took charge of the captured Indian women and children who were being taken to Yreka and returned them to the Rogue River, where he released them to the new territorial governor, John P. Gaines, who had come to make peace with the Indians.[37]

It may seem surprising that Joseph Lane, who had negotiated a peace treaty the previous summer, played no part in restoring peace a year later. By this time, however, Lane was no longer a territorial official. He and the chiefs with whom he had previously negotiated apparently exchanged words from one side of the river to the other. The chiefs complained that whites would not leave them alone; and Lane in turn urged them to cease fighting. But it remained for the new territorial governor to make a second treaty. These negotiations resulted in a treaty that eleven chiefs signed, promising to keep the peace, to remain on the north side of the Rogue River, and to follow the orders of an Indian agent who would be assigned to them. Several bands, however— the Shasta and Grave Creek Indians— refused to meet with the governor and would have nothing to do with making peace.[38]

THE MILITARY EVENTS in the summer of 1851 were a setback to the negotiated peace between Lane and Chief Joe. But negotiations following the summer fighting expanded diplomatic ties. And as more white miners and a few settlers began to move into the region, Rogue River Indians experienced increasing personal contacts with whites, enlarging the scope of middle-ground relationships.

Alonzo A. Skinner took up duties as the first Indian agent for southern Oregon in the fall of 1851. Agent Skinner’s first meetings with Indians in the Rogue River Valley region went well; he found the Indians cooperative and friendly. He made contact with most, if not all, of the leaders of the region’s Indian bands. He told his superior Anson Dart, Superintendent of Indian Affairs for Oregon, that he believed the Indians would keep the peace if whites showed “a little forbearance and discretion.”[39] Whites with whom he talked expressed a similar willingness to put past difficulties behind them, if the Indians kept the peace.

From the Indians' point of view, there probably seemed to be little choice but to abide by the terms of the summer agreement with territorial governor Gaines. Maj. Kearney's regulars and volunteers had soundly punished the Indian forces. Whites were beginning to settle in the Rogue River Valley; by early 1852 about twenty-eight Oregon donation land claims had been filed. After the June fighting, it was time to recover and gather food. Pioneer historian Frances Fuller Victor has pointed out that "Rogue-river Indian politics" oscillated between a "peace party" and a "war party." But fighting was also a seasonal activity; the Indians appear to have fought against whites in the same seasonal pattern as they fought against each other.[40]

Rogue River Indians had reason to be anxious about their situation. Some white miners had begun prospecting on the Rogue River and its tributaries in areas understood to be reserved to the Indians by the new treaty, and white settlers threatened Indian food resources. The *Oregon Spectator* reported an altercation over the eating of an Indian acorn supply by a white man's hogs. Indians demanded a hog as compensation, and the white man drew his pistol and discharged it, causing one of the Indians to shoot at and kill him.[41] In late summer when acorns, which grew abundantly on oak trees in the hot valley climate, matured, Indians gathered them as a winter food resource. If, as this incident seems to indicate, the acorns were stored in an underground cache, they would have been susceptible to invasion by hogs rooting in the ground for food. By December, when this incident occurred, Rogue River Indians had begun to worry about their food supply. They were approaching the winter months when they typically ran short of food; they could not afford to have their winter food reserves consumed by a white man's hogs.

Another incident that occurred about the same time illustrates the growing ambiguities of Indian relations with whites in the Rogue River Valley.[42] In September or October 1851, a white man named Worthington Bills and his father staked a gold-mining claim on the Rogue River near the site of Chief Sam's village. They persuaded the chief to let them settle on several thousand acres of land and to assist them in holding onto it against other whites. The bargain was sealed by the marriage of the younger Bills to the chief's niece "according to the Shasta method," even though Bills already had a white wife and children elsewhere. Chief Sam promised to protect the Bills family from other miners, and he was about to order an attack on the Bills' family's white enemies when someone convinced him that Bills had lied about his life being threatened. Indian Agent Skinner placed Bills under arrest, but he escaped, and when Skinner offered a reward, Chief Sam's people soon captured him. The story illustrates the ambiguity of middle-ground relationships, and how difficult it was for Indians to know which whites to trust.

By early 1852 James A. Cardwell, along with three friends, had returned from Yreka and taken up a donation land claim on the site of what became the town of Ashland. They established the Ashland Sawmill on the stream that runs through present-day Lithia Park. Thomas Smith and several other men had already staked claims in November and December 1851, a little farther south along the trail to Yreka. Cardwell and his partners made a small payment for use of the land to a band of Shasta Indians who lived on the stream and whose chiefs were known to whites as Tipsu (also Tipsey) and Sullix (Chinook jargon names meaning "hairy or bearded" and "angry"). Cardwell recalled that there were about a hundred people living in the Indian village, thirty-five "fighting men" and the rest women, children, and older men. Tipsu would soon gain a reputation among whites as a hostile and dangerous Indian leader. But anthropologist Nan Hannon has pointed out that in his early and brief relationship with Thomas Smith, Tipsu sought to avoid conflict. After a skirmish between Tipsu's band and Klamath River Shastas, Smith gave Tipsu medical treatment that Tipsu believed saved his life. Thereafter, he considered Smith to be a trusted friend, and he turned to him for advice on how to deal with other whites.[43]

Shortly after Cardwell's arrival, Tipsu's people and friendly Butte Creek Shastas fought a three-day ritual battle against Klamath River Shastas, who demanded the return of horses that they had paid in compensation for what they expected to be the loss of Tipsu's life after an earlier skirmish. Tipsu had recovered with Smith's help, and the Klamath River Indians wanted their horses back. After the ritual combat, involving several hundred Indians, the two opposing Indian groups ran out of food, so they came to Cardwell's place to requisition what he had. Narrowly escaping injury after trying to resist their demands, Cardwell sought the help of Indian Agent Skinner, who brought Chief Sam along with him to Cardwell's place. Skinner made "a short speech to Sam and then Sam began to talk to the Indians." Within a few minutes the hostile Indians began to leave, and Cardwell had no further trouble with Tipsu's band for a while.

This experience, like Cardwell's earlier one on the Rogue River, demonstrated the personal influence of Takelma chiefs Joe and Sam over other bands; but they did not exercise any direct control over them. It is likely that whatever influence they possessed depended upon their band size and strength and the desire of other band chiefs to stay at peace with them. As the gatekeepers at the northwest entrance to the Rogue River Valley, chiefs Joe and Sam also had an advantage due to their strategically important geographical position. In general, however, the individual bands pursued their own interests as best they could, often allying themselves with local whites against other bands.

WHITE MINERS PROSPECTED for gold along stretches of the Rogue River in 1851, especially at Big Bar, the location of Chief Sam's winter village (just upstream from present-day Gold Hill at the north end of the Rogue River Valley), hoping for a big gold strike. It came in December 1851 on Jackson Creek in the southwestern corner of the Rogue River Valley. Within a month, one hundred to one hundred fifty miners were working the wealth-producing gulch on Jackson Creek. A mining-camp town, at first called Table Rock City, then Jacksonville, sprang up on Jackson Creek. The influx of miners added their numbers to a white population that by the end of 1851 numbered at least twenty-eight men who had established land claims and two men who operated ferries on the Rogue River. White women and children began to arrive in the valley in early 1852. Pioneer historian A. G. Walling wrote that 1852 was the year the tide of immigration to Oregon began to be "diverted to the Rogue river valley." In 1853, "159 wagons came ... accompanied by 400 men, 120 women, and 170 children ... [along with] 2600 cattle, 1300 sheep, 140 loose horses and forty mules." In earlier years these emigrants would have passed through southern Oregon on their way to the Willamette Valley. But in 1852 and 1853 some of these pioneer families began to choose the Rogue River Valley as their destination.[44]

It is not surprising that in 1852 Indians and whites experienced renewed tensions. However, a careful check of Indian attacks shows that most of them occurred not in the Rogue River Valley itself but at the two gateways on the northwest and southeast. Of a total of 181 whites killed by Indians in southern Oregon and northern California in the period 1850-56, as reported in the late 1850s, only 17 occurred in the Rogue River Valley. Thirty-six whites lost their lives at the northwest entrance in the vicinity of Evans Creek, Grave Creek, and Cow Creek. Another 82 lost their lives on the southern approaches of the Siskiyou Mountains and Klamath-Tule lakes corridor (the Southern Route or Applegate Trail). Sixty whites were killed in southern Oregon and northern California in 1852, more than in any other year, but none of these deaths occurred in the Rogue River Valley.[45]

In early June, a white miner, Calvin Woodman, was killed on a tributary of Scotts River in northern California. Informed by Shastas that Woodman had been killed by "an Indian from Rogue River, in company with one from Shasta Valley," Elijah Steele led a party of white miners across the Siskiyou Mountains in pursuit. The murderers were believed to have fled to the Rogue River Valley for refuge with Chief Sam's people at Table Rock. Two Shastas who knew the identity of the murderers accompanied Steele. Another volunteer company led by Benjamin Wright, a white miner and reputed Indian fighter about whom more will be heard later, went in search of the fugitives up the Klamath River.[46]

When Steele reached the Rogue River Valley with his Shasta guides and white volunteers, he received an alarming report that "the Indians of Sam's and Joe's tribe were gathered in arms near Table Rock on Big-bar, on Rogue river, in large numbers." A volunteer company of miners also had massed on the south bank of the Rogue River to engage them. The confrontation at the Rogue River had started over a grievance between Chief Sam and white settler George H. Ambrose (later to become the local Indian agent), who had built a house only a few miles from the chief's village. Chief Sam demanded payment of a beef for Ambrose's use of the land. The chief also was said to have made a proposal to exchange two Indian children, a horse, and some money for Ambrose's two-year-old daughter. According to Indian Agent Skinner, Ambrose believed the chief would take the child by force if he did not agree to the exchange. At about the same time a party of whites camping near Ambrose's house was visited by fifteen or twenty angry Indians, who harangued them about the killing of Indians in Shasta Valley. Before leaving, the Indians threatened retaliation for white mistreatment of Indians in the Rogue River Valley. With Indian threats ringing in their ears, the whites made haste for Jacksonville, where a volunteer company quickly organized and headed for Chief Sam's village near Table Rock.[47]

By the time Steele's party of ten or twelve men arrived at the Rogue River, Indian Agent Skinner had already begun negotiations with the chief over those matters of concern to whites in the valley. Chief Sam agreed to meet with the white volunteer company and said he wanted to avoid a fight. On the morning of June 17, Skinner brought the Indians down to the north bank of the river. But his efforts to mediate failed, and within a few hours fighting began between Indians and whites. Agent Skinner reported that "the firing became pretty general upon both sides; many who were opposed to commencing the attack thinking it now necessary to fight in self-defence." Steele stated that he ordered his men to open fire in self-defense, and that they killed thirteen Indians.[48]

Pursuit of the fleeing Indian warriors lasted for two days until Chief Sam agreed to stop fighting and make peace. Whatever the exact terms negotiated by Agent Skinner, the chief apparently agreed not to cause any more trouble for whites that summer. By late July, Skinner reported that "the greater portion of the Indians are still encamped near the agency [Skinner's house and land claim], and appear entirely friendly." However, they were impatient for "their promised presents," and Skinner gave them two beef cattle to help replenish their exhausted food supply. Skinner wrote that it "will be quite impossible to keep them quiet much longer," unless promises of payment for their land were kept.

The action at Big Bar in June 1852 showed that although Indians and whites were involved in an increasing number of interpersonal encounters and that some progress toward the creation of a middle-ground existed, that middle-ground was extremely fragile. The incident ended major hostilities in the Rogue River Valley that summer, but Rogue River Indians showed signs of desperation. Steele later recalled that Chief Sam told him "that if the Shasta and Scott's river tribes had broke out as he had sent them to do," he would not have negotiated peace but instead have "killed all of the [white] men and kept the women and horses for themselves."[49] Steele, a white peacemaker, was not one to exaggerate Indian threats. But whites and Indians still had a way to go before engaging in all-out, prolonged war. According to pioneer historian Walling, at the conclusion of the fighting in June 1852, whites decided "that in view of the fact ... the Indians had already suffered much damage [thirteen lives], and the cause of the difficulty did not warrant a war of extermination, it would be best to talk."[50] This reflected Walling's belief, based on pioneer reminiscences, that whites still hoped in 1852 to keep hostilities within limits, no doubt because of their uncertainties about the outcome of a full-scale Indian war involving all the bands in southern Oregon and northern California. Chief Sam and his people also seemed to be willing to continue to work at keeping peace.

Despite the rise of war-party sentiments among Rogue River Indians in 1852, events were still manageable short of full-scale war. Both whites and Indians looked for ways to cope with the uncertainties of their situations. Rogue River Valley Indians had made an effort to develop personal relationships with whites. Chief Sam had tried to establish ties with a friendly white family (the Bills) and the less-welcoming Ambrose family. There were efforts to seek compensation for white use of Indian land in lieu of fighting. Negotiations quickly followed limited warfare. Indian Agent Skinner took action to mediate and negotiate several grievances. On Cow Creek, in the South Umpqua River drainage, too, Indian chief Miwaleta counseled his people to keep the peace with white farmers and miners.[51]

Whites also resorted to legal action against Indians. By doing so, whites in theory accorded to them the same legal rights that they themselves enjoyed, much as they had done in the Whitman massacre trial, even if in practice trial procedures involving Indians usually were a sham. Benjamin Wright and his party intercepted the accused murderers of white miner Calvin Woodman on the Klamath River and took the two Indians to Scott's Valley where, in the presence of Scott's Valley and Shasta Indians, white miners convened a meeting and conducted an informal trial. Surprisingly, as a result of the two Indians' testimony, only one was found guilty and hung; the other one was released. According to Steele, "the Indians were satisfied and peace restored."[52]

This was only the first of several reported instances of ad hoc white legal proceedings used to deal with Indians accused of killing whites. In December 1852, a local Indian band killed eight miners on Galice Creek. When the chief and some of his men later showed up at Vannoy's ferry with a sizeable quantity of gold dust, they aroused suspicion. A later pioneer chronicler stated that "as there were no courts yet organized in that part of the territory, they were brought before a citizens jury, tried, convicted and sentenced to be hanged."[53] Whether an alleged last-minute confession of guilt was true or not, this and other summary trials of Indians showed that whites wanted to give their acts of retaliation against Indians an appearance of legality. Some whites may have wanted to "exterminate" Indians, but that would have exposed them to the charge of savagery. The need for law and order in their relationships with each other constrained whites in their dealings with Indians, as long as Indian attacks on whites remained scattered and fell short of coordinated warfare.

Summer warfare by Rogue River Indians ended at Big Bar in June 1852, but in August the Modocs of northern California attacked wagon trains coming to Oregon over the Applegate Trail from the Humboldt River. These attacks resulted in the largest loss of white lives in southern Oregon in any single period of encounters and increased tensions between whites and Indians in the Rogue River Valley. Charles S. Drew later estimated that thirty-nine persons were killed by Modocs in the fall of 1852, but the number may have been twice that. At the end of a fall campaign against the Modocs, Fort Jones was established in northern California with a small company of U.S. Army regulars. Up to this time the closest army outpost had been Fort Orford on the Oregon coast, which was separated from the inland valleys by a mountain barrier.[54]

Benjamin Wright emerged as the principal leader of retaliatory white volunteer expeditions against the Modocs. Although his initial actions in southern Oregon made him an Indian adversary, other aspects of his personal life placed him in the role of cultural intermediary, and made him a key figure in the history of middle-ground relations in southern Oregon. Wright developed an early reputation as an Indian fighter, considered at the time to be the equal of "Kit Carson and other celebrated frontiersmen."[55] He came to northern California in early 1851, like nearly everyone else, for the gold. But he moved between white and Indian worlds as Indian fighter and "squaw man," a pejorative term used to refer to white men who lived with Indian women. He was later sub-Indian agent on the south Oregon coast. By the time of his death in early 1856, at the time of the Rogue River War, Wright had become one of the most notorious and controversial figures in the history of the region. The fact that his parents were Quaker and family respectable seems at odds with his reputation as an Indian fighter, but it may have had a bearing on his later performance a sub-Indian agent. Men like William R. Fanning, who rode with Wright on some of his adventures, recalled that "he seemed to take pride in looking and acting as much like an Indian as possible. He had glossy black hair, which he wore long, falling in waving tresses on his shoulders, and this with his suit of buckskin, made his resemblance to an Indian very striking when his back was turned."[56]

Wright was born April 7, 1829, in the town of Milton, in Wayne County, Indiana. In 1847, at age eighteen, following his mother's death, he left home and traveled over the Oregon Trail with an emigrant wagon train led by Joel Palmer, who later served as Superintendent of Indian Affairs for Oregon from 1853 to 1856. This partially helps to explain how Palmer knew Wright and why he hired him in 1854 to be a sub-Indian agent for the Port Orford-Gold Beach district. Benjamin Wright's name appears on the muster rolls for the Cayuse Indian War of 1847-48. However, there are no documents or reports of him in the period between the Cayuse War and his arrival at Scott Bar in the spring of 1851.[57]

In the early history of Siskiyou County, Wright was linked both to R. B. Snelling, whom miners elected "County Judge" at Scott Bar in 1851, and to Elijah Steele, a trained lawyer and later Superior Judge of Siskiyou County, who became a much-respected person among both whites and Indians. Wright assisted Snelling by making arrests and hunting down escaped prisoners; he was referred to as "captain of the Government" in Francis Reinhart's account of early Scott Bar days. Elijah Steele, who became a leader in trying to keep peace between whites and Indians, also employed Wright as early as 1852 to interpret for him, "he talking the Indian language well," Steele later wrote.[58]

These are the few known biographical facts behind the legend of Ben Wright as Indian fighter that began in 1851. At that time Modocs had been raiding Shasta Valley ranches for horses and cattle. By late summer white ranchers organized a party of volunteers to try to recover the livestock and to kill Modocs in retaliation. As a participant in this volunteer company and later ones, William R. Fanning recalled that "by a unanimous vote we decided to send for Ben. Wright, who had been living at Cottonwood [a mining camp on the Klamath River],

Benjamin Wright. (Oregon Historical Society, OrHi 1711)

some twenty miles [north] from Yreka. He came at once upon being informed of the opportunity to hunt redskins, and was pressed to take command of the company. This he declined to do, saying that he preferred to do his fighting in the ranks." Wright brought with him "two Oregon Indians" to help in tracking down the Modocs; another Indian (Klamath or Umatilla) accompanied Wright in 1852.[59] Wright was twenty-two years old at the time. Fanning's account shows that he already had a reputation as an Indian fighter, even though there are no documented stories of his exploits prior to 1851. It is also clear that Wright had been living with Indian companions, who may have been working with him at the Cottonwood mining camp.

The 1851 war party against the Modocs lasted until snow fell in November. Fanning told of Wright's skill in tracking down Indians (with the help of his Indian friends), his fearlessness in sneaking up on Indian camps, and his bravery or foolhardiness, in charging headlong into combat with Modoc warriors. The party killed at least fifteen to twenty Indian men, captured upwards of thirty women and children, who were later released, and recovered some of the ranchers' livestock. They had to give up killing more Indians when they ran out of food and winter weather worsened.[60]

In defense of Wright's and the other volunteers' conduct against the Modocs, Fanning wrote: "It was not our intention to harm the women and children, and though Wright is charged with ruthlessly murdering Indians, the statement is entirely incorrect. I was with him not only in this campaign, but also the next year [1852], and we always had the most positive orders from him to refrain from injuring the women and children, nor did he ever molest them when it could possibly be avoided." By comparison, Fanning pointed to the evidence of Modoc Indian atrocities: "The bones of men, women, and children blanching among the rocks" and "tufts of human hair, torn from the heads of innocent women and children" scattered about their camps.[61]

Wright's ruthlessness was elevated to legendary proportions during the 1852 fall campaign against the Modocs, following Modoc attacks on emigrant wagon trains. A party of nine packers was killed at Bloody Point (on the northeast side of Tule Lake along the Southern Route or Applegate Trail from the Humboldt River in Nevada); there was only one survivor. A volunteer company under Wright's leadership (twenty-seven men in all) headed for Tule Lake to retaliate. Meanwhile, an emigrant wagon train came under Modoc attack in the same area. When Wright's party arrived, the Modocs scattered, but Wright's men followed after them in hot pursuit. Fanning estimated that upwards of forty Modoc men were killed. In searching the area nearby among the tule reeds, Wright's men found twenty-two bodies of whites; a volunteer company from Jacksonville found fourteen more a few days later. Some of the bodies were found horribly "mutilated and disfigured," including those of women and children.[62]

Wright's company remained in Modoc country until the last emigrant trains had passed through in October. Wright and eighteen other men determined to stay longer and hunt down Modocs. (It is worth noting that Wright's brother William came to Oregon in 1852, although it is not known whether he came by the Southern Route.) Under pretext of peace negotiations, Wright persuaded the Modocs to camp and eat with his men in mid-November. Warned by a friendly Indian that the Modocs planned to attack Wright's men first, Wright, struck first and killed as many Modoc warriors as he could. Forty-seven Modoc warriors were killed; two escaped (Curly Headed Doctor and John Schonchin) to seek revenge in 1872-73 during the Modoc War.[63] Victorious, Wright and his men returned to Yreka with "Indian scalps dangling from their rifles, hats, and the heads of their horses." It was probably at the conclusion of this campaign that John E. Ross, the commander of a Jacksonville volunteer company that historian Hubert Howe Bancroft referred to as an "Indian butcher," observed that the long pole at the center of Wright's tent in Yreka sported an Indian scalp or two.[64]

The returning victors soon turned to carousing and celebrated for a week with stories of valor and displays of scalp trophies until more sober Yreka citizens stopped them. Even those who appreciated their efforts to exterminate the Modocs had had enough of the victory celebration. But the 1852 campaign against the Modocs exceeded acceptable limits of behavior in a more basic way. Alerted to the massacre, military officials feared that whites had begun a war of extermination that would lead to a coalition of Indian bands in northern California and southern Oregon. (Along the California side of the border from the coast eastwards lived the Tolowa, Karok, Shasta, Modoc, and Northern Paiute Indians.[65])

As a result of heightened tensions, an infantry company was ordered from the Columbia River barracks to southern Oregon. Brevet Brigadier General Ethan A. Hitchcock, Pacific Division Commander, believed that the "treacherous massacre" by Wright seriously endangered Indian-white relations in northern California and southern Oregon.[66] The campaigns of 1851 and 1852 against the Modocs made Wright a "notorious" figure in the eyes of U. S. Army officers whose primary interest was to keep the peace among whites and Indians, while it made him a hero to many white miners and settlers. Although companies that were organized to kill Indians never lacked for volunteers, Wright's conduct pushed retaliation to the extreme of extermination, a position supported by some irate miners and white settlers, although some ranchers and miners benefited from the employment of Indians.

But Wright was not simply an Indian killer; paradoxically, he also lived among Indians. He belonged to a border world of white men who lived with Indian women. Some of these relationships lasted only as long as the gold held out in a mining district; others were more permanent. For many Indian women, living with a white man was the only way to survive after the death of so many Indian men.

The term "squaw man" entered into common usage in the 1850s. Whatever the origins and original meaning of the term "squaw,"by the nineteenth century "squaw man" had come to be used by whites to express their prejudice against sexual unions between white men and Indian women. Historian William T. Hagan has traced the usage of "squaw man" from the 1840s to the development of concern among Indian agents later in the century about the influence of white men married to Indian women living on reservations.[67]

As early as 1855, local citizens complained that white men living with Indian women among the Klamath Indians were causing trouble. Oregon Superintendent of Indian Affairs Joel Palmer expressed irritation at the end of the Rogue River War in July 1856 that "a few *squaw men* and reckless disturbers of the peace" [Palmer's emphasis] had interfered with the process of removing Indians from the south coast. In 1857, Lt. George Crook became equally frustrated with white men "living with squaws" on Smith River because they encouraged Indians to leave a nearby reservation. Writing about Indian reservations, historian Francis Paul Prucha noted that such white men "everywhere ... were a discordant element, backed the chiefs in resistance to change, and earned the enmity of the [reservation] reformers."[68] By the 1870s, the political enemies of whites sympathetic to Indians used the term "squaw man" as a racial insult or epithet. Elijah Steele, who served briefly as Indian agent for the northern district of California in the early 1860s and befriended Indians, found himself forced to counter charges that "I have or had half-breed children in the Lava Beds or elsewhere, or that I have had intercourse with squaws, or that I was a spy in favor of the Indians."[69]

Steele recalled that Wright lived with an Indian woman who provided Wright with information that enabled him to capture Indians believed to be guilty of murder.[70] His relationship with this nameless Indian woman was important to Wright's role in the Shasta Valley area as a tracker and law-enforcement officer. Wright also lived among other men who lived with Indian women. Henry L. Wells in *History of Siskiyou County* (1881) wrote: "Along the Klamath and about Cottonwood there lived in the winter of 1853-4 a number of squaw-men, among whom were Tom Ward, a gambler, and Bill Chance, a member of the Ben. Wright party. They had squaws belonging to Bill's band of Shastas, who made for their headquarters a large cave near Fall Creek, on the north bank of the Klamath, some twenty miles above Cottonwood."[71] Because of "ill-treatment they had received," the women left the white men and went back to their own people. When the white men pursued them, a battle took place at the cave; four of the whites were killed and others wounded. In the process of negotiating peace with Bill's band, A. M. Rosborough, Elijah Steele, and friendly Shasta Chief Tolo heard of the band's grievances. The Indians "complained bitterly" that "they had been whipped, shot, and hung, because, forsooth, they had stolen a few horses occasionally; their squaws had been taken from them without compensation, and disease had been spread among them, until they could bear it no longer and had determined upon revenge."[72]

The truth of such charges was well documented by many white observers of Indian-white relations in northern California. It was common for some, perhaps most, white miners, who had chosen to live with Indian women, to take them by force and to scare away or kill their husbands and relatives. Wright belonged to this rough company of men; but in the account of fighting between Bill's band and Wright's friends, there is no mention of Wright or of the Indian woman who lived with him.

In his study of Indian-white relations in northern California, historian Albert L. Hurtado has remarked that it is impossible to know how many white men cohabited with Indian women or entered into common-law marriages with them. In the written accounts of white miners, he found expressions of aversion to Indian women for several reasons. "Even in the rough-and-ready 1850s miscegenation was frowned on in mining communities," he observed. "Not only was it incongruent with Anglo-American racial and sexual ideals, many whites thought it downright dangerous."[73]

In the period from 1851 to 1853, Benjamin Wright belonged to a group of single white men who lived between white and Indian worlds. Their relations with Indian men were often violent and brutal, but they also accepted younger Indian men as companions who would work for them, drink with them, share Indian women with them, and even ride with them in war parties against other Indians. By living with Indian women, they began a process of racial intermixing that continued into the post-gold-mining years of the late nineteenth century. This joining of the lives of Indian women and white men, whether forced or voluntary, constituted another dimension of the middle-ground in southern Oregon as well as northern California.

Chapter 4
War, Peace, and White Settlement, 1853-54

IN THE THREE YEARS FOLLOWING Joseph Lane's negotiations with Takelma Chief Joe (Apserkahar), a first wave of white gold miners and settlers arrived in the upper Rogue River section of southern Oregon. The resulting interactions with local Indians created a fragile middle-ground of Indian-white relationships. Brief military skirmishes between Indians and whites dominate the historical record, but days and months of peaceful interactions outnumbered those of warfare. In the summer of 1853, the man who would carry the major responsibility for trying to build on previous negotiations, and who would serve as a key cultural intermediary over the next three years, made his first assessment of the situation in southern Oregon. Joel Palmer, newly appointed federal Superintendent of Indian Affairs to succeed Anson Dart, reported in June 1853 that relations between Indians and whites in the Rogue River country had reached a critical stage.[1]

Palmer made his first trip to Oregon in 1845. Like Benjamin Wright, Palmer had grown up in a Quaker family; and later as a young man, newly married, he had moved to the Quaker settlement of Laurel in Indiana's Whitewater Valley, a little south of Milton. It was from there in 1845 that he first set out for Oregon. He had a background of service as an Indiana legislator, and also worked as a canal-construction contractor, and a farmer. After moving permanently to Oregon with his family in 1847, he quickly became a territorial leader. During the Cayuse War he served in the important position of commissary general, with responsibility for supplying militia forces. At the same time, the territorial legislature appointed him superintendent of Indian affairs and a peace commissioner (together with Henry A. G. Lee and Robert Newell) to the Cayuse Indians. He went briefly to the California gold fields, then returned to Oregon and settled with his family on a donation land claim on the Yamhill River, where he and his friend Cris Taylor

Joel Palmer. (Oregon Historical Society, OrHi 362)

built a house and a store, and platted the town of Dayton. Palmer turned his attention to farming, sawmilling, and other business activities until he received his federal appointment in the spring of 1853.[2]

Palmer had the physical strength, commanding voice, and confident bearing of a born leader, and earned the respect of both whites and Indians. Although he had only three months of schooling as a boy, he developed excellent writing skills that shine forth in his account of his Oregon Trail experience as well as in his official government letters and reports. His written reports complemented his actions in trying to work out a humane solution to Indian-white conflicts. Having grown up as a Quaker (late in life affiliating with the Methodists), his humanitarian concerns and standards of moral conduct reflected his Christian faith.[3]

Palmer inherited the commitments of his predecessors and the limitations of federal Indian policy at the time of his appointment as Superintendent of Indian Affairs. Oregon's first Indian agent, Dr. Elijah White, had served from 1842 to 1845. Both Henry A. G. Lee and Joel Palmer had served temporarily as Indian agents during the Cayuse War, and then the position remained vacant until Joseph Lane's appointment as territorial governor and Indian superintendent ex officio in 1849.[4] Lane believed that removal of Indians from the influence of whites was essential to their survival. He argued that "the cause of humanity calls loudly for their removal from causes, and influences so fatal to their existence." He said that Indians should be relocated to a "district" that was "removed from the settlements [of whites]." The Oregon Indian Act of 1850 had included the objectives of Indian land purchase and removal. By November 1851, Anson Dart, the first Superintendent of Indian Affairs for Oregon, and appointed Indian Commissioners had negotiated a total of nineteen treaties involving land purchases and establishment of local reservations.[5] But the United

States Senate rejected the treaties the following year, and they remained unapproved when Palmer took over as Superintendent in 1853.[6]

A federal policy of Indian relocation onto reservations grew out of popular and scientific ideas. The underlying rationale for relocation dated back to the Indian Removal Act of 1830, which gave the president of the United States authority to set aside land west of the Mississippi River (not included in any state or organized territory) as a new home for eastern Indians. By the 1830s, white scholarly views of American Indians had grown increasingly pessimistic. According to historian Robert E. Bieder "the view that Indians had degenerated from a more advanced state of civilization had received wide acceptance." A lively public debate took place in public and academic settings in the 1840s and 1850s between "monogenists," who believed that all human beings belonged to one species, and "polygenists," who believed that they belonged to different species. Polygenist thought encouraged more pessimistic and racist views of Indians. One strand of polygenist thinking held that, although God had created different species, he intended whites to be superior over "darker races." Although Christian morality suggested that Indians could be helped by missionary education, the idea of Indian mental and moral inferiority cast doubt on the feasibility of such efforts.[7]

The idea of removing Indians from white settlements satisfied those who believed efforts to assimilate Indians was a lost cause and contrary to God's will. But humanitarians, who had not lost faith in the power of education, also believed that cultural reeducation of Indians on a reservation was "a final opportunity" to save them.[8] Joel Palmer's views on removing Indians from the corrupting influences of whites needs to be seen against this background of intellectual and political debate over the possibilities for Indian assimilation into white society. His actions to remove Indians from their homelands in order to prevent their extermination demonstrated his belief in the humanitarian optimism of the monogenists, rather than in the fatalistic and religiously motivated racism of polygenists. By contrast, the idea of the inevitability of Indian extinction helped to justify white miners and settlers in killing Indians.

Palmer took office just as reservation policy was about to be implemented in the new state of California and the newly created Washington Territory. California's new superintendent of Indian affairs, Edward F. Beale, proposed that military posts be established on reservations and that temporary reservations be moved as white population increased. Congress approved "five military reservations from the public domain in the State of California, or the Territories of Utah and New Mexico ... for Indian purposes" in the spring of 1853. Isaac I. Stevens, appointed in March 1853 to the positions of governor and superintendent of Indian affairs for Washington Territory, also reflected the emergent consensus on reservations and Indian policy. He wrote in September 1854: "It is obviously necessary that a few reservations of good lands should be set apart as permanent abodes for the tribes," where "each Indian" could have a homestead and which would be off-limits to occupation by whites. Stevens insisted that "the location and extent of these reservations should be adapted to the peculiar wants and habits of the different tribes."[9]

IN THE SPRING AND EARLY SUMMER of 1853, it appeared to whites in the Rogue River Valley that the Indians had begun "to court" their friendship. Only two incidents of violence were reported between December 1852 and June 1853. Indian chiefs Sam (Toquahear), Joe (Apserkahar), and Tipsu were frequently seen in Jacksonville. Pioneer historian Walling wrote that several pioneer residents of Jacksonville, including several women, had commented to him on the "unvarying courtesy and gentleness of the principal chiefs." They were even "favored guests in private houses." According to Walling's pioneer informants, "nearly all the Rogue Rivers were in the habit of coming into Jacksonville, where they begged food, fraternized with the lowest whites, and were friendly to all."[10] This is further evidence of expanded interpersonal relationships that went beyond those originating in negotiations between Indian and white military leaders. Tipsu, however, complained to his white friend Thomas Smith that on one occasion when he and his son had returned some stray cattle to their white owner, he had been given a shirt as reward, but he had not been shown the proper respect of being invited to dinner. Also on this or another occasion, a white man had struck Tipsu with a pole, injuring his arm. He did not strike back, considering the white man's behavior unworthy of retaliation, according to Smith. It was Tipsu's "unexpected dignity," anthropologist Hannon has suggested, that made him seem untrustworthy and dangerous to whites. As a result of these and other clashes, Tipsu visited Smith for the last time late in the spring of 1853 to tell him that he was moving his people to the Applegate River Valley. However, a younger chief, called Sambo by whites (Indian name unknown), stayed behind in the upper Bear Creek Valley.[11]

The surprisingly casual attitude of whites toward Indians became apparent when war broke out in August 1853. Many whites lacked arms and ammunition to fight because they had traded them to the Indians.[12] The reason, according to pioneer historian Walling, was that "Indians often came into possession of their guns, horses, ammunition and other valuables through the sale of their women."[13] Walling felt embarrassed to write publicly about what he regarded as a pioneer secret, but he remarked that "it is useless to disguise the fact." The number and significance of unions between Indian women and white men was underscored after late summer warfare, when a group of about a dozen Indian women who lived in Jacksonville served as emissaries to the Indians who were fighting and tried to persuade them to make peace.[14] The exchange of daughters by their fathers for white guns and other items was consistent with the Takelma custom of parents arranging marriages for daughters with or without their consent in return for items of wealth (e.g., dentalia) and utility (e.g., baskets, food, etc.).

As Rogue River Valley Indians moved freely between their villages and white settlements—talking with whites, working for them, gambling with them, and sometimes living among them—they saw their land being transformed by quiet but industrious farmers. Although gold miners posed the greatest threat of sporadic violence, the single white men and white families who worked the land were the greater threat because of their increasing control over Indian food resources—the oak trees, root grounds, and grazing land for deer and elk. When war broke out in August 1853, about a dozen of these settlers' homes went up in flames. The new middle-ground between Indians and whites rested on conflicting emotions of a desire for peace and, on the Indian side, a bitter sense of injustice at white theft of food resources.

One settler, America Rollins Butler, wife of Ashmun J. Butler, kept a diary of her family's start in the Rogue River Valley. She was twenty-seven years old in the summer of 1853; a few years earlier she had been a schoolteacher in Illinois before marrying her husband. She and Ashmun came over the Applegate Trail to Yreka in 1852, and by late February 1853 had crossed over the Siskiyou Mountains and taken up a land claim on Bear Creek. On May 20 Mrs. Butler wrote: "Mr Butler breaking prairie Cousin John and John Chatfield are hoeing potatoes as to myself I am maid of all traids sweeping dusting churning ironing baking bread and pies diswashing etc."[15] With this simple entry, Mrs. Butler described some of the activities, along with house and fence building, that signaled the permanence of white settlement. From her house, she watched the regular passage of pack trains through the valley. Occasionally the Butlers took in boarders who stopped to investigate the valley's prospects. The permanence of settlement also shows up in Mrs. Butler's references to such community activities as an election, a formal ball, Sunday church, and a Fourth of July celebration.

The first sign of Indian trouble that summer appeared in Mrs. Butler's diary on August 4. "The Indians are becoming very hostile in this valley," she wrote. "They have killed one man and two oxen without cause or provication at the present time they are hostile yet pretending friendship." The next day Mr. Butler went to Jacksonville and came back late. Mrs. Butler feared for his safety, after hearing of two more men who had been killed by Indians. By August 6 she wrote of "families ... leaving their homes for safety." Her men rounded up their cattle. By the next day she wrote that the "Indian trouble has come to open warfare." A battle had taken place in which two white men had been wounded and seven Indians killed. "Great excitement prevails," she wrote. "Our people are act very rash which will cause much trouble." A few days later she noted: "Strong threats are made of exterminating all the Red mans tribe." She also commented that "our men act with a great deal of indecision." Each day she followed the tide of battle, reported numbers of houses burned, men wounded or killed, and the arrival of supporting forces, even though Mrs. Butler's men were not themselves involved in fighting Indians.[16]

Through Mrs. Butler's eyes it is possible to experience the suddenness with which Indian-white warfare began in the summer of 1853 and the indecisiveness with which both sides went to war. In June, white miners hung Chief Taylor and four of his men, then killed others on Galice Creek. On Cow Creek, in the South Umpqua River drainage, white settlers John Catching and William H. Riddle stopped white volunteers from further killing of Cow Creek Indians. But other than these violent incidents, Indians and whites avoided outright warfare until August. War finally broke out unexpectedly over an Indian man's loss of his wife to a Mexican—just another one of the "Boston people as all Americans were then called by the Indians."[17]

The incident, later recounted in several versions, illustrates the important role played by Indian women. Joseph Lane related that the Indian, named Peoosecut (also Peousicut), sold his wife to a Mexican gambler. When the Mexican failed to pay him, Peoosecut tried to take her back, but white miners prevented him from doing so. Angered by this, Peoosecut went back to his band chief, Tipsu, and persuaded him and others to attack white families. Pioneer historian Walling's informants gave him two accounts of this story. In one account, Peoosecut's wife was "enticed or abducted" by the Mexican; when Peoosecut tried to recover her, his life was threatened, and he subsequently went on a rampage of killing. In the other version, the Mexican bought the Indian wife, but she ran away to reunite with Peoosecut, leading the Mexican and his friends to go to Peoosecut's camp and forcibly take her back. This precipitated an attack on a Bear Creek farmer, Richard Edwards, who lived near Ashland, the event recorded by Mrs. Butler in her diary on August 4.

Over the next two days, two more white men were killed in the vicinity of Jacksonville, and two more wounded. Over the next week, houses and other buildings were burned and whites and Indians engaged in small skirmishes. By this time nearly all the Indians in the valley had been drawn into the fighting. On August 7, Captain B. R. Alden, 4th U.S. Infantry, received word of the trouble at his Fort Jones, California, outpost. Although only ten of his men were healthy enough to march and fight, he left immediately with "25 muskets, 5 carbines, and 600 rounds of ammunition."[18] He recruited eighty volunteers in Yreka and reached Jacksonville on August 9. There he enrolled two companies of volunteers, and a third independently recruited volunteer company joined them at Camp Stewart on August 11 near Table Rock, making his total force about two hundred men. Capt. Alden estimated the Indian forces concentrated at Table Rock to be about "250 warriors, 150 of this number being armed with rifles and well supplied with ammunition." His plan to attack the Indian forces was temporarily delayed by news of more attacks in the valley itself. Many of the volunteers rushed back to protect the white settlements, and chased the Indians into the Applegate Valley. On August 15-16, Mrs. Butler noted in her diary that volunteers had headed back to Table Rock and that they had separated into "small companies and start out in scouting parties."[19] Two days later she reported that fifteen white men had been killed and six wounded in skirmishes.

Meanwhile, other white reinforcements arrived. Joseph Lane heard of the fighting on August 17 at his home in the Umpqua Valley. He gathered together ten men and reached Camp Stewart on August 21.[20] As Mrs. Butler accurately noted on August 22: "general Lane took command on monday and started in persuit of the Indians." Lane, his men, and the forces mobilized by Capt. Alden concentrated on the main Indian force located north of Table Rock. But, as noted by Mrs. Butler, scattered attacks continued against farms in the Rogue River Valley and against packers on the Applegate River in the period August 21-26. On August 21, she wrote: "The Indians have again atacked Dunn's house killing one man and wounding three others; burning his barley and oats." For Mrs. Butler, her family, and friends, however, daily routines continued. The day after the reported attack on Dunn's farm, Mrs. Butler wrote: "Mr Butler and Detriall have gone to town John and Bethell are cutting corn Taylor is gathering cucumbers Silcuit is gritting meal and I am sewing."[21]

The decision of the Butlers to remain at their homestead is surprising. They were one of only three families in the local neighborhood that did not leave. Did they consider the possibility of attack remote? Were they most concerned about protecting their crops? What kind of relations did they have with local Indians? There are no answers to any of these questions in Mrs. Butler's diary. Despite the fact that, as she wrote, "many are prophesying bad luck to us in lives and property," they stayed at home.

Perhaps the Butlers' decision illustrates the ambivalence felt by some settlers toward the Indians. Pioneer historian Walling told a story illustrating that ambivalence. Members of Tipsu's Siskiyou Shasta band, led by the young sub-chief Sambo, were thought to be responsible for attacks on settlers near Ashland. Twelve white settlers, including Thomas Smith, Tipsu's friend, attacked Sambo's group, driving off the Indian men and taking hostage the Indian women and children. They were removed to the house of a Mr. Alberding and Patrick Dunn, where a temporary stockade had been built and other white settlers, including five families, had come for safety. A few days later, Sambo and his warriors surrendered and were kept inside the stockade fortification. According to Walling, the white settlers "having ample confidence in the good faith of their savage guests, no great precautions were taken to guard against surprise." About a week later, Sambo's men attacked, killed, and wounded several persons. This was the attack at Dunn's place mentioned by Mrs. Butler on August 21. Later, on August 25, she noted that of the six whites wounded at Dunn's place, two had died, in addition to one person who was killed during the attack. After this incident, the remaining Shastas fled the upper Bear Creek Valley for the Applegate River area.[22]

Considering the risk, why were the whites so trustful of Sambo and his warriors? What might otherwise appear to have been foolhardy behavior looks different when considered in the light of what happened at the end of summer warfare. Joseph Lane, Capt. Alden and his army regulars, and volunteer companies pursued Indian forces north of Table Rock. In the decisive battle on August 23, the white force under Lane's command suffered three killed and five wounded; the Indians had eight killed and twenty wounded (seven of whom were known to have died later). An armistice was declared and the Indians agreed that within a week they would meet to negotiate a peace treaty. The Indian forces numbered about "two hundred warriors, well armed with rifles and muskets, well supplied with ammunition," but according to Lane, Chiefs Sam and Jim told Lane "their hearts were sick of war."[23]

Despite fear that the Indians might renew warfare, the two sides kept the armistice. What is more surprising, "Indian ponies and American horses were turned loose to browse, and the Indians furnished a relief party to assist in bringing in the American wounded." Indian women packed water to Lane's soldiers from the spring that Indians controlled.[24] The conduct of the Indians after the armistice shows the abrupt change in behavior that occurred when fighting ended. Indians could be fighting, as Charles Blair put it, like "bloody looking Savegges" one minute and friendly the next. This behavior reflected more than a tradition of limited warfare. It also showed the basic uncertainty of Indians about whether to join the "peace party" or "war party" of their own people. Pulled by conflicting forces of honor and fears of suffering great losses in battle, Rogue River Indian chiefs and warriors behaved unpredictably.

Whites, too, were divided in their attitudes. Charles Blair admitted that some of the northern California volunteers left the Rogue River Valley "with the ca[lcu]lation of never goin Indian fighting again."[25] Mrs. Butler, who certainly wanted Lane's force to quell the Indian uprising, nevertheless deplored cold-blooded killing of Indians. On August 28 she wrote: "The white men have treacherously decoyed six Grave Creek Indians in with pretents of peace unarmed and shoot them then two of the white men were afterwards shot by the Indians." On September 4 she wrote that "whites have acted so treacherously with they ar afraid to trust them." Despite the recent uprising, Mrs. Butler still felt compassion for the Indians. Although she apparently had no direct encounters with Indians herself, she obviously participated in a middle-ground of moral consideration about how Indians and whites should behave toward each other.[26]

Divisions among Indians existed before, during, and after the summer warfare, complicating Indian interactions with whites. One version of how the 1853 warfare started concluded that the Indians "matured plans for a renewal of hostilities on a large scale" throughout the summer. Charles S. Drew, who held this view, drew attention to reports that Indians had been digging through rubbish piles in Jacksonville for pieces of "lead, or other metal that they could mould into bullets."[27] But in fact Indians had been divided over whether to go to war. A few weeks after the summer warfare of 1853 ended, Mary, Chief Joe's daughter, whom Lane had given her American name, came to Lane's tent under cover of darkness and told him how Peoosecut and Chief Tipsu's band had started the conflict. When whites fought back, Chief Tipsu had hurried to Joe's camp for protection. According to Mary, he told Chief Joe that "all the Indians would be killed if they did not band together and fight for their lives and their homes."[28] Chief Joe replied that "he had done nothing to make the white people mad and could not see why he should fight and proposed to go to Jacksonville and have a talk with the whites." But when whites on horseback appeared in the valley below his campsite, he decided that it was too late to talk and retreated with his people into mountain country north of Table Rock. Whites gave Chief Joe credit for having tried to avoid fighting, thereby reflecting their willingness to distinguish between friendly and hostile Indians.

We can only guess at the debate that took place among Indian leaders once warfare began. Historian Walling suggested that the "minor bands had been worse treated by the whites than had the Table Rock Indians" under chiefs Joe and Sam and were eager to fight. These smaller bands included those living on Butte Creek, the Applegate River, and Grave Creek. Raids on farms in the period August 11-22 indicate that many

Indians felt the time was right for such an attack. James W. Nesmith later said that "at the commencement of hostilities the [white] people of Rogue river valley were sadly deficient in arms and ammunition," and that the Indians actually had the advantage.[29] Capt. Alden's forces were especially vulnerable from August 11-16, when Indian raids in the valley had drawn away many volunteers. But Takelma chiefs Joe and Sam, who actually may have had a superior force at the time, did not attack.

The uncertainty of Indian military leaders was highlighted by the action of the dozen or so Indian women who passed between white and Indian camps trying to prevent an even larger, full-scale war. E. L. Applegate wrote that "these women were given comfortable quarters at the encampment of the soldiers, were supplied with saddle ponies and went every day from the camp of the soldiers to that of the Indians and labored to dissuade the natives from their contemplated general assault upon the whites."[30] Whites respected them afterwards for the role they had played in averting further white casualties. They had served at the time as cultural intermediaries trying to preserve a tenuous middle-ground in the face of warfare, and some of them extended that middle-ground into the future through their continuing relationships with white men.

Up to the signing of a "treaty of peace" on September 8 by chiefs Joe (Apserkahar), Sam (Toquahear), and Jim (Anachakarah), whites were uncertain the Indian bands would cease fighting. Lane wrote immediately afterwards that the treatymaking had been helped by the arrival of Captain Andrew J. Smith, who came with reinforcements, dragoons (mounted soldiers) from Port Orford. Lane observed that "his troop served to overawe the Indians." By September 10, a company of volunteers under James W. Nesmith arrived together with regular officer Lieutenant August V. Kautz, Fourth Infantry, his men, and a twelve-pound howitzer, which added to the show of force. A second treaty, which was signed on September 10 with the major Indian bands, established the terms of land sale and transfer from the Rogue River Indians to the United States. Indians ceded all lands from a mile below the mouth of the Applegate River west to the Cascades and from the Siskiyou Mountains to a line just north of Upper and Lower Table Rock. These were lands of chiefs Sam, Joe, and Jim's people on the Rogue River, and of chiefs John, Limpy, and George's people on the Applegate River. Chief Tipsu's Shasta band was left out; so, too, were bands farther west along the Rogue River and on the Illinois River. The treaty also included installment payments of sixty thousand dollars in goods, less fifteen thousand for indemnities, and it established a temporary "Indian reserve" on the north side of the Rogue River in the vicinity of Lower Table Rock. The reserve boundary enclosed land between the Evans Creek drainage and Rogue River, an irregular-shaped area about twelve miles by fifteen miles at the outer limits. The reserve was about one hundred square miles in size; and the ceded land amounted to about nineteen hundred square miles. Much of the ceded land was mountainous country, but it also included the best land for growth of native plants as well as for agriculture.[31]

While the treaty of September 10 officially brought about four hundred Indians onto the reserve, it left a little over five hundred Indians outside it. Of the number outside the reserve, perhaps seventy-five to one hundred could be considered fighting men,[32] and they continued to become involved in violent skirmishes with whites in the fall of 1853. Sometimes whites started the incidents, at other times Indians did. Pioneer historian Walling concluded, that "whites as a class were content with the treaty and obedient to its provisos, [but] there was a considerable minority who lost no opportunity to manifest their contempt of the instrument and their disregard of its obligations." Only three days after the treaty had been signed, Applegate Valley Indians fought a white company of thirty men. Walling described several incidents of white atrocities at Grave Creek and on the Applegate and Illinois rivers that persuaded Indians they were still in danger, and that led them to acts of reprisal.[33]

These incidents of violence in the fall, however, did not alter the recognition by white and Indian leaders that the summer war of 1853 and subsequent treaties marked the end of one era and beginning of a new one. Lane, in later years, wrote to Nesmith: "Old John and Adam, and all others except Jo's and Sam's people fought you hard [in 1855-56], but the Rogues, proper, never forgot the impression we made upon them in the great Council of September 10, 1853."[34]

The scale of warfare in the summer of 1853 was different from previous summers. Walling reported that about fifty Indians had lost their lives in the fighting in 1851; Steele reported killing thirteen Indians in the 1852 encounter, and probably as many more also lost their lives that summer.[35] A careful tally of casualties for the months June-October 1853 shows that at least sixty Indians were killed in fighting, or from being hung. Perhaps a third of these lost their lives in June and the rest in August; at least ten were hung. Fifteen Indians died in the major engagement with the white volunteers north of Table Rock, where eighteen whites also lost their lives.[36] Mrs. Butler's running tally of white dead and wounded in August 1853 totaled thirty-four people. Three deaths of whites occurred during the August volunteer engagement. Total reported deaths of both whites and Indians in the Rogue River Valley-Illinois Valley-Grave Creek region probably approached at least one hundred to one hundred twenty persons. These numbers far exceeded the casualties of earlier summers.[37]

In addition to the number of dead, the August Indian uprising also released a degree of savage brutality among whites that had not been evident before. Probably because of the lower ratio of whites to Indians, fewer incidents of brutality against Indians had taken place in the Rogue River Valley than in northern California prior to August 1853. Reports that whites slaughtered Indians right and left during the August fighting exaggerated the scope of white retaliation, but accurately highlighted the savagery of particular incidents. Benjamin F. Dowell described his unsuccessful attempt to prevent the hanging of an innocent Indian boy in Jacksonville in early August.[38] Matthew P. Deady, then U.S. District Court Judge and later Oregon Supreme Court Justice, recounted the story, also referred to by Mrs. Butler, of Indians lured into a log house for food and then killed by whites as they were eating.[39] In the summer of 1853, incidents of this nature were still sufficiently rare to be talked about and remembered, but they occurred with greater frequency during the next three years.

DESPITE THE VIOLENT SUMMER CONFLICT, treaty negotiations that took place in early September provided another opportunity for the reinforcement of middle-ground relations between Indian and white leaders. Joseph Lane and Chief Joe (Apserkahar) were again the key figures. On September 10, Lane took a small group of about fifteen to twenty men to negotiate a treaty with Chief Joe and his people. The group included Superintendent of Indian Affairs Joel Palmer and Indian Agent Samuel H. Culver, along with military officers Capt. Andrew J. Smith, Lt. August V. Kautz, and Oregon political figures James W. Nesmith, Lafayette Grover, and Matthew P. Deady, as well as several others. The composition of Lane's party reflected the expanded federal and territorial administrative scope of negotiations. Although Lane would draw upon his personal relationship with Chief Joe to help make the negotiations a success, the implementation of this summer's negotiations would clearly be in the hands of military and Indian Affairs officers. Lane's party went unarmed, which Nesmith later claimed put their lives in great danger. Lane trusted in his relationship with Chief Joe, established in the summer of 1850.[40]

Matthew Deady recalled that the treaty council was held "on a narrow bench of a long, gently sloping hill, lying over against the noted bluff called [Lower] Table Rock."[41] Nesmith remembered being surrounded by "seven hundred fierce and well armed hostile savages, in all their gorgeous war paint and feathers."[42] Nesmith may have exaggerated, but nearby Indian camps would have included women and children. Deady recalled seeing "above us on the hillside ... some hundreds of dusky warriors in fighting gear, reclining quietly on the ground."[43] According to Lafayette Grover, the Indians were "drawn up in the form of a horse shoe" with the Indian chiefs at the top and warriors on either side of them with "rifles loaded & capped in their hands."[44] Grover also recalled that when they arrived at the treaty site "everything looked very solemn and morose, & there was not a word said to us, or to each other .... It looked very black, and dangerous." Echoing Grover's view of the solemnity of the Indians, Deady noted that "Indian Joseph, tall, grave, and self-possessed, wore a long black robe over his ordinary dress."

Treatymaking was delayed by the absence of Chief Jim (Anachakarah), a subordinate chief, descended from the Umpqua Indians. While they waited for him, Indian leaders passed around a ceremonial peace pipe. Some Indians began to display their wounds from the fighting. Lane's party took this as a sign that the Indians seriously wanted to make peace. When Chief Jim arrived, everyone became silent and he delivered an eloquent half-hour oration. Then an Indian runner entered the treaty council and told of the killing of an Applegate River Indian by a white volunteer company. According to Nesmith's account, Lane took charge of the situation and, "with his arm bandaged in a sling" from a wound he had received in the earlier fighting, stood up calmly and promised that the white men responsible would be punished. Grover recalled that Chief Joe then said: "We sent for you to come here, and to leave the soldiers behind ... We told you to come without arms, that we wanted to make peace ... We could kill you all now [as whites did the Applegate Indians]. But ... the Indian is nobler than the white man."

The several accounts of this historic negotiation complement each other by explaining what made it possible for Joseph Lane and Chief Joe to understand and negotiate successfully with each other. Both leaders showed qualities of courage, a sense of honor, fairness, and trust, all reinforced by the personal bond established in the summer of 1850. But neither man negotiated alone. On the white side, Joel Palmer's ideas as superintendent of Indian affairs, as well as federal Indian policy and treaty precedents, shaped the outcome of the treaty council. All the major Rogue River chiefs had to agree to the treaty. In addition, Indian consent was subject to a participatory process. Deady described the involvement of the gathered Indian warriors as well as chiefs: "After a proposition was discussed and settled between the two chiefs, the Indians would rise up and communicate the matter to a huge warrior who reclined at the foot of a tree quite near us. Then the latter rose up and communicated the matter to the host above him, and they belabored it back and forth with many voices. Then the warrior communicated the thought of the multitude on the subject back to his chief; and so the discussion went on until an understanding was finally reached."

At Table Rock, as at treaty councils elsewhere, the terms of treaties had to pass through several stages of translation. James W. Nesmith, who served as "Interpreter" at the Table Rock council, described the process as one in which speeches made by Lane and Palmer were translated into Chinook Jargon and then into Takelma. The Indian chiefs who signed the treaty were Joe (Apserkahar or Apsakahah, Horse-rider), Sam (Toquahear or Kokohawah, Wealthy), Jim (Anachakarah or Anachaharah), John (Tecumtom or Tecumtum, Elk Killer), and Lympe or Limpy (no other name given).[45] The Indian chiefs probably understood the treaty's basic terms. Indians would receive some compensation for the loss of their land. They were supposed to live within a designated area within the Rogue River Valley. And if they did not follow the terms of the treaty, they would be subjected to a prolonged and perhaps fatally destructive war with whites. Although some of the Indians present at the negotiations may have thought of this treaty as just another truce, chiefs Joe and Sam never did make war again. The smaller bands of chiefs John and Limpy, as well as the non-signatory bands, renewed warfare over the next few years.

After the treatymaking ended, Chief Joe's daughter Mary came to Lane and told him that Peoosecut of Tipsu's band had started the war, and urged Lane to have him killed. With directions from Chief Joe's people, Lane and his interpreter, Robert B. Metcalfe, who had once lived with Chief Tipsu's band, found the chief and convinced him to agree to the treaty terms. Lane promised to bring "a shirt, pantaloons, coat & shoes for him, and shirt and pantaloons for each one of his braves." Lane did not find Peoosecut, but later he was arrested for murder, tried, and hung. The following spring, Tipsu's band became involved in an attack on a pack train on the Siskiyou trail to Yreka. Pursued by army regulars with the help of a contingent of Deschutes Indians, Tipsu sought help from his old enemies the Klamath River Shastas under Chief Bill, but they killed and scalped him.[46] In seeking out Peoosecut and Chief Tipsu, Lane fulfilled an obligation to Mary, Chief Joe, and their people, as well as to his own.

The treaty of 1853 was different from the earlier treaties that had concluded summer clashes in the previous three years. These had been informal truces, whereas the treaty of 1853 was a formal treaty negotiated by agents of the United States government and resulted in the transfer of Indian lands as well as the cessation of hostilities. Moreover, the 1853 agreement established a temporary Indian reserve in the Rogue River Valley that forced treaty Indians to live within a more restricted area. At the conclusion of previous summer warfare there had been no formal means for enforcing treaty terms, but the 1853 agreement required treaty Indians to submit complaints of injuries to the Indian agent. In addition, Fort Lane was established on September 28, 1853, on the south side of the Rogue River, just outside the Indian reserve. Although consisting of only "three depleted companies of the second infantry" (perhaps less than a hundred men), it substantially increased white ability to retaliate against Indian attacks. With the transfer of Indian land to white control, creation of an Indian reserve, and establishment of a U.S. Army fort in the Rogue River Valley, all elements of federal Indian policy finally converged in southern Oregon.[47]

From an Indian military point of view, the summer of 1853 marked the last chance for a loosely coordinated offensive against white settlement by all the Indian bands. After the treaty negotiations, war and peace factions among Indians became permanent divisions between the bands. Leadership of opposition to white settlement passed from chiefs Sam and Joe to leaders of smaller outlying bands, especially Chief Tipsu in the Siskiyou foothills and Old John (Tecumtom or Tecumtum), a chief in the Applegate River Valley (who had close ties to the Klamath River Shastas). Middle-ground relations between Indians and white leaders also changed. In the period 1850-53, Joseph Lane had played a dominant role in dealing with the Indians. He personalized relations, playing the role of cultural intermediary for whites, as Chiefs Joe and Sam did for the Rogue River Indians. After the summer of 1853, Indians had to deal with less well-known Indian agents and officers of the United States army, who became the new white cultural intermediaries of a legal and political middle-ground created by treaty.

THE WHITE EMIGRANTS on the Southern Route who arrived in southern Oregon in 1853 had left their old homes in the east long before the summer warfare in the Rogue River Valley began. The John Beeson family reached Clear Lake (close to the Oregon-California border, southeast of Klamath Falls) on August 21. A company of U.S. Army dragoons was camped there to protect emigrants against Indian attack. Seventeen-year-old Welborn Beeson wrote in his diary: "The soldiers gave us late Papers. The news from Rouge River, give d[r]eadful account of the Indians war burning houses and Mascre'g the people. The old chief declares he will have his valley back or die fighting."[48]

Perhaps six to seven hundred men, women, and children entered Oregon in 1853 on the route that led northwest from the Humboldt River through the Black Rock Desert in the northwestern corner of Nevada to Goose Lake and Clear Lake in northern California and then to Lower Klamath Lake in Oregon. The route opened by Jesse Applegate and others in 1846 was as difficult as ever, but it had become clearly marked, and there were soldiers and volunteer militiamen along the way to protect new arrivals from Indian attack.

The Beeson wagon train passed over the Cascade Mountains west of the Klamath Lakes and reached the Rogue River Valley on August 30.[49] From settlers at Mountain House, the party learned that Indians and whites were fighting in the valley. Settlers had gathered together for protection. Welborn wrote: "We passed several houses and farms, but they were all deserted having fled to the Fort for protection from the Indians the Fort is just across the little creeck from Alberts, owned by Mr Jacob Wagner, all the Citizens of this part of the Valley are collected in it."[50]

Despite the Indian threat that continued until a treaty of peace was signed on September 8, Welborn and his family liked the looks of the valley in the vicinity of present-day Talent where they decided to stop and make a home. Welborn noted that the cattle there were "very fat," and they immediately turned theirs loose to graze on the rich grass along Bear Creek. Local farms had abundant tomatoes, melons, and other garden crops. In less than a week John Beeson bought a farm for $1,500. It had "1/3 acre potatoes 1 acre of corn, and sundry other garden stuff," Welborn wrote. The farms of the Robison, Anderson, and Wagner families adjoined theirs. The Beeson farm included three fenced acres of crops and "a good log house 32 ft long and 16 wide, divided into two rooms, each 16 ft square."[51]

In the fall, Indians began to live under the terms of the Treaty of 1853 that had established an Indian reserve north of the Rogue River near Lower Table Rock. The reserve officially extended west to Evans Creek, but most of the Indians on the reserve were concentrated in the historic territory (now Sams Valley) of Chief Sam's people near Table Rock. Superintendent Palmer and his agents, as well as the army regulars stationed at Fort Lane, now had responsibility for keeping Indians on the reserve and whites away from it, in order to keep the two populations separate. The Treaty of 1853 was based on the principle of separation of Indians and whites. White settlers and miners demanded to be protected from Indian attacks; Indians struggled to stay alive. Lack of provisions for the Indians on the reserve inevitably led to hunting and gathering forays off the reserve, which sometimes ended in theft of food and property from white settlers and miners. As a result, whites talked more about Indian removal and even "extermination."

The ratio of whites to Indians had changed significantly by the fall of 1853.[52] Oregon Donation Land Claims in Jackson County for the three years 1851-53 increased from eight to 53 to 129. For Jackson County, 1853 was the peak year of filings; only 91 were filed in 1854 and 34 in 1855. Single males filed about half the claims. However, newcomer John Beeson wrote that when he arrived with his family only "a very sparse settlement of whites" was at the south end of the valley and mostly Indians lived at the north end. There were many more miners than there were settlers, even though some miners had also taken out land claims. Pioneer historian Walling estimated that the 1853 migration on the Southern Route numbered 400 men, 120 women, and 170 children, a total of 690 persons. Even though most of the newcomers to Oregon passed on through to the Willamette Valley, their arrival in early fall added substantially to the white population of the valley. It seems likely that the Rogue River Valley settlement population numbered four to five hundred men, women, and children by late 1853, exclusive of the large mining population of several thousand men. Jacksonville's population was estimated at three to four hundred people. If these pioneer estimates are correct, then white settlers and townspeople about equaled the Indian population of the valley, and, together with the miners, easily outnumbered them.[53]

White-Indian warfare in the summer of 1853 made many settlers consider moving on to places like Coos Bay on the Oregon coast or to the Willamette Valley. At the same time, new emigrants on the Southern Route, like the Beeson family, began to arrive in late September and early October. America Rollins Butler, whose family took up a land claim in early 1853, wrote in her diary: "Quite a number of emigrants have arrived this week and a great many of our citizens are leaving for Coose Bay our Indian difficulties will be quite a draw back to this valley Provisions are so cheap that it wont pay expenses." All through summer, the Butlers suffered from fever ("ague"), probably malaria. Some members of the Butler family were "tired of farming and tired of the country and have got Coose Bay fever." By October three of the six men in the Butler family had left.[54]

But most settlers stayed in the Rogue River Valley. On October 10, the same day that four emigrant wagons and about a hundred cattle passed by the Butler farm, Mrs. Butler wrote in her diary that "the farmers are all anxious to put in largely of wheat some are putting in a hundred acres this fall." By late October a neighbor had returned from the Umpqua Valley with seventy-five hogs, and threshing and sacking of oats was underway. In November the Butlers got the help of neighbors to raise a new house frame. Mrs. Butler had to feed twenty people at the house-raising dinner that followed. The Butler household had also grown by eight men in addition to family members. Later that month, Mrs. Butler's husband was busy "putting muslin windows in [the new house] so this gloomy weather we will not be in perpetual darkness."[55]

The building of a farming community rapidly transformed the Rogue River Valley landscape. But the new emigrants had mixed feelings about their situation. One of the new arrivals, S. H. Taylor, wrote back to his hometown newspaper in Watertown, Wisconsin. What impressed him most about Oregon was the difficulty of life for new arrivals. He told his friends back in Wisconsin that "more than half" of the emigrants "regret having come here." On the other hand, he praised the helpfulness of the previous year's emigrants toward people like himself. And although the land was dry and needed irrigation, farmers had success growing wheat, oats, and barley. Cattle did well on the valley grassland.[56]

The John Beeson family, along with others, stayed in the Rogue River Valley. In the fall of 1853, the family began the hard work of building a permanent home and farm. In the next few years, John Beeson became an outspoken advocate of fair treatment for the Indians of southern Oregon. But his primary concern in 1853 and 1854 was to build a home for his family and to plant crops in order to survive. The Beeson family's daily life illustrates how settled the Rogue River Valley was becoming in the aftermath of the 1853 summer war.

John Beeson and his wife Ann Welborn had immigrated to the United States from England in 1830. Their only surviving child, Welborn Beeson, was born in 1836 after they had settled in LaSalle County, Illinois.[57] The family farmed in Illinois for nineteen years before beginning the overland trek to Oregon. During that time John Beeson was a temperance-reform lecturer; he also helped fugitive slaves escape to the north on the underground railway. He was known in LaSalle County as a radical abolitionist.[58] Welborn Beeson, who began his daily journal in 1851 at age fifteen, made an entry shortly before leaving Illinois that highlighted his father's abolitionist activity: "Father came to me in the field he told me It was two young men from below Grandville they had brought a poor slave from the land of bondage on his way to Canada his name is William Carey. Oh when will the laws of the United States become human enough to Abolish slavery."[59] Welborn Beeson's expression of support for the abolition of slavery suggests the moral foundation of the Beeson family's pro-Indian sympathies. The Beesons found that injustice toward Indians paralleled the injustice of slavery. They also discovered that many pro-slavery southerners had migrated to Oregon as settlers and miners.

From September through November 1853, Welborn and his father spent many days splitting rails for fences. The Beesons bought a cast-iron plow and beginning October 20, they "broke praria" with four yoke of oxen. From time to time Welborn and his father made trips to Jacksonville to sell cabbages, onions, potatoes, and pumpkins. On Sunday, October 30, the Beesons had a church meeting at their house for the first time, and many settlers in the neighborhood attended. Plowing continued through November and December. By December the family began to get mail from back east, including six issues of a phrenological journal and five issues of water-cure journals for John Beeson. Several school meetings took place at what was called "Wagner's Fort," and by mid-December settlers in the neighborhood had decided to build a schoolhouse. Although Welborn does not tell us how many people had settled on Wagner Creek near present-day Talent by late fall 1853, three years later he recorded that forty-two men, women, and children lived there.[60]

Welborn made no mention of contacts with Indians during the fall months of 1853, but he and his father discovered the location of several "Indian ranches" or campsites on the creek that ran through their farm.[61] It bothered John Beeson's conscience that he had settled on Indian land. His sensitivity to the plight of Indians had been awakened by contacts along the Oregon Trail. He later wrote in his book condemning white treatment of Indians in southern Oregon: "We had no sooner got west of the Mississippi river than I had a foreshadowing of a work to do for the Indians."[62] Along the creek where he settled with his family, he observed that "there were still remaining the excavations, the poles, bark, and coverings of their wigwams, and the fresh ashes of their fires." These reminded him of "being an interloper or usurper of homes which others ought to possess, or for which they ought to be paid."[63]

January 1854 brought freezing temperatures and snow. The Beesons worried about being able to feed their cattle. Rail splitting and fence building continued. On January 18 the Beesons got word that on the way to Yreka some Indians had attacked a white party, killed five men, wounded others, and stolen their mules.[64] A few days later they heard that Indians had been discovered at a cave on the Klamath River and attacked by whites. By January 31, the Beesons learned that the whites had been beaten back by the Indians and that the Indians refused to make peace. "Bravo for the Indians," Welborn wrote in his diary. He then went on to record fighting between Indians and whites near Crescent City on the coast.[65] Whites hung an Indian boy there, provoking Indian retaliation. Welborn hoped that the Indian boy's killers would be found and hung too. On February 10, Welborn noted that an Indian had been hung in Jacksonville and that "most of [the Beesons'] neighbors went." Two weeks later, on February 26, an Indian woman came to the Beeson house. The Beesons fed her, and she finally made them understand that she needed matches to start a campfire.[66]

In March, the Beesons continued their work of splitting rails and building fence. They also helped their neighbors with plowing. By mid-March they planted potatoes, corn, melons, onions, tomatoes, and "other garden stuff." Welborn and two friends began panning and sluicing for gold on the creek. On May 15, the neighborhood men raised the schoolhouse. Two days later, Welborn's father went to Jacksonville, where he traded thirty pounds of cheese for one hundred pounds of flour.[67] The summer months brought forth a bountiful harvest of wheat, potatoes, and garden crops. By the fall of 1854, the Beesons were able to purchase new clothes, harness for their oxen, a new yoke of oxen, a new stove for the house, and a wagon. They also built a bedroom onto their house and began to fence in a "large wheat field." There is no indication that Welborn's father had started to speak out publicly on behalf of local Indians. He was involved in farming; he attended regular church meetings; and by late fall he had begun to lecture on water-cure treatment and to organize temperance meetings.[68]

The emigrants who arrived in the Rogue River Valley in the fall of 1853 apparently had little or no trouble with Indians while getting settled during the following year. But they also had limited contacts with Indians, judging from Welborn Beeson's diary. John Beeson was only an indirect participant in middle-ground relations between Indians and whites, even though he was sympathetic to the Indians' plight. But Beeson's success in transforming his small piece of the Rogue River Valley into fenced farmland threatened the Indians' survival just as much as the success of white farmers less conscious of Indian rights.

Chapter 5

Uncertain Peace, 1853-55

THE TREATIES NEGOTIATED with upper Rogue River Indians at the end of summer fighting in 1853, and with the Cow Creeks immediately after, thrust Superintendent of Indian Affairs Joel Palmer into the middle of Indian-white relations in southern Oregon. At first his attention focused on the Rogue River Valley, but it soon turned to the coastal zone for two reasons. As Palmer looked for a way to separate Indians and whites, the north-central Oregon coast, as yet unsettled, seemed ideally suited for a reservation. At the same time, the southern Oregon gold rush carried whites across the mountains to the coast, causing increasing uncertainty for coastal Indians.

In the year after treaty negotiations with the upper Rogue River Indians, Palmer still had to negotiate treaties with coastal Indians and the non-reserve Indians in the Rogue River Valley area. In addition, he had to administer treaties negotiated by Joseph Lane with a majority of the upper Rogue River Indians. However, Palmer viewed the Table Rock reserve as only a temporary expedient. Even in late June, before the summer fighting had begun, Palmer wrote that western Oregon Indians would have to be removed from "reserves in the heart of the settlements" and "guarded from the pestiferous influence of degraded white men, and restrained by proper laws from violence and wrong among themselves."[1]

Palmer, as an early white pioneer and leader of the 1845 migration to Oregon, was as biased as any settler on the question of the right of whites to settle on Indian land. His experience of living in the Willamette Valley and of trying to mediate grievances between white settlers and the small population of Indians who lived there had left him skeptical that Indians and whites could live together. He observed that as roots and game grew scarce, Indians resorted to "petty thefts." He also believed that most Indians were "exceedingly indolent and improvident," especially given to gambling away what little they owned, and thus being taken advantage of by "unprincipled whites." These observations, although prejudiced, also were perceptive as to the

Indians' vulnerability to white dishonesty. Palmer, the humanitarian, concluded that "a home remote from the settlements" must be found for Indians, where the government could provide them with "comfortable houses," teach them how to farm, instruct Indian children, and make "an honest and determined endeavor ... to save and elevate a fallen race."[2] Palmer looked to the north-central Oregon coast with its small river valleys and abundant natural resources for a site on which to relocate southern Oregon Indians.

In the fall of 1853 Palmer saw two major obstacles to continued peace: one was the "conduct of evil-minded whites," and the second was the fact that treaties negotiated with various Indian bands had not been ratified. The unratified treaties caused Indians to have a "want of confidence" in the United States government. Palmer knew that negotiation and ratification of treaties was essential to smoothing the way for white settlement. He warned that without "Government" action a "general indian war" could result.[3] But he also criticized the practice in negotiating with Indians of making promises that could not be met, and of gathering them together in a single place "to be paraded, petted and feasted at the public expense." He believed that they should be negotiated with on their own territory at a time of year when their resources were depleted. He gave credit to Joseph Lane "for the explicit and fair dealing which has always characterized his intercourse with the indians." Lane "avoided making them promises beyond his confidence of being able to perform."[4]

Palmer depended upon his Indian agents to report on conditions of Indian-white relations in their districts and to mediate disputes. He had Indian agents for the Rogue River and Umatilla Indians; sub-Indian agents for the Willamette Valley, Clatsop Plains, and Port Orford; and special agents assigned to the Umpquas, Coos, and Coquilles. Believing in the importance of their jobs, Palmer urged the Commissioner of Indian Affairs in Washington, D.C., to raise their pay. He noted that sub-Indian agents received "barely the pay of a common laborer and insufficient to secure the services of competent and reliable men."[5]

The southern Oregon coast seemed especially important to Palmer in late 1853 and early 1854 because of the recent discoveries of gold on coastal streams and tributaries (Chetco, Rogue, Elk, and Sixes) and on coastal beaches. There was an increased population of white miners from just north of the Coquille River (at the mining camp of Randolph City) south to the Chetco River. The presence of miners of "reckless and desperate character" and "affected with such feelings of hostility to the indians" posed a serious threat to local Indians. Palmer did not receive funds to visit the southern Oregon coast until the spring of 1854. He reached the Rogue River in mid-May, where he negotiated a treaty. Soon after, Congress ratified the treaties Palmer had made with the Cow Creek and Rogue River Indians. In historian Terence O'Donnell's words, it was "the best news he had so far received as superintendent." [6]

ALTHOUGH COASTAL INDIANS' CONTACTS with whites had been limited to a few coastal and HBC explorers and fur trappers, the Jedediah Smith expedition, and American missionaries Jason Lee and Gustavus Hines, their isolation ended in 1850. The California gold rush stimulated a new interest in coastal as well as inland northern California and southern Oregon. In the spring to early summer of 1850, a group of men organized a joint-stock company—Winchester, Paine, and Company—and launched an exploring expedition named the Klameth or Klamath Exploring Expedition that left San Francisco on the schooner *Samuel Roberts* to investigate the southern Oregon coast. The objectives of this business venture were to find a good harbor, lay out town sites, and explore inland along the Rogue River (called the Klameth River on early maps, thus the name of the expedition) in search of gold.[7]

In late July 1850, the Klameth Exploring Expedition entered the Rogue River. Albert Lyman, aged twenty-four and captain of the schooner *Samuel Roberts*, described some characteristics of the Rogue River Indians he met.[8] He found that Indians near the mouth of the river were numerous, friendly, unfamiliar with whites, and lacking in trade items. He described them as "mostly naked or wrapped in a deer skin. Some had a closely woven conical cap made basket fashion and the chiefs had a deer skin cap with feathers on top. They paint their faces with black and red and wear pearl ornaments in their nose & ears. Some have feathers stuck through the perferature in their nose. Their Bows and arrows are of very nice workmanship." Lyman saw only "two old muskets among them." Some of their arrows had iron points, others flint. Their knives were made of copper or iron. "Their canoes," Lyman wrote, "are rather rude being square at each end."[9] Lyman's description of lower Rogue River Indians provides evidence of white trade items, but few in number, suggesting that contact with white coastal traders had been infrequent.

Uncertain about the attitude of lower Rogue River Indians and dissatisfied with site opportunities, the Klameth Exploring Expedition sailed on to the Umpqua River, arriving on August 2, 1850. Lower Umpqua Indians, descendants of the Kalawatsets who had attacked Jedediah Smith's party in 1828, approached the *Samuel Roberts* in canoes. Lyman observed that "they appeard very different from the indians of the Klameth [Rogue River] having seen much more of the whites. They were most of them provided with shirts, coats & pants & were much more respectful in their demeanor." Lyman also commented that their canoes were "very gracefully shaped and are made from a log of wood though very light and handy."[10] The white trade items noted by Lyman reflected over twenty years of middle-ground relations with HBC traders at Fort Umpqua and along the Umpqua River west to the coast.

After anchoring his schooner upstream near what became Scottsburg, Lyman continued on by canoe to Fort Umpqua (located across the river from present-day Elkton), which he described as follows: "There was formerly a great business carried on here in furs with the indians, but at present it does not amount to much. Mr. Gagnier is assisted by one white man and a few Kanakas [Hawaiians] and indians. He cultivates about 50 acres of land and raises wheat & corn, potatoes & most all kinds of garden vegetables. He has a few apple trees which bear well. Mr. Gagnier has an indian wife and one son." By August 27, when the *Samuel Roberts* weighed anchor to return to San Francisco, four townsites had been laid out on the Umpqua River. Lyman wrote that one was located "at the mouth of the river called Umpqua, one at the head of navigation called Scottsburg, one near the fort called Elkton, and one at the forks of the river 30 miles from the fort called Winchester."[11]

In June 1851, a year after the Umpqua town sites had been established, another business entrepreneur, William Tichenor, captain of a coastal schooner, landed a small party of nine men at Port Orford.[12] Between 1792, when Vancouver stopped briefly, and 1851, when Tichenor anchored in the lee of Cape Blanco, attitudes of local Indians toward whites apparently had changed. Tichenor's men landed on June 9 and, fearing the Indians they met, immediately built a defensive breastwork of logs on an offshore rock that became known as "Battle Rock." Tichenor left for San Francisco in the *Sea Gull* for more men and supplies, leaving behind the small group of men and an old cannon. The first fighting between south coast Indians and whites since the Jedediah Smith expedition massacre at the Umpqua River was about to begin.

The next day, a large war party of Indians gathered, perhaps numbering a hundred, and attacked. The white adventurers used pine boards as shields to protect themselves as best they could, but several were wounded. As Indians charged the eroded ridge of Battle Rock, the white defenders fired their cannon, killing about seventeen Indian attackers. After hand-to-hand skirmishing, the rest of the Indians retreated.

At the conclusion of this first day of fighting, Indians carried away their dead. Fighting ceased for fourteen days, then a second and larger force of Indians, perhaps numbering several hundred, attacked the white position. After holding off the Indian force through the afternoon and with ammunition running out, Tichenor's men left their crude fortification and fled for white settlements they knew lay to the north.

At the Coquille River the escaping party came upon a large Indian village, which they quickly left behind, because the Indians there also seemed hostile. Continuing north, they were helped by Indians on Coos Bay and finally reached the white settlement of Umpqua City at the mouth of the Umpqua River on July 2, 1851, a little over three weeks after their landing at Battle Rock. Tichenor returned to Port Orford in mid-July with sixty-seven men and supplies. The new party built two blockhouses that marked the beginning of the town of Port Orford. But the new settlement's survival was tenuous until the following year.[13]

In late August 1851, twenty-three men led by civilian William G. T'Vault left Port Orford to explore for a route to the interior Oregon-California trail. The party started up the Rogue River, but soon felt threatened by lower Rogue River Indians. Within two weeks the party found itself lost and running short of food. Thirteen men of the party returned to Port Orford. The remainder continued exploring, by following an Indian trail over the mountains to the south fork of the Coquille River. Upper Coquille Indians took the ten white men downstream to within a few miles of the mouth of the river, where there was a large Indian village. When the whites stepped ashore, they were attacked. Five men of the expedition were killed; T'Vault and four others escaped.

On September 14, the day of the attack, Lieutenant August V. Kautz arrived at Port Orford to establish Fort Orford and give U.S. Army protection to coastal settlers. Within a few years, Fort Orford consisted of quarters for officers and soldiers, a hospital, store houses, guard house, and officers' messhall. The attack on the T'Vault party prompted the temporary dispatch in late October of three companies of U.S. Army foot soldiers and dragoons or cavalry to reinforce the small garrison of twenty dragoons at Fort Orford, bringing the number of U.S. Army troops on Oregon's south coast to about one hundred fifty.[14]

The newly arrived U.S. Army soldiers left Fort Orford in November to fight the Coquilles in retaliation for the killing of T'Vault's men. Tichenor later related that a blockhouse was erected "on the bluff commanding a view of the large Indian vilage and the [Coquille] river. A howitzer was brought to bear upon the village; shells thrown, clearing the ridge of the natives and causing great terror."[15] Shortly thereafter, a battle took place at the junction of the middle and south forks of the Coquille River between the soldiers and upper Coquille Indians.[16]

In December, the three U.S. Army companies temporarily assigned to Fort Orford returned to San Francisco. Replacement dragoons left for Fort Orford on the schooner *Captain Lincoln* in January 1852. Due to bad weather, the schooner was blown north of Port Orford to Coos Bay, where it ran aground on a sand bar off the channel entrance. Aboard the transport were about thirty men and supplies. The location of the shipwreck was described by Henry H. Baldwin, a member of C Troop, 1st Dragoons, as being two miles north of "Kowes" or "Kowan" bay. Pioneer historian Orvil Dodge concluded that the wreck occurred on the ocean side of Coos Bay's north spit "nearly opposite the present site of Empire City."[17]

Shelters made from the ship's spars and sails were erected to protect men and supplies from the weather. Indians from nearby villages across the bay soon arrived to investigate. As so frequently happened in contacts between Indians and whites, something turned up missing, in this case a revolver. An Indian suspect was apprehended, tied to a pole on which the United States flag had been raised, and given twenty-five lashes with a "raw-hide." After this initial incident, however, relations improved. Baldwin wrote that the "old chief, named, Hunness" (actually a variant of the village name Hanisich, thus Hanis Coos Indians) came on his second visit with "a long pack-train of squaws laden with fish of all kinds, wild geese, ducks, elk and venison." In return the Indians were given "hardtack, rice, tobacco and lots of old dragoon pants, shell jackets, capes, skirts, boots and shoes, which pleased them extremely well, especially the jackets, which were decorated with grand yellow lace and a multitude of bright brass buttons."[18] Although the Hanisich village chief acted as spokesman for the Coos Bay Indians, Indians from other villages also visited the white camp.[19]

News of Camp Cast-A-Way reached several white outposts. Baldwin reported that within a few weeks several Americans and an HBC representative visited them from the Umpqua River to offer help. Assistant Quartermaster of the Pacific Division Morris S. Miller sailed from San Francisco to Fort Orford and then proceeded overland to Coos Bay in order to salvage the wrecked ship's cargo. During his two-month stay on Oregon's south coast, Miller had an opportunity to observe the Indians from Fort Orford to the Umpqua River. In his report, he wrote as follows:

> *There has been but little intercourse as yet between the Indians and the whites along the route from Fort Orford to Kowes river, and the use of ardent spirits is still unknown to them. They evinced throughout the most friendly disposition, aiding us readily with their canoes in crossing the rivers, bringing wood and water to the campfire, and considering themselves amply remunerated for these services by a small quantity of hard bread.*
>
> *They are full of curiosity with regard to the whites, particularly desirous of procuring clothing, and much disposed to barter; offering even their children in trade. In the vicinity of Fort Orford they are aware of the value of coin, but in other places their currency is small shells strung together, and called "sirvash." They are humble and peaceably disposed, being armed entirely with the bow and arrow; and, in my opinion, no difficulty need be apprehended from them, unless it originate in aggressions of the whites.*[20]

Miller's observations indicated a readiness on the part of the Coos Indians to establish good relations. They also indicated that the Coos had been less involved in trading through the HBC's Fort Umpqua than their northern neighbors. On the whole, the wreck of the *Captain Lincoln* seems to have resulted in peaceful exchanges between C Troop and local Indians. But it brought Coos Bay to the attention of white gold miners, settlers, merchants, and sea captains, as well as to the rest of the southern Oregon coastal zone.

The discovery of gold on Jackson Creek in the Rogue River Valley in late 1851 had led to exploration for gold along the entire Rogue River drainage, with its many tributaries leading toward the coast. By the spring of 1853 gold miners from Jacksonville had worked their way down the Rogue and Illinois waterways to the mouth of the Rogue River. The town of Ellensburg, later Gold Beach, was one of several clusters of log cabins built on the Rogue River's south shore. At the same time, discovery of gold on the beach just north of the Coquille River brought a rush of miners and the construction of a temporary mining camp called Randolph City near a creek the miners named Whiskey Run.[21]

Where Whiskey Run Creek trickles into the ocean, two brothers of French-Canadian and Indian ancestry, John and Peter Grosluis, discovered gold, probably in the winter-spring of 1852-53.[22] The first whites to settle on Coos Bay arrived in the spring through fall of 1853, establishing the town of Empire City. By 1854, gold mining on the beach at Whiskey Run had attracted a mining population of perhaps a thousand men. Pioneer wife and mother Esther Lockhart recalled that "practically everybody deserted Empire City [on Coos Bay] and rushed to the gold mines," including her husband Freeman Lockhart. In a narrative of her life recorded by daughter Agnes Ruth Sengstacken, she described the scene: "At Randolph the ocean beach was staked off into 'claims' for miles, and rough boarding houses and log cabins sprang up like magic. Of course all the activities of a frontier mining camp flourished, including the dance hall, the saloon and the poker table, where the gambler played with his cocked revolver beside him."[23] During the winter of 1854-55, stormy weather and heavy seas eroded the beach, and the gold-laden black sand disappeared. The gold rush at Whiskey Run ended as abruptly as it began, but not before it had thoroughly disrupted life for the Indians living on the lower Coquille River.

Inland on Coos Bay and the Coquille River, whites were anxious about how the local Indians would react, but boldly asserted their right to settle there heedless of whether treaties with Indians had been negotiated or ratified. Esther Lockhart described her experience of settling with her husband on or next to an Indian village (located on upper Coos Bay at present-day North Bend): "For the first few weeks all went smoothly enough, if we may except the theft of the 'washing.' The Indians were friendly, too friendly, in fact, for their calls at the cabin with requests for food became too frequent. I did not dare to refuse their demands, for I realized that we were in their power. Still, we did not fear them. Gradually, however, there came muttering of discontent from among them."[24]

About six weeks after the Lockharts settled at North Bend, "a band of fifty or sixty natives, in war paint and feathers, armed with bow and arrows" showed up at their cabin. They demanded that the Lockharts leave, which they finally did a week or two later, fearing for their lives.[25] However, once they were back in Empire City, on the ocean side of the Coos Bay peninsula, local Indians were not a problem. "The Indians always seemed to enjoy supplying the white people with sea-food, wild game and berries, in those days rarely appearing to want money for their wares. They much preferred to have some of the newcomers' clothing or some other article from the belongings of the palefaces."[26]

In the spring of 1855, a few settlers located farms in the Coquille Valley, near the south and middle forks of the Coquille River. Russell Cooke Dement, whose family moved there when he was seven years of age, recalled that his family got along well with local Indians. Although the family temporarily moved back to Empire City during the Rogue River War of 1855-56, the Dements left almost all their possessions behind. "We would have been perfectly safe to have stayed," Dement wrote. "The Indians didn't molest a thing we left."[27]

The Indian-white encounters at North Bend described by Lockhart might have resulted in white retaliation ending in bloodshed, but at the time, whites were few in numbers and hesitant to provoke warfare. Indians and whites on Coos Bay established peaceful middle-ground relations, both economic and interpersonal. Historian and ethnobiographer Lionel Youst notes that many of the nineteen men of the Coos Bay Commercial Company, who established Empire City in the area of three Indian villages, married Indian women.[28] This was in contrast to the initially hostile interactions between Indians and whites at Port Orford and on the lower Coquille River. Relations between Indians and whites on Coos Bay remained peaceful, even through the Rogue River War of 1855-56, in which Coos Indians did not participate.[29]

BUT IN EARLY 1854, Superintendent Palmer's fears of increasing Indian-white conflict became reality elsewhere on the coast. On January 28, at the mouth of the Coquille River, approximately forty white miners, working beach placers north of the Coquille River, massacred Nasomah Indians living in three encampments on both sides of the river.[30] George H. Abbott, who was elected captain of the expedition against the Indians, described the massacre site: "The Indian village is in three different parts, situated on both sides of the river, about one and a half mile from the mouth." Abbott divided his force into three elements, one of which attacked each of the village sites. The Nasomahs numbered about seventy-five persons. Indian sub-agent F. M. Smith reported that "the Indians were aroused from sleep to meet their death, with but a feeble show of resistance; they were shot down as they were attempting to escape from their homes; fifteen men and one squaw were killed; two squaws were badly wounded. On the part of the white men, not even the slightest wound was received. The houses of the Indians, with but one exception, were fired and entirely destroyed. Thus was committed a massacre too inhuman to be readily believed."[31]

The attack on the Nasomah village sites was preceded by public meetings at the Randolph City mining camp on the beach north of the Coquille River. Formal resolutions were drawn up in a ritualistic show of democratic legalism prior to the use of vigilante violence. This was consistent with conventions of frontier mining communities in the American West. But a resolution requesting the intervention of Agent Smith was drawn up and sent to him on the day prior to the attack, leaving no time for him to make the trip from Port Orford to the Coquille River in time to mediate.[32]

In defending their attack, the white miners referred to as the Indians' "insolence," incidents of theft, and the discharge of a gun by the local Indian chief near the ferry-house. When Agent Smith later questioned the chief, he found that the chief had been shooting at ducks, and that the ball from his gun had probably ricocheted. The chief admitted, however, that some of his men had threatened white men, stolen possessions from them, and used their horses without permission. Whites in self-justification insisted that the Indians had "declared war" and were "on the eve of commencing an outbreak against the whites."[33]

In the middle of February, whites on the Chetco River initiated a second massacre of coastal Indians. It grew out of a dispute over control of a ferry across the river. Although in competition with Indians over ferrying business, a white man, A. F. Miller, insisted that he be allowed to build a house in an Indian village on the river's south bank, which he did. On the morning of February 15, Miller and eight or nine of his friends attacked the Indian village in which he had built his house. Thirteen Indian men were shot as they emerged from their houses; two more died from house fires started by two Indian women friendly to Miller. According to Joel Palmer, women and children were allowed to escape. Indians in a second village on the north bank of the river returned fire on the white attackers, but eventually they were forced to flee to the hills, and their lodges were burned down too. Twenty-three Indians including several women were killed. The two massacres of Indians that occurred in early 1854 on the Coquille and Chetco rivers provoked strong humanitarian reactions from Palmer and his local Indian agents. In reporting to Joel Palmer on his investigation of the Coquille River incident, Agent Smith used the strongest words he could find to express his revulsion. "I grieve to report to you that a most horrid massacre, or rather an out-and-out barbarous murder, was perpetrated upon a portion of the Na-son [Nasomah] tribe ... by a party of forty miners."[34] Agent Smith found no justification for the miners' action. He concluded that the Indians have no desire to be hostile but that they might be pushed to it by "*savage* white men."

In May, Joel Palmer investigated the Chetco River massacre scene himself. He was particularly incensed at the whites' duplicity before the attack: "What adds to the atrocity of the deed is, that shortly before the massacre, the Indians were induced to sell the whites their guns, under the pretext that friendly relations were firmly established." He reported to his superior, Commissioner of Indian Affairs George W. Manypenny, that it was a "horrid tragedy" and that there seemed to be no way to punish the responsible parties. "Arrests are evidently useless, as no act of a white man against an Indian, however atrocious, can be followed by conviction."[35] Palmer wrote that Miller was "subsequently arrested and placed in the custody of the military at Port Orford; but on his examination before a justice of the peace, was set at large on the ground of justification, and want of sufficient evidence to commit."[36] He also observed that while there were "miscreants" who "slaughter these poor, weak, and defenceless Indians with impunity," there were also "many well-disposed persons in that [Port Orford] district whose sense of justice and humanity revolts at such inhuman scenes; but through fear, or some other cause, they are silent."[37] Port Orford District sub-Indian agent Josiah L. Parrish also attested to the innocence of coastal Indians, who had been victims of white attacks. "Within the last six months four of their villages have been burned by the whites ... Many of them have been killed merely on suspicion that they would arise and avenge their own wrongs, or for petty threats that have been made against lawless white men for debauching their women ... I believe, in no single instance have the Indians been the first aggressors."[38]

In September 1854, following on the heels of the two coastal massacres, Palmer appointed Benjamin Wright as special sub-Indian agent to handle affairs in the Port Orford district, which extended from the Coquille River on the north to the Chetco River on the south.[39] Wright had developed a reputation as an Indian fighter as a result of his earlier attacks on Modoc Indians in northern California. Even in the 1850s, Wright seemed to be an unlikely choice for the job, and historians have wondered about the appointment ever since.[40] Joel Palmer had a reputation as a friend of Indians. Had Wright, the twenty-five-year-old Indian fighter, undergone a change of heart?

Josiah L. Parrish, a religious man who served as the sub-Indian agent for the Port Orford district before Wright, commented years later on Wright's character: "He was a frontiersman of the roughest kind, and he mingled with the Indians in a way that I never did." Wright had worked for Parrish as a guide, so he knew him first-hand. Parrish recalled: "I had no other white man with me in the Port Orford District." He told historian Hubert Howe Bancroft that Wright had bragged to him about how he tricked the Modocs into thinking he wanted peace and then slaughtered them.[41]

Wright fit the mold of the white hunter-hero frontiersman. This mythical, but also real, character type was well known to Americans both in literature and in life. In stories of men who willingly left white settlements behind to hunt and live among Indians, American colonists created a new kind of hero. Hunter heroes, in historian Richard Slotkin's words, "could engage in struggle with Indians, and yet emerge as spiritually regenerate heroes of Christian civilization." However, there was always a danger that the hero might lose "the integrity of his ... white soul" and never return (becoming a "racial renegade") or return corrupted by the experience.[42]

San Francisco journalist William V. Wells met Wright in October 1855, only four months before Wright was killed and scalped. He included this description of him in a travel story written and published after Wright's death.

> *While on the route [to Coos Bay from Port Orford] we met Ben Wright, the sub-Indian agent, an experienced hunter and trapper; whose life has been passed in the mountains and on the Western frontier. He was a man of some thirty-two years [actually twenty-six years], with black curling hair, reaching, beneath a slouched Palo Alto hat, down to his shoulders; a Missouri rifle was slung across his back, and he rode a heavy black mule with bearskin machillas. Altogether he was a splendid specimen of a backwoodsman, of noble stature, lithe as an eel, of Herculean strength, and with all the shrewdness and cunning acquired by a lifetime passed among the North American Indians.*[43]

There is evidence that Wright had in fact been chastened by the response to his campaign against the Modocs and other Klamath country Indians. One fact stands out about Wright's experience in northern California. In the two years in which the black-legend of Wright the Indian fighter became fixed, Wright worked closely with R. B. Snelling and Elijah Steele, men who stood for the establishment of law and order in the mining districts of Siskiyou County. As crude as the miners' courts and early trials may seem to us now, they represented an effort, however weak, to prevent theft and murder between white miners, and sometimes between whites and Indians. Steele spoke to Wright after the 1852 Modoc massacre and criticized his action: "At the time others, as well as myself, told Wright that the transaction [Modoc massacre] would at some time react fearfully upon some innocent ones of our people."[44]

During the Cayuse War, in which eighteen-year-old Wright had served, Palmer had been Commissary General, in charge of providing the arms, food, and other war supplies. Although he was a friend of

Indians, Palmer recognized the necessity at times of going to war against them.[45] Despite Wright's reputation, Palmer in the fall of 1854 needed someone who was fearless, who spoke some Indian languages and/or Chinook jargon, and who had close friends among whites, Indians, and mixed-bloods. He turned to Wright almost in desperation. Wright had served as a packer, interpreter, and guide on Palmer's spring trip through southern Oregon.[46] In August, three of Palmer's sub-agents had resigned because of personal problems, inadequate compensation, and increasing difficulties in Indian-white relations.[47] Since the conclusion of the 1853 summer war in the Rogue River Valley, Indian-white relations had become increasingly tense. Nearly a fourth of the Indians there on the reservation died during the 1853-54 winter, probably from malaria and pneumonia. On the coast, white attacks on Indian villages showed that the situation was out of control. So Palmer appointed Wright, known as an Indian-killer, to succeed Parrish, a Methodist minister, and charged him "to preserve amicable relations between whites and Indians and among the Indians themselves."[48]

Palmer's September 1854 report on Indian affairs in southern Oregon, despite its bleak outlook, still reflected some signs of peaceful middle-ground relations between Indians and whites. He noted that starving Umpquas had been "kept from perishing by the limited assistance afforded by a few humane settlers." It was later reported by the Indian agent of the Willamette Tribes, John H. Miller, that many Umpqua and nearby Kalapuya Indians "acquired considerable property by trading and working for whites."[49] In the Port Orford district, Parrish reported to Palmer that "some of the young men are employed by the whites as domestics." U.S. Army doctor Rodney Glisan also noted in his journal that Indians "around the white settlements will occasionally hire themselves out for a few hours or days at a time."[50]

After talking with Palmer, but before receiving his appointment, Wright faced his first challenge—renewed conflict between Indians and whites on the Chetco River. His first official letter to Palmer, which he wrote on September 17, 1854, only two weeks after his appointment, related the circumstances behind the killing of three Chetco Indians by whites. As a result, Illinois River and Deer Creek Indians had joined with the Chetcos and threatened retaliation. They asked Wright what to do, and he advised them "to keep out of the way of the whites, and not fight the whites, as they said they had been governed entirely by what I had before told them, which was to take to the mountains when the whites commenced killing them."[51]

Two months later, Wright reported negotiating peace between several different Indian bands. He also reported that he had persuaded the Chetcos to come out of the hills and to rebuild their homes with the agreement of local whites. He predicted a hard winter for Indians of the district, because they had been interrupted in their harvest of salmon by heavy rainfall and high water that had destroyed their fish dams.[52]

By February 1855, Wright was trying to prevent clashes along the Smith River between Indians from his district and whites from Crescent City, who were making plans to attack the Chetcos after a successful massacre of Smith River Tolowas. Wright met with them and warned them of "fearful consequences" if they crossed over into his district. He clearly prided himself on his ability to prevent further bloodshed, and Palmer approved of his actions.[53]

After concluding a treaty with the Coos, Lower Umpqua, and Siuslaw Indians on August 17, 1855, Joel Palmer arrived at the Rogue River on August 26 to negotiate with the Rogue River Indians.[54] He explained that he came "with a view of forming a treaty with them for the purchase of their possessory rights to the soil, and their removal to an Indian Reserve to be set apart for them higher up the coast [on the Siletz River]." Dr. Glisan, medical officer, and Lt. August V. Kautz, commanding officer, at Fort Orford, met Palmer at the treaty grounds, "a beautiful myrtle grove" on the south bank of the Rogue River three miles upstream from the river's mouth.[55]

Dr. Glisan described the Rogue River Indians he saw at the council grounds: "In this whole council you couldn't perceive two Indians dressed precisely alike. One man's apparel consisted of simply a coat; another, of drawers; a third, of pants; a fourth, a jacket; a fifth, a soldier's uniform; a sixth, a pair of boots and a breech-cloth, and occasionally you might see one dressed *a la American* (naked)."[56]

It was Ben Wright who had gathered upwards of twelve hundred Indians for the council. When a fight broke out between a white man and an Indian, resulting in the white man being shot in the shoulder, it was Wright who placed the Indian under arrest and then protected him from a white mob. Reporting on Wright's action, Dr. Glisan wrote: "Wright stood in the door [of a small hut], and by his determined manner and strong arguments, managed to keep them at bay until the arrival of a detachment of fifteen U.S. troops."[57] A number of white men in a boat killed the prisoner and another Indian the next day while they were being taken downstream to be tried at Gold Beach, but not before the soldiers in charge killed three of the whites. It seems clear from Glisan's report that Wright and the soldiers stationed at Fort Orford were doing all they could to keep peace between Indians and whites in an equitable way, and despite the difficulties, by September 8 Palmer had concluded treaties with the coastal bands in southern Oregon.

ALTHOUGH THE WORST clashes between Indians and whites in 1854 and early 1855 occurred in the coastal zone of southern Oregon, the tentative middle-ground established by the treaties of 1853 in the upper Rogue River Valley had eroded substantially in the same period. The conditions for erosion are reflected in the Beeson family's successful establishment of their farm and in John Beeson's evolution from settler to Indian advocate.

The year 1855 began with three feet of snow in the Rogue River Valley, and the Beesons' cattle and horses suffered from lack of forage. John Beeson chaired a Methodist prayer meeting at the neighborhood schoolhouse, where the Beesons and their neighbors made a New Year's resolution to work toward enactment of a prohibition law for the Oregon Territory. The temperance cause was uppermost on John Beeson's mind.

The Beeson men spent most of January feeding the family's livestock, chopping firewood, and splitting rails for fencing. By January 26, Welborn and his father had begun plowing with a new "breaking plow" and four yoke of oxen. Father and son killed and cleaned fifteen chickens that John took to Jacksonville to sell for cash. By the end of the month John had sown the first wheat seed of the year.

On February 5, John went to Jacksonville for jury duty, but Judge Matthew Deady did not show up, so he returned home. The next day he began transplanting apple tree seedlings. Between February 8 and 10, John and Welborn hauled over 241 rails to their property line, and over the next several days Welborn fenced in their wheat field while John plowed. On Sunday, February 18, John preached at the

John Beeson. Drawing from A Plea for the Indians *(1857, 1858)*

neighborhood church meeting; other neighbors preached on alternate Sundays. John preached again on March 4 on the topic of sabbath obligations. His sermon set off a debate that caused some people in attendance to leave the meeting in exasperation at what Welborn wrote was his father's effort "to prove that the Sabbath was made for man and not man for the Sabbath."

On February 19, Welborn noted that two Indian women passed by the farm. Later in March, he met some Indians on his way to Ashland. But apparently these were uneventful encounters, worth mention only because he seldom saw Indians.

By late March the Beesons began preparing their garden, and then planting potatoes, corn, and peas. John received more "Water Cure" and "Phrenological" journals in the mail. Two "Methodist Bretheren" stayed with the Beesons over a weekend for a two-day church meeting that included preaching and "exhortation."

April began with dam building, ditch digging, and roadwork. During the work on a ditch for irrigation to their fields, Welborn and the crew "dug up the remains of an Indian long dead and decayed." Construction of the ditch continued through the month. Welborn and some of his friends also went on a three-day camping trip in the nearby hills, where they hunted grouse, pheasant, and squirrels. Welborn made no mention of meeting Indians, and there was nothing in his diary to suggest that the young men considered themselves to be in any danger.

John Beeson made a trip to Jacksonville, as he did regularly to sell butter, eggs, and potatoes from the farm. At the end of the month, Welborn went along, and the two of them stopped at the Robinson House hotel (later the Union Hotel and afterwards the United States Hotel), located on the main street of town. They heard Joseph Lane, who was campaigning for reelection as Oregon's Territorial Delegate to Congress (and who won in the June election). Welborn observed: "He is a red faced man with W[h]iskey roses all on his nose. He is a Demicrat." At the time, Lane was fighting charges of overindulgence in alcohol while on the job in Washington, which was the reason for Welborn's partisan comment.[58] As Republicans, the Beesons were not sympathetic to Democrats because of increasing controversy over the extension of slavery into new western territories. John Beeson ran for the Territorial legislature in this election on the Republican ticket, speaking out against slavery and for the rights of African-Americans and Indians.[59]

In May, John and Welborn continued hauling rails to fence more of their land and planted potatoes, corn, pumpkins, and beans. In late May, John went to a "political meeting," preparatory to the upcoming election. Rail hauling continued nearly every day or so in June (June 6—307 rails; June 7—143 rails; June 8—145 rails; June 9—298 rails) until by July 7 the fence around the Beeson property had been finished, as Welborn wrote proudly—"6 rails high." By late July wheat harvesting began. Threshing started in mid-August, with ten men and ten mules helping on the Beeson farm. Threshing continued on neighboring farms through the rest of the month. On September 8, John and Welborn went to a nearby mill and traded pumpkins for lumber to build a corral and stable. On Sunday, September 16, the family celebrated John Beeson's fifty-second birthday. He no doubt felt proud that the new home and farm, after two years of hard work, was well established.

The first mention of Indian trouble in Welborn's diary entries for 1855 appeared on August 2. It is a cryptic note that his father had gone to Jacksonville and heard that there had been some Indian attacks in the Applegate Valley. Then on September 26, news of a major attack in the Siskiyou Mountains reached the Beesons. A man and boy (Calvin M. Fields and John Cunningham) were reported killed and two men (Oatman and Dan Briton) escaped. This attack on the road between Jacksonville, Ashland, and Yreka (in northern California) occurred on September 24. Later, blame was placed by Charles S. Drew on "Rogue

River Indians from the Table Rock Reserve, aided, probably by Indians from the Klamath Lake Country."[60] The four men were hauling a wagon loaded with flour and pulled by oxen. Welborn joined a search party looking for Cunningham, and afterwards he helped make a coffin for Fields. The Indians killed about thirteen oxen and drove off eleven more; they also stripped the dead men's bodies of clothes and took other items. A party of about thirty volunteers and thirty-six soldiers went out after the Indians. The next day Welborn helped search for the lost oxen.[61]

After the excitement of Wednesday and Thursday, Welborn went with a friend on Friday to an "exhibition at Mr. Oatman's tavern": "They used the Drummond light to lighten the room. They had panaramas of scenes in Europe, besides several droll scenes." There was a quarterly church meeting on Sunday; and on Monday, John again went to Jacksonville for jury duty. On the farm, Welborn kept busy husking corn and hauling pumpkins in from the field. But on Wednesday, October 3, Welborn "went a hunting Indians." He evidently went on his own, but instead of finding Indians, he came upon two neighbors. Much to Welborn's amusement, this encounter led to a rumor that Welborn had found three or four Indians. The next night a party of volunteers went out looking for Indians, but when they actually met some, the volunteers became frightened and hurried home. Welborn noted, by contrast, that on the other side of the Siskiyou Mountains, on Cottonwood Creek, a dozen Indians had just been hung.

John Beeson's concern for Indians after his arrival in the Rogue River Valley developed gradually. As an abolitionist, he reacted with anger to the fact that men from Missouri and southern states regarded Indians as even less than "Niggers."[62] Where Beeson built his home, there were remains of Indian campsites, which made him feel guilty. He also grew "sensitive to the daily reports" of Indian-white conflict, which reached a new peak of intensity in the late summer and early fall of 1855.

During the "Court-week" that began October 1, John was in Jacksonville for jury duty.[63] He talked with a Mr. Jones, who lived down the Rogue River (about seven miles) from the Table Rock Indian Reserve, and who complained that his farm had become an encampment for Indian men. Their wives and daughters had been taken by a company of white men camped farther downstream (another seven miles or so). Beeson suggested that he bring his problem before the grand jury. When the grand jury responded that it lacked jurisdiction, Beeson suggested going to the court, sheriff, and Indian agent. In mid-week, so-called Major James A. Lupton (Major L in Beeson's book), newly elected Jackon County representative to the territorial legislature, came to Jacksonville and, according to Beeson, "addressed the citizens," urging them to join volunteer companies to attack several Indian encampments.[64] Mr. Jones, in the meantime, had failed to get help from the judge and sheriff. Indian Agent George H. Ambrose (who supported volunteer action against Indians off the reservation) told him "to order the Indians off [his land], and if they would not go to shoot them." Jones listened to Major Lupton and agreed to "help muster a company to act in concert for a general massacre." Beeson tried to dissuade him, but without success, and returned home "full of sad reflections."

On Sunday, October 7, a community meeting was held and Major Lupton's plan was favorably received—even by "two Methodist Preachers and other leading men."[65] On Monday, October 8, the day for the killing of Indians to begin, Beeson attended a Methodist Quarterly Meeting. It was at this meeting that Beeson apparently made his first public protest speech on behalf of Indians. He appealed to fellow Methodists as Christians and in the name of "a living Gospel of love." He warned of the danger to their families if Indians retaliated. But when he had finished: "No voice responded to the appeal, and the meeting closed; for no one had independence enough to speak his thoughts."[66] Later, Beeson learned that some people had agreed with him, "but the pressure of public opinion prevented open expression." Beeson was convinced that if elders and leading church members had opposed Major Lupton's planned massacre, it could have been prevented.

Two years later, after being forced to leave the Oregon Territory, John Beeson published a book condemning white treatment of Indians in southern Oregon. It was entitled *A Plea for the Indians; with Facts and Features of the Late War in Oregon* (New York, 1857).[67] In this book Beeson advocated protection of Indians and their rights as human beings, and he told of the events in the fall of 1855 that led up to the Rogue River War of 1855-56 and his part in it. In October 1855, Beeson's role as an advocate for Indians was just beginning. It was erosion of a limited middle-ground between Indians and whites that aroused Beeson to his late-hour defense of Indian rights.

Chapter 6

The Rogue River War, 1855-56

THE MILITARY ASPECTS of the Rogue River War provide a context for events significant to a continuing story of middle-ground relations between Indians and whites in southern Oregon. But the military operations of U.S. Army and Oregon territorial volunteers alone, the focus of most historical accounts, do not throw much light on middle-ground relations. We can follow these relations better from three different points of view. One focus involves the humanitarian efforts of Superintendent of Indian Affairs Joel Palmer, Brevet Major General John E. Wool, and John Beeson to control war objectives and public opinion in order to protect the hostile Indian bands from annihilation. A second involves the Indian people caught up in the war and their uncertainty about whether to make peace or to continue fighting. And a third involves two cultural intermediaries—Benjamin Wright, sub-Indian Agent for the Port Orford District and Enos (Thomas), a mixed-blood leader of hostile lower Rogue River Indians.

There were increasing numbers of clashes between Indians and whites throughout Washington and Oregon territories in the fall of 1855. White volunteer companies and U.S. Army regulars engaged Indians in fighting on several fronts. The attack on Rogue River Valley Indian villages that John Beeson had protested against before the Methodist Quarterly Meeting started the Rogue River War on the upper Rogue River. The first major battle of the war came at the end of October. By December the forces on both sides temporarily stopped fighting. In January, volunteer companies renewed the search for remnant bands of Indians on the upper Rogue River. A coastal Indian uprising at the mouth of the Rogue River occurred in late February, but major fighting on the middle Rogue River (between Grave Creek and Illinois River junctions), where the main Indian force wintered, was not renewed until March. Then, the U.S. Army launched a major campaign which, reinforced by volunteer company attacks, lasted through May 1856. Despite the collapse of middle-ground relations, Indian and white cultural intermediaries played an important role in limiting the fighting and preventing it from becoming what the more reckless whites wanted it to become—a war of Indian extermination.

Indian women and children were the first major casualties of the war. The October 8 attack by Lupton's volunteer militiamen on two Indian encampments near Fort Lane took the lives of more women and children than of men.[1] In his chronicle of white fatalities, Charles S. Drew argued that these were Indians who had left the Fort Lane reservation and "dared the Indian agent to make the attempt to compel them [to return]."[2] Drew stated that sub-Indian agent George H. Ambrose and Captain Andrew J. Smith tried to get them to return to the reserve, but when they defiantly refused, the volunteers attacked. Drew wrote in defense of the vigilante group: "The attack was commenced while it was yet too dark to distinguish one Indian from another, and by this reason it so happened that several squaws and children were killed. None were killed after it became light enough to distinguish the sexes."[3]

Agent Ambrose, who was there before and after the massacre and who was therefore the most reliable witness, highlighted the vulnerability of Indian women.[4] He described two attacks on the morning of October 8, one on Chief Sambo's band (two miles from Fort Lane) and the other on Chief Jake's band nearby. At Chief Sambo's camp, he found two women dead (one had been shot and the other had died "a natural death"); another woman and two boys had been wounded. At Chief Jake's camp, Ambrose found twenty-three "dead bodies," a boy reported "two women floating down the river," and Ambrose thought it "quite probable several more were killed whose bodies were not found." According to Ambrose, the Indian men of the villages actually heeded his warning of the day before and had started to Fort Lane. The old men and women were going to follow on the day they were attacked. Of the twenty-three dead bodies he counted, fifteen were women and children and four were old men.

News of the massacre spread rapidly and non-reserve Indians quickly organized to counterattack, no doubt fearing that their people might be next to be attacked by white volunteers. This was not the usual time of the year when Indians took up arms against whites. With winter coming on, the resort to arms reflected a total loss of confidence in the capability of the army regulars to control the attacks by civilian volunteers. The men of Chief Jake's band who had gone to the reserve joined the hostile Indians (see Appendix 2, Table 1). In the next several

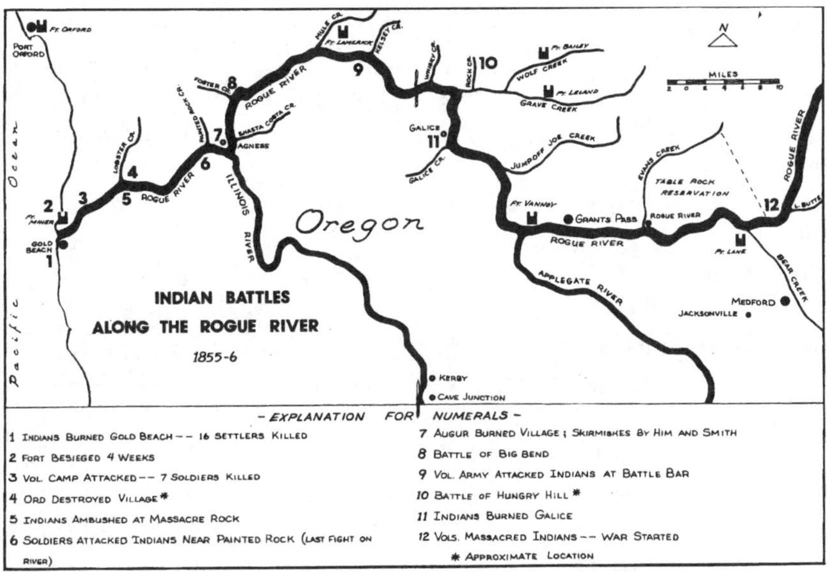

Map of Rogue River War battle sites. Map by Kathy Hartman from Indian Battles Along the Rogue River 1855-1856 *(1972), courtesy of Frank K. Walsh.*

days hostile Indians killed approximately twenty white men, women, and children living down the Rogue River from Fort Lane between Evan's ferry and Grave Creek.[5] As they continued west downstream toward the coast, attacking white homesteads and mining camps, Indian women and children accompanied the "warriors."[6] Agent Ambrose highlighted the significance of the massacre of Chief Jake's band and subsequent Indian killings: "The whole [white] populace of the country have become enraged … and I apprehend it will be useless to try to restrain those [hostile] Indians in any way, other than to kill them off. Nor do I believe it will be safe for Sam and his people [on the Table Rock Reserve] to remain here."[7]

Old John (Tecumtom or Tecumtum), a chief of one Applegate River band with close ties to Klamath River-Shasta Valley Shastas, left the Table Rock Reserve and became the principal leader of the hostile Indians. John Beeson, in his book, documented the reason for Old John's decision to go to war. When the husband of Old John's daughter had tried to rescue his wife from white men who had taken her captive, he was shot. Nothing was done by whites to punish the guilty party or parties. Then one of Old John's sons was accused of murder and taken by military escort to northern California for trial by a white jury. He was acquitted, but on the trail back to the Applegate Valley, while still accompanied by soldiers, he was murdered. The incident had the effect, Beeson wrote, of "strengthening his [Old John's] resolution to be his own defender," because he felt he could not rely on white soldiers for protection.[8]

The Indians on the Table Rock Reserve under Chief Sam (Toquahear, also Kokohawah, translated as Wealthy) did not participate in the Rogue River War.[9] (Chief Joe, or Apserkahar, had died in early November 1854.) The reserve Indians numbered 314 people, 81 men and boys over twelve years of age; and 233 women, girls, and boys (twelve and younger).[10] A census of the "hostile" bands taken in November 1854 showed a total of 522 persons, of whom 147 (28 percent) were men, 200 (38 percent) women, and 175 (34 percent) boys (97) and girls (78). Although this census probably underestimated the number of women and children (to be discussed later in this chapter), it reflected the fact that the Rogue River War was waged against far greater numbers of refugee Indian women and children than of Indian men.[11]

There is evidence that the hostile Indian bands had anticipated white attacks and prepared to resist. According to Capt. Smith, who was in charge of Fort Lane: "A large majority of the Indians are well armed with good rifles, of different descriptions, procured through their squaws, from a reckless class of whites that infest this region."[12] Capt. Smith reported to his superior officer that most of the white settlers were unarmed and that he intended to provide some of them with old musketoons from his armory. In fact his own soldiers carried muskets inferior to rifles being used by some Indians.

Charles S. Drew, in defense of white volunteers, insisted that Indians acquired rifles through ambushes and raids against white parties passing through southern Oregon. But if Capt. Smith was correct, as he had reason to be, then the best guess is that the rifles were traded for sexual favors, as payment for Indian women living with white men. As discussed earlier, these were sometimes forced relationships involving the murder of Indian husbands and family members, and sometimes exchanges made willingly by Indian fathers and husbands for material gain, with at least the passive consent of Indian women.

After the attack on October 8 by Lupton's white volunteer company on two Indian camps, Capt. Smith and Superintendent Palmer immediately spoke out against the renewal of warfare. Capt. Smith in a letter to U.S. Army, Department of the Pacific, headquarters at

Benicia, California, characterized it as a "war of extermination."[13] Supt. Palmer was even more emphatic: "The existence of a war of extermination by our citizens against all Indians in southern Oregon who, by recent acts, appear to evince a determination to carry it out, in violation of all treaty stipulations and the common usages of civilized nations."[14]

Capt. Smith's hostility to volunteer militiamen had been provoked most recently by demands of the justice of peace in Yreka, and northern California Siskiyou County volunteers. The volunteers had insisted that Capt. Smith and Indian Agent Ambrose turn over several Indians (one of them the son of Old John, or Tecumtom of Applegate Valley) for trial on charges of murder. These Indians, who lived on the Table Rock Reservation, were accused of having massacred about twenty whites on the Klamath River in July. White volunteer militia had tracked them back to the reserve. Capt. Smith and Agent Ambrose refused, fearing an uprising of the Indians on the reservation if they let the volunteers have their way.[15]

The only extended Indian narrative of the war—one told by Galice Creek Athabaskan descendant Hoxie Simmons to University of Washington anthropologist Melville Jacobs in the 1930s—treats the Klamath River Indian attack as the initial incident of the war. In this story a Shasta Indian, Klamath John, tricks the white volunteers from Siskiyou County into thinking that Indians from the Table Rock Reserve massacred whites on the Klamath River when actually the Shastas did. However, the upper Rogue River Indians, upset with white action against innocent Indians, joined the Shastas: "That's why the Rogue River Indians caused more trouble. Whites and Klamath River Indians [Shastas] fought in the Siskiyou Mountains. The Klamaths [Shastas] declined in numbers. The Rogue River and Applegate Indians [led by Chief John] 'took pity' on them, and joined in fighting whites on the Rogue River."[16] The Hoxie Simmons narrative portrays Indians as the initiators of action, and as acting together to expel whites from their homeland, not as victims of white attacks. This, ironically, also was the prevailing white view of events and justification for aggressive action against hostile Indians.

Despite their united front against the Siskiyou County volunteers, Capt. Smith and Agent Ambrose disagreed over the Lupton volunteer company massacre and subsequent Indian retaliation. Smith put the blame squarely on whites: "During the summer and fall ill-disposed whites have been threatening the Indians that belong to this reserve to commence a war of extermination."[17] Ambrose, on the other hand, blamed hostile Indians: "No longer any doubt exists but that this must be a war of extermination against all the chiefs and leaders of these hostile bands.""[18] Under the pseudonym "Miner," Ambrose wrote publicly in support of exterminating hostile Indians.[19] His position directly contradicted Palmer's October 13 orders to his agents for handling hostile Indians in southern Oregon: any Indian who joined the hostile bands was to be regarded by his agents as an enemy and denied reservation sanctuary, but if apprehended was to be delivered over to civil or military authorities.

The onset of war created panic among whites from the upper Willamette Valley to the Rogue River Valley and south coast, quieting more cautious and humane voices. It had been commonly argued before October that white settlers stood more to lose than to gain from a general war. That was the position Capt. Smith and Agent Ambrose had taken in August, when they tried to protect a fragile middle-ground by refusing to turn over Indians to Yreka volunteers. Beginning in October, the challenge for those concerned about the fate of Oregon and Washington Indians was how to prevent a general war from becoming a war of extermination, ending any middle-ground whatsoever.

On the coast of southern Oregon, Robert W. Dunbar, Collector of Customs at Port Orford, reported in October and November on steps sub-Indian agent Benjamin Wright was taking to deal with fearful and angry whites and Indians:

> *When Ben reached the coast he found everything in the wildest confusion. At Randolph they had cached their effects and were leaving for protection: all down the coast the same excitement existed, and now there is but two white men between here and Coquille—all have come to Port Orford for safety. At Rogue River those 'fire-eaters' are in a perfect fury of excitement; have built defenses, armed, and threatens to attack the Indians, or to go by force and disarm them, and all this is kept up by a set of graceless scamps at Rogue River, who have no higher desires than to murder the defenseless Indians for pastime. Up to this time no act of violence has been done. By the advice of the cool-minded [Ben Wright] they have been deterred.*[20]

Three years earlier Wright had ridden with some of these same men and participated in the massacre of the Modocs. Now, he was a key cultural intermediary trying to maintain peace between whites and Indians.

Meanwhile, Oregon territorial governor George Curry called up a volunteer militia force. Civilian volunteers participated with U.S. Army regulars in the first major military engagement in the war—the Battle of Hungry Hill (October 31-November 1, 1855). It took place on the divide between Grave Creek and Cow Creek. Whites described the hostile Indian force as numbering three hundred against a white force that varied in later estimates from four to six hundred army regulars and volunteers.[21] But the 1854 census of 522 "hostile" Indians (147 men, 200 women, and 175 children), although probably inaccurate, indicates that about three-quarters of the Indian force were women and children. Therefore, when 1st Lt. Jonathan Withers described the Indian defense at the Battle of Hungry Hill, he probably described the work of women and children as well as of men: "The Indians are supposed to have numbered 300. They were posted securely on a steep hill, covered with forest, and had cut down trees to form obstructions to any attack."[22]

Anthropologists have recognized the participation of Indian women in warfare among southern Oregon and northern California Indians. Leslie Spier, who talked to Klamath informants in the 1920s, reported that Klamath women went along with war parties. In addition to cooking and paddling canoes, he believed that they sometimes fought with the men using short spears to help "catch [enemy] women and children and to slay the aged."[23] Edward Sapir, writing about Rogue River Takelmas, noted that women joined in the war dance, and "often accompanied the men in the fight."[24] But his informants indicated that women's participation in war was restricted to guarding slaves and cooking. Among Shastas, women often served as advance scouts, visiting an enemy camp under the pretext of seeing a relative, but actually to determine the strength of the enemy. Women also served as messengers and negotiators to reestablish peaceful relations again when fighting ended.[25]

One of the most singular accounts of Indian women's participation in warfare involved Mary, the daughter of Takelma Chief Joe (Apserkahar). When white volunteers and army regulars under Lane's leadership fought Rogue River Valley Indians in the summer of 1853,

Mary was observed to be on the Indian front line. One correspondent wrote to the *Oregon Statesman*: "I have been told that during the battle, 'Mary,' wife [actually daughter] of one of the chiefs, stood up encouraging the warriors, telling them to take good aim—save their ammunition—bring down a Boston [white man] every shot. Mary is a noble looking woman and has much influence with the tribe."[26] This battlefield incident was remembered incorrectly by former white volunteer Cyrenius Mulkey as having occurred at the Battle of Hungry Hill (October 31-November 1, 1855).[27]

Later in November, after the Battle of Hungry Hill, 386 volunteers and fifty U.S. Army regulars attacked an encampment of about two hundred Indians, probably half of them women, children, and old men, located at Battle Bar on the south side of the Rogue River below Grave Creek. On the whole, these attacks proved futile, but they did force hostile Indians to establish winter encampments along the middle Rogue River between Grave Creek and the Illinois River.

IN EARLY NOVEMBER, Joel Palmer wrote to Gen. Wool, seeking U.S. Army help in protecting the Indians of southern Oregon:

> *Believing, as I do, that the cause of the present difficulty in southern Oregon is wholly to be attributed to the acts of our own people, I cannot but feel that it is our duty to adopt such measures as will lead to secure the lives of these Indians, and maintain guaranties secured them by treaty stipulations. The future will prove that this war has been forced upon these Indians against their will, and that, too, by a set of reckless vagabonds, for pecuniary and political objects, and sanctioned by a numerous population who regard the treasury of the United States a legitimate subject of plunder.*[28]

Superintendent Palmer and Capt. Smith at Fort Lane articulated an interpretation of the war's origin that Gen. Wool supported in his communications to Washington, D. C. and in his public statements. This interpretation, however, outraged white proponents of war. Supt. Palmer placed himself in a worse political position than he had been in before the war began. In early 1855, rumors circulated that Palmer had abandoned the Democratic Party (to which he owed his appointment) for the American or Know-Nothing Party, a third party based on opposition to foreign immigrants, Catholicism, slavery, and the temperance movement.[29] In Oregon, the Know-Nothings challenged Democratic control of the territory, but lost in the June 1855 election. When the war began, Know-Nothings in southern Oregon scrambled to control the volunteer companies.[30] By employing Know-Nothings in the Indian service, Palmer alienated fellow Democrats.

Historian E. A. Schwartz has emphasized the importance of political rivalry and the role of the Know-Nothings in starting the Rogue River War.[31] He has highlighted the role of local Rogue River Valley political figures Benjamin F. Dowell and Charles S. Drew, who switched from the Democrats to the Know-Nothings in 1855 and drummed up enthusiasm for a war against the Indians. But in the June elections, Democrats won three of four seats to the territorial legislature from Jackson County. James A. Lupton, who led the volunteer-company attack and massacre that started the war, was one of those newly elected Democratic legislators. Initially, the Know-Nothings were successful in organizing volunteer companies, but the majority of volunteers were probably Democrats. Asahel Bush, editor of the *Oregon Statesman* commented that "less than one-third of the men in the field" were Know-Nothings. There is no question that the *Oregonian*, with its Know-Nothing and Whig editorial policy promoted the cause of Indian extermination. In its October 20 issue, the *Oregonian* declared: "This idea of humanity to Indians in this country is preposterous, if not criminal."[32] But pressures on Gov. Curry to call up volunteers occurred first as a result of fighting in the Yakima country of Washington Territory. Gov. Curry issued his first call for northern volunteers on October 11 and for southern volunteers from Lane, Linn, Douglas, Umpqua, and Jackson counties on October 15.[33] Know-Nothings put pressure on Gov. Curry to take strong action, but by the time he issued calls for volunteers, most Democratic Party loyalists as well as Know-Nothings supported a general war (editor Asahel Bush and District Court Judge Matthew P. Deady notwithstanding). Political rivalry promoted war, but Democrats and Know-Nothings showed equal eagerness to fight. Palmer's criticism of the war made him a target of both Know-Nothing and Democratic attacks.

Gen. Wool's reactions to Indian-white conflict in Oregon and Washington territories was crucial to the peace- and treatymaking efforts of Superintendent Palmer. Without the U.S. Army regulars under Wool's command stationed at Fort Jones in northern California, and Fort Lane and Fort Orford in southern Oregon, there would have been no one to stand in the way of so-called exterminationists. Local political leaders, courts, humane citizens, federally appointed Indian agents, and territorial officials were powerless to prevent genocidal acts. The role of U.S. Army regulars in providing some protection for southern Oregon Indians seems contradictory to the history of their later nineteenth-century involvement in Indian fighting. But as historian Robert M. Utley has pointed out, Indian policy after the Civil War came to be dominated by western politicians who favored the use of force, even if it meant extermination, to solve the Indian problem. Gen. Wool deserves to be considered as the first of the "humanitarian generals" in the West.[34]

Brevet Major General John E. Wool took command of the U.S. Army's Department of the Pacific in January 1854.[35] But he brought with him nearly a half-century of military experience with federal Indian policy. From 1816 until 1841, he had served as inspector general in a small U.S. Army (only six thousand men in 1821), making many tours of Ohio, Missouri, and Mississippi Valley military outposts, and becoming one of "the nation's best-informed soldiers regarding United States military strength."[36] In 1837, by which time Wool had achieved the rank of brigadier general, he was assigned to oversee preparations for the removal of Cherokee Indians from their homeland in northern Georgia, Alabama, southeastern Tennessee, and western North Carolina.[37] This assignment gave him first-hand experience in negotiating the conflicting demands of state governors, volunteer militia companies, frontier settlers, Indians, and Army regulars. Gen. Wool's efforts to protect Cherokees brought him into conflict with the state governors and legislatures, President Andrew Jackson, the war department, and commissioners appointed to negotiate with the Cherokees. He was finally forced to subordinate his actions to civil authorities, but not before being court-martialed and exonerated. In his defense he told the military tribunal: "My crime has been ... in listening to [an Indian's] complaints and redressing his wrongs."[38] Wool distinguished himself in the war with Mexico, and commanded the army of occupation afterwards.[39]

Gen. Wool brought this background of experience with him to his new command. Although several forts had been built to help protect emigrants on the Oregon-California Trail, U.S. Army regulars under Wool's command in California, Oregon, Washington, and parts of Utah and New Mexico numbered less than two thousand.[40] Wool's attention immediately turned to the problem of Indian-white relations in California.[41] He staked out a position for dealing with Indians to which he adhered until he relinquished command in February 1857: "Indians can only be restrained by a decided, steady, and firm, but just course. They should be protected in all their rights, and punished whenever they violate the rights of others."[42]

When war began in late 1855 in southern Oregon, Gen. Wool considered Gov. Curry's ordering up of eight companies of mounted volunteers provocative and unwarranted.[43] He viewed it as a blatant raid on the national treasury, having as its primary objective the relief of a temporary economic depression in Oregon. Gov. Curry refused to comply with local commander Major G. J. Rains' request that volunteers be placed under military control. When James W. Nesmith, appointed by Curry to command the Oregon Mounted Volunteers, requested artillery support for a campaign against Indians in eastern Washington, it was Wool's turn to refuse. He replied that he had "no authority either to employ or to receive volunteers in the service of the United States."[44] Although Oregon's territorial governor was the first to mobilize volunteers, Washington's territorial governor, Isaac I. Stevens, also called for volunteers, but initially placed them under U.S. Army command.[45]

It is not surprising that during the course of the war Palmer and Wool found themselves at odds with Oregon's territorial officials. From the start, Palmer and Wool agreed on most issues—responsibility for the war, the role of volunteers, and reservation policy. They were joined in their humanitarian protest against the volunteer actions in the war by a most unlikely ally—the settler turned Indian advocate, John Beeson.

John Beeson returned to work on his farm for the rest of the month of October and November. Warfare between Indians and white volunteers and army regulars took place downstream along the Rogue River. Beeson and other residents of the Rogue River Valley were surprised that the hostile Indians retreated and fought defensively. Beeson later wrote in his book, *A Plea for the Indians*: "Had the Indians been disposed to destroy and slaughter all they could, there would have been hardly a house in the Valley; and it was often a subject of remark, that they did so little damage."[46] It would have been especially life threatening for whites if Chief Sam's people on the reservation had not remained at peace. But in the absence of fighting in the Rogue River Valley, the Beesons and other farm families were left to carry on with their normal activities at this time of year—digging up potatoes, plowing, sowing winter wheat, and chopping wood. All of November was taken up with putting in wheat. The Beesons celebrated Christmas by going to a neighborhood dance. The next day Welborn took his mother for a sleigh ride over three inches of new snow. The Indian war was temporarily forgotten, and, in fact, military actions had ceased because of the weather and the season.

But the war continued to occupy John Beeson's thoughts as the year 1856 began. He later wrote that he talked to volunteers who felt ashamed at their conduct. Some of them had left the ranks of the volunteers in disgust, particularly in view of the basically defensive behavior of the Indians. But the majority of the volunteers continued, hoping to be reimbursed by the federal government for their service, while being fed and mounted at the expense of the territorial government. Beeson believed that most volunteers were taking advantage of the situation for the money, as well as to kill Indians. Local merchants who provided supplies for the volunteer companies also stood to profit from a continuation of the war.

In January, "the citizens living on Bear Creek" resolved to call a meeting to try to end the war through negotiations. Beeson wrote of his involvement: "I engaged the largest room that could be found, and procured the printing of hand-bills, calling for a meeting at the Robinson House [in Jacksonville], at 2 o'clock, P.M. [on January 22]. In posting them round town, such was the opposition that several were torn down before my face."[47]

When the meeting took place, the strength of the opposition to Beeson became painfully evident. Beeson may have organized a committee to arrange for the meeting, but his was a lonely voice of protest on behalf of the Indians. He wrote of it later in his book:

> *The meeting gathered slowly. It was not till after 3 o'clock that many were present; and I had to regret the absence of every one of those who had specially promised to attend. Several speeches were made in favor of war; and then I endeavored to give a brief account of its origin, its management, and its present and probable results; of the advantage of peace, and the ease with which it might be established.*
>
> *A Reverend Doctor, from New Orleans, argued for continued war, and utter extermination; and another gentleman agreed to make a treaty, but only to massacre all the Indians as soon as they had signed it. My remarks, including several interruptions, occupied nearly two hours; and when the vote was taken, the party who were for war promptly spoke, while some of those who were on the opposite side refused to vote either way. So the meeting broke up, with but one voice raised in behalf of peace.*

After the meeting, a gentleman came up to Beeson and offered to forward his speech to the Commissioner of Indian Affairs in Washington, D. C. This offer may have been the only support Beeson received.

AFTER BEING ICE BOUND for three weeks at Fort Vancouver, in what must have been one of the Pacific Northwest's coldest winters, Gen. Wool returned to San Francisco. With reports in hand from various quarters on the excessive expenditures and ineffectiveness of Gov. Curry's volunteer army, Wool had become uncompromising in his view of the cause of the war and its reckless expansion by Oregon's leaders. "In Oregon, as well as in the northern part of California," he wrote, "many whites are for exterminating the Indians. This feeling is engendered by two newspapers that go for extermination, and is more or less possessed by the volunteers, as well as others not enrolled under the banner of Governor Curry. As long as individual war is permitted and paid for by the United States, and which is expected by all the citizens of Oregon, we shall have no peace, and the war may be prolonged indefinitely, especially as it is generally asserted that the present war is a God-send to the people."[48]

At the end of January 1856, the Oregon territorial legislature urged the president of the United States to remove Gen. Wool from his command of the Department of the Pacific. In support, the legislature reported that Wool had discouraged merchants from selling supplies to the volunteers. It also reported that he planned to try to prevent the Oregon Territory from being reimbursed by the federal government for expenses (what pro-war advocates called "just claims") incurred in trying to protect the citizens from Indian attack.[49]

At the same time as the territorial legislature was making its appeal, one of the principal supporters of the war in the Rogue River Valley, Benjamin F. Dowell, a University of Virginia-educated lawyer, wrote a letter to his brother in Virginia explaining his pro-war position. From 1853 to 1856, Dowell had worked as a packer, delivering supplies to volunteer companies.[50] In early 1856, he returned to law practice, specializing in the representation of whites seeking Indian-war claims from the federal government: reimbursement for volunteer service, provision of supplies, rent of horses, etc. He was later publisher of the *Oregon Sentinel* (1864-78), a Jacksonville newspaper. He no doubt expected the letter to his brother to be published in eastern newspapers, where he hoped it would gain support for the war and justify the war claims of the volunteers. His letter is a rebuttal to Supt. Palmer and Gen. Wool, who charged that whites were responsible for "commencing the war" and for "the purpose of plundering the Treasury of the United States."[51]

Dowell told his brother that he would be the last man "to aid and assist to prosecute an unjust war." He wrote that he was "as much opposed to extermination of the red race, as Gen. Palmer and Gen. Wool." However, he said, innocent whites were being killed and hostile Indians needed to be shown the "utter folly" of taking up arms. For that reason he supported the Oregon legislature's memorial condemning Wool and Palmer's position and requesting their removal. He argued that most Oregon citizens were "lawabiding" and not "vagabonds." He accused Palmer of changing position, first having advised Gov. Curry to call up volunteers and then opposing their use. "The truth is," he wrote, "the good citizens of Oregon not only in this war, but in all our indian wars have risen in mass, from a sense of justice, against the Indians for self-protection."

The private and public statements of Palmer, Wool, and Dowell framed the white historical debate over the war. Palmer's moral and political critique of war was repeated and developed more fully in Gen. Wool's later verbal war with Washington's Governor Stevens. It was the core of John Beeson's book, *A Plea for the Indians*, which found a receptive audience among eastern humanitarian reformers.[52] Dowell's arguments, on the other hand, can be found reflected in the public statements of Oregon and Washington territorial governors, Curry and Stevens, as well as Oregon's territorial delegate to Congress, Joseph Lane. In the spring of 1856, Lane did all he could to secure funding for the war, and he accused the hostile Indians of waging a war of extermination.[53]

A FORCED REMOVAL of Indians from southern Oregon at Superintendent Palmer's direction began on February 22, 1856 to protect the Indians on the Table Rock Reserve from white attacks.[54] About four hundred friendly Indians left the reserve under escort and headed for a reserve site on the Yamhill River in the upper Willamette Valley—the Grand Ronde Reservation. A Coast Reservation centered on the Siletz River Valley and extending south for one hundred miles along the coast almost to the Umpqua River had been designated for the removal of coastal and hostile Rogue River Indians.

Meanwhile, sporadic fighting resumed on the lower Rogue River. A small company of white volunteers under the command of John Poland was camped at Big Bend (near Illahe) on the lower Rogue River. On January 25, U.S. Army medical officer Rodney Glisan reported that "a party, consisting of two white men and a Canadian Indian" were attacked by hostile Indians resulting in the death of the two white men. Only the Canadian Indian escaped to bring news of the attack.[55] The "Canadian Indian" was named Enos (also spelled Enas and Eneas), and described by whites as a "half-breed," "renegade," and "traitor." Enos, a mixed-blood, was, like Benjamin Wright, a man living between white and Indian cultures. He told whites at the mouth of Rogue River that John Poland, captain of the volunteers at Big Bend, had sent him to get ammunition. But he rejected offers of company on the return trip to Big Bend, and he never arrived there. Whites suspected him of "double dealing" and getting additional ammunition from "squaws" to assist the hostile Indians.[56]

Benjamin Wright returned to Port Orford from Portland on February 2 aboard the steamer *Columbia*. He and another Indian agent, accompanying the volunteers under Poland's command at Big Bend, began to urge Indians who wanted to avoid war to move downstream away from hostile bands. By February 10, Poland's volunteers were headed toward the mouth of Rogue River with a large group of friendly Indians, stopping at a Tututni village about three miles upstream on the north side of the river. Whites felt optimistic that the plan of separating friendly from hostile Indians would work.

Most of the volunteers went farther downstream to attend a Washington Birthday celebration "ball" or dance on the evening of February 22, leaving only about ten men behind. At the same time, Wright received a message that Enos, at the Tututni village, "desired Wright to come up immediately, as he wished to have a talk with him." Enos was well known to Wright. For several months, at least, Enos had served as a guide and interpreter for the army and for Wright on the lower Rogue River. He was described in a newspaper report as a large man, nearly blind in one eye, and with a facial scar from an arrow wound (perhaps to the bad eye).[57] By this time Wright probably knew that Enos had taken the side of the hostile Indians, and feared, as Dr. Glisan wrote, that the friendly Indians would be "led on by that rascal Enas, who from having been employed so much by the army as guide, has a perfect knowledge of this country and its most assailable points."[58]

William Tichenor, founder of the town of Port Orford, recalled hunting with Enos the previous fall: "In the first part of November [1855], I went up with Enos, a great renegade [it] proved afterwards, hunting in the Indian country. Every Indian village and camp we came to they were busy making arrowheads and arrows, and they could not conceal that they were aching for a war."[59] Tichenor had returned to Ellensburg (Gold Beach) at the mouth of the Rogue River and warned that war was imminent.

One of the most detailed insights into the connection between Wright and Enos in 1855-56 came from pioneer Con Hillman, who served as an officer in the Southern Oregon Volunteers during the Rogue River War. According to Hillman, Enos was one of Wright's "confidants." Hillman described him as "a Canadian Indian ... who spoke good English":

> *This Indian lived mostly with Wright, but spent a portion of his time with the Indians. Having a wife belonging to the Tootootney tribe, which lived at the mouth of the river and within a mile of Wright's house and office, he could thus be at both places daily, and in undisturbed intercourse with both parties. He was a smooth tongued and smiling Indian, to all appearances an innocent and kind individual, but really deep, crafty and dangerous. He had obtained a partial control of the Indians in the immediate neighborhood and was looked to by them as a chief and guide when the proper time for an outbreak should occur.*[60]

Another pioneer, O.W. Olney, noted that Enos had been in Wright's service "for several months" and though "kindly disposed towards the whites" he had "manifested a greater affection for the captain [Wright] than for anyone else." Enos' wife "persistently asserted that she had disowned her people, and had been in turn disowned by them, and would stand ready at all times to aid in the execution of any plan that promised material damage to her unfriendly kin." As a result, Enos and his wife won Wright's trust, and he "took the plotting pair of savages into his confidence and his councils."[61]

Enos's past is hard to trace. He is supposed to have been a guide to John Charles Frémont, but Frémont's report of his 1843-44 exploring expedition to Oregon and California makes no mention of anyone with that first name or variants (Enos, Eneas, Enas, Ignace, or Iness).[62] These names are also absent in the reports of subsequent expeditions. However, it is possible that Enos may have been one of the "two Indians" that Frémont hired in late 1843 to guide his expedition from The Dalles to Klamath Lake. He wrote that "one of whom had been there [Klamath Lake], and bore the marks of several wounds he had received from some of the Indians in the neighborhood; and the other went along for company."[63] The physical description of the first man fits that of Enos.

The reference to Enos' service with Frémont is not the only possible clue to his background. Enos is an equivalent, phonetically, of the name Ignace, and that name appears in the literature on Canadian Indians of

Iroquois origin. A number of Iroquois entered employment with the North West Company in the early 1800s.[64] Historian Robert Ignatius Burns points out that when Jesuit missionaries baptized Indians they gave them new names, for example "Eneas or Aeneas for Ignace."[65] Enos may have grown up in the community of retired HBC servants and their white-Indian children in the upper Willamette Valley, called French Prairie. The records of the St. Paul parish, established in 1839, include many people with the name Ignace.[66] Francis Reinhart, a gold miner who ran a small ranch and store two miles north of Mussel Creek between Port Orford and the Rogue River, recalled Enos's ties to local *métis*. Allix and Frank Purrier, John and Peter Grosluis[louis], and Antoine Murain, who were his neighbors, had come from French Prairie in the upper Willamette Valley, and had been successful in gold mining on the south coast of Oregon. Reinhart met Enos and another French Canadian neighbor, Francis Richards, at a Mackinoo [Mickonotunne] village on Rogue River in the spring of 1855.[67] Enos is also known to have returned briefly to the French Prairie area after the Rogue River War ended.

WRIGHT AGREED to Enos's request to talk with him at the Tututni village, and left with John Poland from the mining community at the mouth of the Rogue River. Wright and Poland were both killed that night or early in the morning of February 23. The volunteers (at first called the Gold Beach Guard and afterwards, officially, Company K, Second Regiment, Oregon Mounted Volunteers) who had been left behind while their fellow volunteers celebrated Washington's Birthday farther downstream also came under attack from several hundred Indians early that morning. The volunteers' camp lay on the north side of the Rogue River across from the south-side "treaty grounds" where Superintendent Palmer had negotiated with lower Rogue River Indians in August 1855. All but two of the volunteers were killed. One of these men, Charles Foster, reported that during the night of February 22-23 he and others had heard noise across the river, where he thought the attack on Wright and Poland took place.[68] After attacking the volunteers, the Indians moved downstream, burning cabins and killing whites who were not at the Whaleshead or Gold Beach all-night dance.

What happened when Wright and Poland were killed is uncertain. Early historian Frances Fuller Victor pointed to the difficulty when she wrote: "No one ever knew the manner of his death, only as it was truly or falsely revealed by the savages themselves, and *boasted of by Enos*" (italics mine).[69] The *Oregon Statesman* (March 11, 1856) reported that Enos and a party of Indians knocked on the door of the cabin where Wright was staying. When he stepped out, an Indian "caught Ben Wright by the hair, others held him, and one cut his head off with an ax." Historian Victor believed that Wright and Poland were killed at an Indian encampment on the south side of the river.

At Gold Beach, some one hundred thirty white men, women, and children retreated to a fortification on the north bank of the Rogue River, where they stayed for about a month. After army regulars came to the rescue, surviving whites searched cabins along the Rogue River to locate and identify the dead. But Wright and Poland were not among the bodies they found. Pioneer historian Orvil Dodge in 1898 suggested that their bodies had been thrown into the Rogue River.[70] Frances Fuller Victor, in a story of Wright's life, published in 1881, wrote: "It was said, on Indian authority, that he was cut to pieces with knives, his heart cut out and roasted, and a part of it *eaten by his Indian wife*, who had told the Mackanotins to kill him in that manner, since they believed he could not be shot" (italics mine).[71] Although Victor admitted that the story sounded sensational, she repeated it with slight differences in *The Early Indian Wars of Oregon* (1894).[72] Whatever the true circumstances of his death, Wright apparently believed to the very end in the possibility of talking the lower Rogue River Indians into remaining at peace. He died trying to preserve a middle-ground between whites and Indians.

Although coastal Indians were divided as to whether to fight or submit, the situation was different in early 1856 than it had been before.[73] Now there was an imminent threat of removal to a reservation, which had already become a reality for the upper Rogue River Indians. For this reason, white pioneer O.W. Olney seems exactly right in his explanation that once lower Rogue River Indians heard from Enos and his Tutuni Indian wife that they were going to be removed to a reservation, according to Palmer's plans, they decided to take Enos's advice and fight.[74] Wright's murder was the first step in a well-planned local Indian uprising.

Enos's motives remain a mystery. Perhaps as a person of mixed Indian-white background, this was the moment of choice he had been postponing all his life, and he finally decided to take a stand on behalf of his Indian heritage. He was obviously a complex man, one who had earned the respect of Indians and whites, but also a man who was capable of deception. Another perspective on Enos came out of an interview with Coquelle Thompson, a Coquille Indian, who talked about him to Elizabeth D. Jacobs (anthropologist Melville Jacobs's wife) in 1935 at the Siletz Reservation. He said that he had heard of Enos as a boy. He referred to him as a "French man who lived with an Indian woman and helped the Indians fight the white people." Thompson remembered that the Indians knew that Enos "wanted gold" and that he "got lots of gold."[75] If true, Coquelle Thompson's story adds another motive to explain his actions, giving further depth to the uncertain middle-ground dimensions of his life.

Enos was unquestionably identified by whites as the major Indian leader on the lower Rogue River at the time of the uprising, even though Chief John (Old John, or Tecumtom) of the Applegate and Illinois River region (with close ties to Klamath River Shastas) became the most important Indian leader in the fighting the next spring. Lower Rogue River Indians may have gone to war even without Enos's leadership, but his access to the white community and knowledge of its affairs must have encouraged them to follow him into war. For whites, Enos's leadership in the burning of nearly all white cabins in the region (estimated at about sixty), and on February 22-23 in the killing of about thirty-one persons (including Wright, Poland, volunteers, and five "sons"), marked him as a war criminal.

No white women were killed in the uprising; however, Christina Geisel and her two daughters were taken captive (her husband and three sons having been killed) but later released in an exchange for four Indian women, blankets, clothes, and provisions.[76]

Few lower Rogue River whites were as fortunate as Thomas Van Pelt, who had a good relationship with local Indians. He tried to warn Wright of trouble after he found that the door of his house had "an Indian lock" or green bush placed against it, to signify that it was protected. His was one of a few houses left unburned, along with "two or three French homes ... *saved through the influence of Enos who was half French and half Indian*" (italics mine).[77]

In the month immediately after the lower Rogue River uprising, Enos led hostile attacks on the "Miners' Fort" or fortification where whites took refuge. The defenders recalled that Enos "could be readily distinguished from the fort by the aid of spy glasses, as he rode a white horse up and down the lines of the Indians violently haranguing them." The siege of the fortification continued for nearly a month, with occasional skirmishes leading to at least six deaths. Another six men lost their lives from drowning in an effort to resupply the fort.[78]

When U.S. Army soldiers reached the mouth of the Rogue River on March 20, Indians besieging the fort retreated upstream. Little is heard about Enos from this point on during the last phase of the Rogue River War. According to Thomas Van Pelt, he wounded Enos in a skirmish at Pistol River, and "the wound that Enos received in the thigh kept him out of the war."[79]

AT MIDNIGHT ON MARCH 8, the steamer *Columbia* arrived at Port Orford with reinforcements. Gen. Wool, who was on board, ordered a three-pronged attack: approximately a hundred soldiers from Fort Lane, a hundred from Fort Humboldt by way of Crescent City, and seventy from Fort Orford were to converge on the Rogue River Indian forces.[80]

At the same time, volunteers called up by Gov. Curry prepared to attack down the Rogue River as well. John K. Lamerick reported to the adjutant general of the Territory of Oregon on January 12 that he had mustered 478 in the northern and 387 in the southern battalions of the southern division of Oregon mounted volunteers.[81] The U.S. Army group from Fort Orford left for the confluence of Rogue and Illinois rivers on March 14. The force consisted of 102 regulars and 15 guides and trappers. Some ten miles from Fort Orford, near Reinhart's ranch, an old Indian woman was taken captive. Dr. Glisan wrote that "she … states that the upper Rogue river Indians, and the coast tribes, have been quarreling, and that the former have gone up the river, taking most of the plunder with them; and that *the traitor Enas* is yet with the latter" (italics mine).[82]

By April, Capt. Smith's company of dragoons from Fort Lane had combined with the coastal army forces. Brevet Lieutenant Colonel Robert C. Buchanan, commander in charge of the U.S. Army regular

Chief John (also Old John; Tecumtom or Tecumtum) of the Applegate River Valley.

forces, complained of a shortage of provisions and rainy weather. On April 28, Capt. Smith's company returned to Fort Orford from a reconnaissance to the Rogue River, after being turned back by a storm that left as much as a foot of snow in places.[83] The combination of bad weather, scarce provisions, and the continued presence of army regulars and volunteers took its toll on the Indians. On April 30, another elderly Indian woman was picked up near Port Orford. Dr. Glisan noted that "she seemed to be in an almost dying condition from disease, fatigue, fear and hunger." The next day, on being questioned by interpreters, she said: "The upper Rogue River Indians, and *Enas*, who had inveigled them into making war on the whites, had basely deserted them—that all their ranches and provisions were destroyed—many of their number killed and wounded, that they were nearly starving, and were desirous of peace, and were willing to come in and submit to anything the troops desired" (italics mine).[84]

On May 8, about 343 regular army soldiers moved up the Rogue River for a renewed spring campaign. By May 15 the regular force reached Oak Flat on the east bank of the Illinois River. The next day, talking began between Lt. Col. Buchanan and Indian leaders. After a week or more, Indian chiefs George (Cholcultah) and Limpy came to Buchanan and agreed to go onto the reservation with their people. Chief George told Buchanan that he would bring along with him the Galice Creek and Applegate Indians, who had been with Chief John (Old John, or Tecumtom).[85]

Capt. Smith went to Big Bend to meet the surrendering Indians on May 26; but the next day Chief John attacked with about one hundred fifty warriors. Fortunately for the army regulars, Chief George had warned Capt. Smith of the attack. Capt. Christopher C. Augur came to the rescue on May 28 and succeeded in driving off Chief John's force, but not before twelve members of the regular force were killed and nineteen wounded. Dr. Glisan concluded that without the "warning from old George, every man in his [Smith's] command would have been butchered."[86] Chief John's skill as a military leader impressed the regulars he fought against. Then-1st Lt. (later Brigadier General) H. G. Gibson wrote that the chief had "forced into a cul-de-sac, a body of regulars not inferior to his own—[and] surrounded them in their rifle pits." Pioneer historian A. G. Walling acknowledged Chief John's military accomplishment: "John developed all the tactics and strategy of a consummate general in his management of these and subsequent charges," and "implicit and thorough obedience characterized the conduct of his warriors." [87] Although finally forced to surrender, Chief John and his warriors for nearly half a year got the better of the U.S. Army regulars and civilian volunteers and successfully employed white military tactics against them.

The bands under the leadership of chiefs George and Limpy numbered 185 men, women, and children. They did not participate in the Battle of Big Bend with Chief John and the remaining hostile Indians, but instead put themselves under Superintendent Palmer's control when he reached the battle site on the final day. For the past several months, Palmer had been kept busy with removal of Indians to the new Grand Ronde Reservation in the Willamette Valley. He had been gone from the south coast for six months until he arrived at Port Orford on May 16. But he played a key role in getting the Indian chiefs to surrender. Sub-Indian agent Robert Metcalfe wrote to a correspondent, "if Palmer had not been there not an Indian would have ever surrendered to Col. B. or any of his command."[88]

While Palmer and Buchanan worked on peace arrangements, Chief John and Enos tried to head off the momentum toward peace. Although Enos does not appear in reports of fighting at Big Bend on May 27-28, Supt. Palmer's pocket diary notes indicate that Enos was still active behind the scenes.[89] Chief John figured more prominently in the Rogue River War as a military leader, but Palmer's notes on Enos's activity as recruiter of warriors and advocate of protracted war point to his importance as a war leader to the end.

At about the same time that Palmer and Buchanan were working to bring an end to the war, John Beeson's anti-war protests drew increased attention. Earlier in the spring he had mailed letters protesting the war to newspapers outside of Oregon. Newspapers in the territory refused to publish them, so he sent them off to the editors of the *New York Tribune* and *San Francisco Herald.* These letters were intercepted by his opponents and read at a public meeting in Jacksonville on May 23, and declared to be untrue.[90] Welborn Beeson wrote in his diary on May 23: "There was an Indignation meeting at the school house against Father on account of his being opposed and writing & talking against the present Indian war ... I am afraid Father will have to leave this country. Public opinion is so strong against him some would about as leave kill him as an Indian just because he has spoken the truth out boldy against the rascality of this Indian war, or rather butchery of the Indians."

The next day Welborn went to Jacksonville and heard threats against his father's life. That evening Welborn and his father went on horseback to Fort Lane, where his father got a military escort to the other side of the "Canyon" (just south of Roseburg) under cover of darkness.[91] Beeson's forced departure silenced the only vocal Indian advocate in the Rogue River Valley. Beeson thought that people who feared and hated Indians could be persuaded otherwise by an appeal to their Christian moral values. Finally, realizing his error, he was forced to flee for his life because he could no longer trust his neighbors and Christian friends even to respect his rights as a free citizen.

Beeson's opponents linked him to Superintendent Palmer and Gen. Wool. Their voices of opposition to the Rogue River War had become particularly painful to supporters of the war by the spring of 1856. Beeson insisted that he had not acted "under the direction of Gen. Wool or Gen. Palmer," and that in fact the only official with whom he had ever talked directly was Capt. Smith, the commander of Fort Lane. But however uncoordinated the relationship between the three men, they articulated an intellectual and moral middle-ground of humanitarian values that helped prevent escalation of the Rogue River War from acts of genocide by individuals and groups (the white volunteer companies) into a genocidal war.

After several more weeks of small skirmishes, coastal Indians began to turn themselves over to the U.S. Army regulars, who made conscious efforts to protect Indians from genocidal action by volunteer companies. By June 11, Lt. Col. Buchanan could report to his superior Gen. Wool that in addition to lower river Indians coming in, some 277 upper river Indians had surrendered. Dr. Glisan noted a few days later that the regulars were on the way to Fort Orford "with two hundred seventy-one upper Rogue River Indians, George and Limpy's bands, and four hundred and thirty-one Coast Indians." Chief John still held out, and there was no report of Enos's whereabouts.[92]

By June 15, Lt. Col. Buchanan and his troops arrived at Fort Orford with more than seven hundred Indians to add to the four hundred already there on the temporary reserve. Several hundred Indians under Chief John's leadership, as well as Chetco and Pistol River Indians, remained to come in. Throughout the Indian removal operation, Lt. Col. Buchanan gave strict orders to his regulars to protect surrendering Indians from white volunteers and local citizens. Dr. Glisan noted that he "issued orders *to shoot any man who attempts to kill an Indian*" [italics mine].[93]

Despite rumors that the Indians on the temporary reserve might make a last "stampede" to break free, and despite the urging of some white men living with Indian women that they do so, Indians remained on the reserve. Collector of Customs Dunbar wrote to Palmer that between Coos Bay and Port Orford "every single man ... is the owner of a Squaw." He considered these men to be an obstacle to removal of Indians to the coastal reservation, and viewed them as "a low miserable set of *white men* ... who prey upon the Indian, coax, buy or steal their women, and if they refuse, they are beaten and abused." There is no way to know how many Indian women lived with white men under coerced circumstances. But we know that some Indian women preferred to remain behind with white men rather than make the long, arduous, and frightening trip to the coastal reservation and away from their homeland.[94] For these Indian women, the white men so sharply criticized by military officers and Indian agents offered an alternative to removal.

The steamer *Columbia* arrived at Port Orford on June 19 in order to transport just over seven hundred of the hostile Indians (the first of two steamer loads of Indian passengers) to the Willamette River and then to the northern half of the Coast Reservation on the Siletz River.[95]

The southern half of the one-hundred-mile-long reservation was to serve primarily as a buffer zone to prevent Indians from returning to their homeland. The Indians were transported to Portland by steamer and to Dayton by riverboats, and then they went on foot and on wagons to the coast reservation.

On June 20, the day before the vessel's scheduled departure from Port Orford, word reached Lt. Col. Buchanan that Chief John was ready to surrender. Capt. Ord was dispatched from the mouth of Rogue River with one hundred ten men to meet him and his band. Word of Chief John's desire to surrender was brought in by three of his sons. According to a correspondent in the field for the *Oregon Statesman*, Enos was with Chief John's people but refused to surrender.[96]

With Chief John's agreement to stop fighting, the Rogue River War for all practical purposes ended. To the white regular soldiers and volunteers, it had been a surprisingly prolonged war. Nowhere west of the Mississippi River had a white armed force previously fought Indians in sustained combat as they did on the Rogue River in 1855-56.[97] The Rogue River War was the first of the Indian wars of the western United States. For Indians it was a bitter defeat, followed by a bitter process of removal. The limited middle-ground of the years 1850-55 had not proven satisfactory for either Indians or whites, but while it lasted it had helped Indians to continue to live in their homeland and it had helped whites avoid the human cost of a full-scale war.

DEMOGRAPHER RUSSELL THORTON, comparing the decline of the Indian population in northern California and southern Oregon in the 1850s with that in other places in the United States, has asserted that "genocide" was more "blatant" there than anywhere else.[98] But how destructive was the Rogue River War? Although earlier historians have given estimates of deaths for individual battles, none have attempted to estimate, even approximately, the overall population decline of the Indians of the region resulting from the war. Only after Indians had been removed to the Grand Ronde and Siletz reservations was an accurate census taken of southern Oregon Indians. That census can be compared with earlier, although less accurate, population estimates to determine how many lives had been lost during the war. By comparing white and Indian casualties, we also can better understand the suffering involved on both sides.

After the Rogue River War, Charles S. Drew, a southern Oregon politician and volunteer officer during and after the war, published a list of white civilians whom he considered to be non-combatants (i.e., white persons who were not "bearing arms against the Indians by whom they were killed") who had been killed by Indians.[99] Drew itemized white casualties by name for the period 1847-57, during which time southern Oregon Indians killed about 111 non-combatant civilians (exclusive of deaths attributed to Modocs, Klamaths, Pitt Rivers, and Shastas in northern California). To the non-combatant civilians must be added volunteer militia and regular army personnel killed in southern Oregon while fighting Indians. One officer was killed in summer fighting of 1851, two soldiers in 1852, and 18 volunteers were killed and 13 wounded (also one regular army officer) in 1853. In late 1855, volunteers and army regulars suffered approximately 24 killed and 43 wounded (of whom volunteers suffered the most with 18 killed and 39 wounded). In 1856, 15 volunteers were killed near Gold Beach and on the lower Rogue River, and the regular army force suffered 11 killed and 18 wounded at the Battle of Big Bend (May 27-28, 1856). This totals 71 white wartime deaths of army regulars and militia volunteers in the period 1851-56 (inclusive of the Rogue River War).[100]

Indian war deaths can be enumerated from recent histories as well as historic documents.[101] In 1851, at least 67 Indians were killed in summer fighting (50 in the Rogue River Valley and 17 at Port Orford), and in 1852 about 13 were killed in the Rogue River Valley and 15 on the Coquille River. In 1853, approximately sixty Indians were hung or killed in summer fighting. In four major massacres of Indian villages/groups (1854-58), no less than 66 persons were reported killed (there may have been as many as ten to twenty more). In the major encounter at Big Bend on the lower Rogue River, Indian losses were unknown to whites and unreported later by Indians. But counts of battlefield deaths were reported for other actions. White reports of Indians killed during the Rogue River War total between 187 and 205, exclusive of the Battle of Big Bend, at which probably ten to twenty more were killed based on earlier casualty reports.

Combined combatant and non-combatant casualties for the years 1851-56 probably totaled 182 whites and between 418 and 446 Indians (see Appendix 2, tables 2, 3, and 4). These Indians deaths are exclusive of about a hundred Indians who died on the Fort Lane Reservation in 1853-54. During the Rogue River War (1855-56), perhaps upwards of 225 Indian men lost their lives (based on the higher estimates of Indians killed that appear in historic documents and that have been referenced in recent histories, as well as an estimate of additional deaths). The total male population of the "hostile" bands from which these men were drawn numbered 595 (147 upper Rogue River and 448 lower Rogue River Indians), according to prewar censuses submitted by Indian agents. However, these censuses probably undercounted men, as well as women and children.

What was the impact of these Indian deaths on the southern Oregon Indian population as a whole? By September 1857, the population of southern Oregon Indians on the Grand Ronde and Siletz reservations was: Shasta and Upper Rogue River Indians—821; Coastal Indians (Coquille River south only)—1,493. This totals 2,314 Indians, out of a total population on the reservations of 4,060 men, women, and children. (For purposes of this comparison, the 444 Coos, Lower Umpqua, and Siuslaw Indians on a temporary Umpqua River reserve will be left out. They were not included in the prewar censuses, and they did not participate in the war.)[102] A year before the war began, sub-Indian agent Samuel H. Culver counted a total of 537 treaty and non-treaty Indians in the Rogue River Valley (after an estimated 25 percent decline in the treaty or reserve Indian population since fall 1853 had reduced their number from about 396 to 297).[103] His successor George H. Ambrose in November 1855 conducted a more accurate census, counting 314 on the reserve and 523 off the reserve, a total of 837. On the coast, in 1854, sub-Indian agent Josiah L. Parrish enumerated 1,311 persons from the Coquille River to the Chetco River.[104] The combined total for coastal (excluding Coos, Lower Umpqua, and Siuslaw Indians) and Rogue River Indians for 1854-55 (using the Ambrose and Parrish counts) was 2,147 (676 men, 814 women, and 657 children). In view of reported deaths on the reservation in 1856 and 1857, we would expect a lower count in 1857 than in 1854-55, even allowing for births. But the census of southern Oregon Indians (exclusive of Coos, Lower Umpqua, and Siuslaw Indians) was 2,314 after the war (579 men, 851 women, and 884 children), a difference of 167, or about 8 percent more.[105] The postwar census shows fewer men, slightly more women, and 227 more children. The main reason for a population figure greater after than before the war probably was due to the difficulty of counting a population that was more dispersed before the war.

Despite the apparently anomalous overall increase in population from the prewar to postwar years, available population figures for particular bands and for males show a decrease after the war. For example, the Mackanotins declined from 177 to 129, or by 27 percent; the Port Orford Indians declined from 272 to 242, or by 11 percent; and the Chetcos declined from 241 to 215, or by 11 percent. Tututni males declined by 55, or 19.4 percent; Chetco/Cheattee males by 56 or 48 percent.[106]

The overall male population before the war can be approximated by combining the Ambrose and Parrish censuses of 1854-55, giving a total number of men on Rogue River and the coast (from the Coquille River to Chetco River) of 676. On the reservations in 1857 after the war, there were 579 men in these same bands. This represents a decrease in the overall male population of 97, or about 14 percent. However, if, as we have established, wartime male Indian casualties probably numbered up to 225, then the postwar male population on the reservation should have numbered about 451, not 579. Adding 225 back to the actual postwar male population of 579 equals a prewar count of 804 males. A loss of 225 from this reconstructed, hypothetical base represents a decline of about 28 percent. "Hostile" Indian males would have numbered 708 using this hypothetical base (88 percent of the total male population of 676 or 228 upper Rogue River and 448 coastal Indians, as counted by Indian agents), and a loss of 225 would have represented a 32 percent decline in their numbers.[107]

These comparisons of censuses taken before and after the war suggest the following conclusions. First, the decline in the "hostile" adult male population as a result of the Rogue River War was probably about 32 percent (after correction is made for possible undercounting of males). Second, the disparity between the prewar and postwar censuses of women, and especially of children, makes it difficult to determine the impact of the war on the populations of these groups. Women and children probably experienced far fewer deaths in the war than men; but there is no way to know how many woman and children died in the war. The postwar enumeration of children showed about a 34 percent increase from 1854 to 1857. (In my hypothetical estimate of the southern Oregon Indian population at the beginning of the 1850s, I have used a 10 percent correction for possible war deaths of women and children.)

The number of Indian male casualties in the war represented a significant decline in the overall male population of the Indian bands of southern Oregon, and especially of the "hostile" bands. Indian women were confronted not only with the loss of their homes and exile to a strange new place (especially those who were removed from the drier inland Rogue River Valley to the wetter coastal Siletz Reservation), but with the loss of husbands and other male relatives. The burden on women of providing for their families (children and older adults) increased enormously. One of many survival strategies for Indian women was to continue, or to take up for the first time, a relationship with a white male as a source of economic support. This was to contribute to a continuing middle-ground between Indians and whites after the war.

Chapter 7

Removal and Resistance, 1856-1860s

THE REMOVAL OF INDIANS from southern Oregon was a traumatic ordeal, involving the uprooting of Indians from their homeland, and their subjection to physical hardship, sickness, and sickness-related deaths. Indians from the Table Rock Reserve, on the upper Rogue River, walked for thirty-three days and 263 miles in cold, wet, winter weather to their reservation destination.[1] Most of the Indians who left from Port Orford were transported by coastal steamer, and experienced the miseries of seasickness and overcrowding to reach the same destination, while others were forced or chose to walk along beaches and rugged coastal headlands for several hundred miles. Within two years, about 205 out of 590 upper Rogue River Indians died of sickness and disease on the Grand Ronde and Siletz reservations.[2] Demographic historian Robert Boyd points out that reservation deaths were from chronic diseases (syphilis, a venereal disease; scrofula, a form of tuberculosis that attacks the lymph glands; and consumption, or tuberculosis of the lungs), rather than epidemic diseases.[3] Although the combined Siletz population (inclusive of Alsea Agency Coos, Umpqua, Siuslaw, and Alsea Indians) was about 2,600 in 1865 (nearly the same as in 1856-57), by 1877 it had declined to 1,085 (due to further deaths, a low birth rate, and people leaving the reservation—about 360 Coos, lower Umpqua, and Coquille left in 1875).[4]

The process of removal itself avoided the far worse possibility that if Indians had continued to live among whites in some parts of southern Oregon they would have been killed individually and village by village as they were in northern California.[5] In southern Oregon in the 1850s, death came to Indians from village massacres, hangings, wartime fighting, and the impact of diseases, especially on the Table Rock Reserve (as reported in 1854 by Palmer and Culver). There were eight deaths and eight births on the way to the Grand Ronde Reservation from the upper Rogue River in March 1856, but no deaths during the removal by land and sea at the end of the war in June-July 1856.

However, deaths from sickness and the physical exertion of removal marches did occur after arrival at the Grand Ronde and Siletz reservations. Courtney M. Walker (whose title was Local Indian Agent Conductor, and who was the official in charge of the Coast Station Indian Reservation) reported to Superintendent Joel Palmer on August 5 that the newly arriving Indians at the reservation were unhappy, fighting among themselves, and dying. "Very many are sick," he wrote, "and many dying every night almost some die, at least 20 deaths since they have been here."[6]

The coastal removal of Indians from Port Orford on the steamer *Columbia* was completed in two trips. One left on June 21 and the other on July 8, 1856, the combined human cargo numbering a little over 1,400 Indians (710 on the first trip and 729 on the second).[7] Chief John's band of about 215 people was marched up the coast overland. But this was not the end of the removal process, because hundreds of Indians were not caught up in this mass removal, including Enos, the mixed-blood leader of the Indian uprising on the lower Rogue River.

William Chance, then an Indian agent, recalled when Enos finally came out of hiding: "Enos arrived [July 26 or 27] at the camp of Taminetse, a To-to-tin [Tututni]. Tayonici, the chief of the Port Orford tribe, informed me of his arrival. I sent a note to Lieut. Sheridan and he sent a file of men and had him arrested. He made no resistance, said he could not keep away. He did not know why but it appeared to him that he had to come to the reservation."[8]

The treatment of Enos by military and reservation officials differed from the treatment of other prominent Indian leaders. Captain DeLancy Floyd-Jones, the officer in charge of the army's "upper post" guarding the reservation, and the person responsible for Enos's arrest, wrote that Lt. Col. Buchanan, who headed the regular forces in the Rogue River War, regarded "the half-breed Eneas" as an "out-law." Superintendent Joel Palmer, despite his sympathies for the Indians, expressed support for the idea of "trial and punishment" for the principal Indian leaders.[9] In fact, he wrote to Indian Agent R. R. Thompson that he favored execution of all Indians known to have killed whites.[10] The difficult question was whether the killing of whites by Indians in wartime constituted collective acts of war or individual acts of murder.[11]

In order to calm the Indians and make transportation to the reservation easier, no Indian war leaders, except for Enos, were singled out for trial. Palmer viewed leniency as a "bitter pill" but necessary to keep peace. When Enos was taken into custody, Palmer wrote in a letter to Walker : "I am gratified with the arrest of the notorious Enaes and have this morning sent a messenger to Judge Willis asking a Special term of the court to try him."[12]

With the approval of Palmer, Capt. Floyd-Jones transferred Enos from the coastal reservation to Fort Vancouver "for safekeeping" pending trial by a "civil tribunal." A decision had been made that a civil rather than military trial was now appropriate. The charges set forth in Capt. Floyd-Jones's letter of August 4, 1856, were "desertion" (from the Gold Beach volunteer company) and "murder and inciting to massacre" (referring to the murder of Benjamin Wright and John Poland, and the "various massacres" that followed). The "witnesses" to these charges included Capt. Floyd-Jones himself, Superintendent Joel Palmer, William Tichenor, Indian Chief Joshua, two other Indians (one from Joshua's band and a Tututni woman), and two other white men.[13]

This last phase of Enos's life highlighted the importance for white leaders of legal ritual (laws and their enforcement, trial, and punishment) in the establishment of white settlements and relations between whites and Indians. Beginning with the 1848 trial and hanging of Indians held responsible for the deaths of Marcus and Narcissa Whitman, whites sometimes subjected Indians to court trial procedures in cases of alleged murder. More often, however, Indians suspected of criminal offenses (whether murder, theft, or other crimes) were killed without legal formalities.[14] The selective inclusion of Indians within a framework of white legal culture reflected symbolic as well as practical objectives. Whites wanted to distinguish between bad and good Indians and between uncivilized Indian behavior and civilized white behavior. The ritual of trial and punishment for murder by hanging also brought whites together in a symbolic act that reaffirmed their own cultural values.[15]

In most of the trial actions against Indians in southern Oregon, Washington Territory, and northern California that began shortly after the first white American settlers and miners arrived, justice was clearly absent, the arrest and trial being merely a ritual preliminary to hanging; but in a few documented cases, Indians were found innocent and/or protected against vigilante action.[16] In Washington Territory, where whites and Indians interacted for a longer period (1854-89) outside of the reservation setting, historian Brad Asher has found that "an Indian accused of killing a non-Indian faced no greater chance of conviction than a non-Indian charged with the same offence."[17] But that was not the case in the 1850s, even in Washington Territory, where hanging was used with or without trial to punish Indian war leaders.[18]

In the spring of 1857, at a time when whites along the southern Oregon coast north and south of Rogue River were still concerned about possible attacks by small bands of desperate Indians, the U.S. Army sent Enos by steamer from Fort Vancouver to Port Orford for civilian trial. Because of stormy weather, the steamer docked at Crescent City to the south, where Enos was held awaiting transfer to Port Orford. Curry County's sheriff, W. F. Riley, accompanied Enos from Fort Vancouver to Crescent City and then to Port Orford.[19]

Never formally tried, Enos (Thomas—his last name recorded in the Curry County records) was hanged on Sunday, April 12, 1857, one of about seven Indians who died that way in southern Oregon from 1853 to 1857.[20] The prime witness against Enos, Christina Geisel, "could not be found ..., so the Justice [of the Peace, William M. Copeland] ordered Sheriff Riley to turn the prisoner loose."[21] After blacksmith William J. Berry freed Enos of his chains on April 11, a mob immediately took control of him.[22] According to Sheriff Riley's son: "Whiskey was given him [Enos] and he partly confessed to having assisted in the killing of his three companions [John Cleninger, Enoch Huntley, and perhaps another man] ... on the way up the [Rogue] river [in January, 1856, prior to the killing of Ben Wright]." Then, as happened to a Coquille Indian hung on May 7, 1856, Enos "was hanged on historical Battle Rock, where his body was buried."[23] The *Oregon Statesman* correspondent who witnessed the hanging noted that Enos "met his fate with perfect indifference," perhaps defiance, if Coquelle Thompson's story about his refusal to divulge the location of buried gold is true.[24]

In addition to Enos, there were still scattered bands of Indians left in the coastal mountains east of Gold Beach. In the fall, after the Rogue River War had ended, William Tichenor, founder of Port Orford, sea captain, and guide for the army throughout the war, contracted for the capture and delivery to the reservation of as many Indians as he could track down in the south coast mountain country. But white men who lived with Indian women opposed his efforts. Unsympathetic to Tichenor, Collector of Customs Robert W. Dunbar wrote to Palmer: "Old Tich is here [at Port Orford] with about 50 Indians and 5 or 6 men to help him, he is in a stew. Men come and take his Squaws, and run them off. Some get married under his nose: he has sent a requisition to the mouth of Umpqua for 25 men [soldiers] to enable him to get his Indians."[25]

Sometimes with the help of detachments of army regulars, Tichenor continued to be employed until the spring of 1858 in rounding up several hundred Indians hiding in the mountains. In the fall of 1857, he gathered up approximately one hundred fifty Indian men, women, and children to remove to the temporary Fort Umpqua reservation. Some twenty Indian "warriors" with their families remained in the hill country. The next spring he persuaded about seventy Indians to surrender, but when the men tried to escape, Tichenor's men killed them. According to sub-Indian agent E. P. Drew, this would end attacks on white settlements by "a lawless, desperate and troublesome band of marauding savages."[26]

With the ending of the Rogue River War almost a year earlier, army officers and men had been reassigned to Washington, California, and elsewhere. The only remaining military presence on Oregon's south coast was Fort Umpqua at the mouth of the Umpqua River. It had been established on July 28, 1856, to block the return of coastal Indians to their homeland. The contingent of officers and men stationed there, which reached 167 men by December 1857, also watched over a large encampment of approximately 444 Coos, lower Umpqua, and Siuslaw Indians who had not participated in the Rogue River War.[27] In the fall of 1859, these Indians were moved north to Yachats; and Fort Umpqua was abandoned in 1862, the second year of the Civil War.

Some Indians in the upper Umpqua River drainage also managed to avoid removal. After the end of the war, about a hundred Cow Creek Indians continued to resist volunteer and U.S. Army efforts to capture them in the mountains on the south fork of the Umpqua River.[28] James P. Day hunted Indians in Douglas County, as Tichenor did in Curry County, but without much success. Historian Stephen Dow Beckham notes that "many [Indians] eluded him and survived as the remnant Indian population of the Umpqua Valley and the Western Cascades." But for the Dick Johnson Indian family near Yoncalla, who owned and farmed their own land, it proved impossible to live among whites. Despite the efforts of white neighbors like the Applegates, who supported the Johnson family's effort to remain on their land, Dick Johnson and his stepfather were shot and killed, and the surviving family

Fort Umpqua on the North Spit of the Umpqua River entrance. From Frank Leslie's Illustrated Magazine *(April 24, 1858), Oregon Historical Society, OrHi 76449*

members removed to the Grand Ronde Reservation. Jesse Applegate Applegate, son of Lindsay Applegate, recalled a confrontation between an Indian agent and the three Applegate brothers: his father Lindsay, Jesse, and Charles. The agent had rounded up about a hundred Indians to take to the reservation. But the Applegates and other white neighbors questioned his authority. The agent then accused them of "interfering with their own government." He finally drew a gun and threatened to shoot Yoncalla chief Halo. Lindsay persuaded him to let Chief Halo and his women remain, but the others had to go with the agent, despite the efforts of the Applegates and other white neighbors to prevent their removal. A band of about eighty Indians (Molalla, Yoncalla, and Umpqua) lived on the North Umpqua, and another band on Rice Creek, into the 1860s or later. Beckham notes that the Cow Creeks "remained free in the remotest parts of their old homeland" on through the century.[29]

THE INDIANS WHO FOUGHT in the Rogue River War, and who then were forced to go to the Grand Ronde and Siletz reservations, left behind no documents and written reports of their experience as whites did. But among the oral traditions of southern Oregon Indians there are a few stories and story-fragments that were passed on to a later generation. In a longer narrative about the war, Hoxie Simmons, a Galice Creek Athabaskan descendant, told about the removal experience.[30] Simmons was born after the Rogue River War, probably in the early 1880s. He learned the Galice Creek language from his mother, and he told his stories to University of Washington anthropologist Melville Jacobs in that language. Jacobs was impressed by the narrative quality of the "historical event texts" he collected from Hoxie Simmons. I have condensed and paraphrased this portion of the Jacobs' translation, except for quotations.

> Then the government soldiers issued rations, blankets, and clothes to them, and killed cattle for them to eat [after they stopped fighting]. Some days later the soldiers "drove men, women and children downstream, some by canoe, others on land, down to Port Orford." All the coastal Indians were gathered at Port Orford. A big boat was filled with some Indians.
>
> Three times they (brought and) landed boatfuls of Indians at Oregon City." Another boat took them from the waterfall there on up the Willamette River to Dayton. From there they went on land to Grand Ronde. The boat also picked up Willamette River Indians. Indians stayed at Grand Ronde a year, and then the southern Oregon Indians were moved to Siletz [actually some were at Siletz by early fall].
>
> There was lots of deer, salmon, and elk at Siletz. The Indians from the Table Rock Reservation who did not fight were also taken to Grand Ronde and then to Siletz. "That was the way the whites were smooth-mouthed." Joel Palmer promised them houses, cattle, and money (a bushel of gold and another of silver). "His voice sounded so sweet." The Indians all agreed. "That is why the Indians have all died here. Whatever Joel Palmer told the Indians, not one thing became true (right)." The Indians who are still alive always speak about that. They say: "When will the government make right what it (said it) was going to do for us?"

Another narrative of removal, by a Coquille, Coquelle Thompson, was told to Elizabeth Jacobs (Melville Jacobs's wife and co-researcher).[31] Thompson was born on the upper Coquille River of the Oregon south coast; he was six or seven at the time of the Rogue River War of 1855-56. His narrative of removal also is part of a longer narrative of the war, but it is much more detailed than Simmons's account. I have again condensed and paraphrased the narrative, except for quotations.

Soldiers [white volunteers] came to the Coquille River in May [1856] from the Rogue River to catch Indians who had killed some white men. Two Indians were hung at the mouth of the Coquille River. A soldier chief got up on a barrel and explained that under white law people are hanged if they kill other white people. It was the first time the Coquille Indians had seen someone hanged according to the white man's law.

The white men decided not to go after a third Indian to hang him. They would catch and hang him later. In June, a treaty was signed. The white men paid compensation in blankets for an Indian boy they had killed, who would not give up his knife to them because he did not want to be captured. The Coquilles didn't want to fight, but the whites thought they did.

In July the Coquille chief decided that his people had to leave their home for Fort Orford. "If we stay here; maybe white people will bother us and we will kill white people; there will be nothing but trouble. We will have to go where they tell us; their government will take care of us." They had to leave canoes and other possessions behind.

A steamer came to Fort Orford. Four to five hundred people got on the boat [actually over seven hundred in each of two steamer loads of Indian passengers]. Joel Palmer was there. An interpreter explained things. Some people thought they were going to be taken out to sea and thrown into the water. "Palmer told us not to be afraid." Indians questioned Palmer about what it was like on the Willamette River. He said that it was like the coast but more open and with plenty of deer, fish, and eels. That made people happy and they were ready to go. The people asked if there were deer, fish, eels, elk, bear, and different kinds of berries. Palmer said yes, "everything you have here is just the same there." The people agreed to go. They left the next day from Fort Orford.

It took all day to get into the boat. "I remember a soldier held my hand. They gave us a good place because my father was a chief. They put us up front in a little place like where the captain stayed." They appointed an Indian who had been to the Columbia River before to watch for the entrance. "If the boat went past the mouth of the Columbia River there would have been war right there on the boat." The Indian on watch signaled when they reached the Columbia River. The boat turned. "Then everybody was glad. They had been afraid they would be taken somewhere else." They got out of the boat at Portland and stayed overnight in a tent near a big lake below Portland. Then the boat was cleaned out. Palmer got off there to go to his home in Dayton.

The next day another boat came and took people to Oregon City (half of them at a time). From there (above the falls) they were taken in small boats to Dayton, where a big camp was set up. They were told not to cook. Bread, meat, and coffee was brought out. Every day more people came by boat and some came by land. "My father came by land because he was a chief. He talked to his people. Just my mother and my mother's sister were on the boat with me. My father's two wives were with him on land." People were tired and slept well. The next morning cannons boomed. Everyone was excited, thinking they were going to be killed. "About ten o'clock that day we start big 4th of July dinner."

People who came overland had to drive cattle. Every night they killed a beef to eat. "Lots of people didn't want to go on the boat." After staying a while at Dayton, white men took us to Grand Ronde. Other people were already camped there, and soldiers were there. "Everything was ready. You didn't have to get wood, or fix grub. You just unrolled your blanket and you were all right—and we had all kinds of blankets. Our people were there and Clackamas and Mollala people. There were soldiers watching them. We stayed there maybe a month. Then everybody wanted to get to Siletz."

It was fall when we came to Siletz. "I remember Chinook Salmon were spawning there." The people who were born here were few, only one or two scattered families. "Smallpox had killed them all." They said that there used to be lots of them here, all along the beach to Newport. Later an agent came, and soldiers built a big log house. The soldiers drilled. The next year oxen teams arrived and Indians were told to work like white men. "There was no school for a long while. The agent and soldiers took Indian women. There were no white women in here at all. The agent treated his women good. He gave his wife's folks lots of government blankets and government grub."

"As soon as we got here—lower farm—they built a sweat house right away. Every group built a sweat house." [Then Coquelle Thompson explained the making of a sweat-house.]

Coquelle Thompson experienced removal as a child, when he was at an impressionable age. In general, the Thompson and Simmons narratives agree on the main facts about the boat and land transfers to the Grand Ronde reservation. Thompson's narrative vividly describes the fear people had of being tricked and thrown overboard to drown at sea. These details can be interpreted as highlighting the hardships of removal. It was difficult as Palmer himself wrote, because of high seas, crowded conditions, and seasickness.[32] But under Palmer's direction, the trip from Port Orford to the reservation was made without loss of life.

Initially, Palmer is portrayed as promising better conditions than people found at Siletz. But Thompson's later recollection of spawning salmon undercuts this earlier hint of criticism. However, the narrative is critical of whites generally. Whites forced their law for dealing with murder upon Indians. They took away their homeland with its abundant resources, and they treated Indians as captives and put soldiers to watch over them. They forced them to give up their traditional way of life and to take up farming. White men took Indian women to live with them (although to the benefit of some Indian families). In concluding, Thompson turned to the remedy of cultural self-help.

A YEAR AFTER THE WAR ENDED, Special Agent of the Treasury Department J. Ross Browne, an investigator of Indian affairs for the federal government, met with Indian chiefs on the Siletz Reservation.[33] The interpretation of the war that emerged from the chiefs' comments focused on treaty promises and whether they had been honored. The chiefs were highly critical of Joel Palmer. Present were "John [Tecumtom or Tecumtum], the Shasta chief; Joshua, the chief of Lower Rogue Rivers; Jackson, Lympy [or Limpy], and George [Cholcultah], and other chiefs and headmen of the southern Oregon tribes."[34] The remarks of Joshua, John, George, and Jim (a lower Rogue River Tututni chief) were recorded. An interpreter told the chiefs that the "President in Washington" wanted to get the facts of what had happened "before and since the war." He knew they were dissatisfied, despite "all he had done for their benefit," and wanted to know why.

Joshua, the first chief to speak, declared that his people had not been "dealt with in good faith." What his people had received did not live up to Palmer's promises. "When we made the treaty, General Palmer told us we were to have a horse apiece; that we were to have nets to fish with; cooking utensils, sugar, coffee, etc., when we came on the reservation. That we were to have a mill to grind our wheat, and make lumber to build our houses; that we were to have everything we wanted for ten years; that we would have a white doctor and plenty of medicines, and none of us would die. That all these things were to be given to us in payment for our lands. That we would not have to work for them, but had a right to them under the treaty." Joshua also spoke of mistreatment by the Indian agent on the reservation. "He troubles our women; he beats them." But the heart of his short speech was the complaint that Palmer had promised more than the government had delivered.

Old John, the Applegate Valley war leader, first complained of how his people were dying on the reservation. "We have no game; we are sick at heart; we are sad when we look at the graves of our families." Then he, too, pointed to the failure of the government to deliver on the treaty. However, he stressed the land issue. "A long time ago we made a treaty with Palmer. There was a piece of land at Table Rock that was ours. He said it should remain ours, but that for the sake of peace, as the white settlers were bad, we should leave it for a while. When we signed the paper that was our understanding; we now want to go back to that country." Chief John noted that conditions on the reservation had improved since the previous year, and his people were no longer starving. But they were still dying. He could wait another year before going back to his country, but no more.

George, chief of Applegate-Galice Creek Indians, reinforced John's remarks. He said, "We sold him [Palmer] all of our country except two small tracts, one on Evans' Creek and one on Table Rock." Palmer had told them then that they could live there five years, before going onto the reservation. (Palmer cut the time short in February 1856, when he had the peaceful Indians moved to the Grand Ronde Reservation to protect them from angry whites.) Chief George had insisted at the time that the two remaining tracts were not for sale—"we only wanted the mountains which were of no use to the whites." Chief George could not understand why the president, "if he is powerful," could not protect them against whites if they returned to their homeland. He also complained that when Palmer had taken their guns, he had promised to return them when they got to the reservation. "We have never seen them since. Has he stolen them?"

Chief John spoke up again, adding that his warriors had fought bravely until overpowered by white muskets and ammunition. A year after the war, his people were too few to fight again. He said that when he stopped fighting, he encouraged other hostile tribes to stop too. His son had carried his message to the Yakimas and Klickitats. He thought that this action showed his good faith, and that the president should let his people go home and escape from the reservation, "where we are all dying."

Jim, a Tututni chief, spoke briefly. His people's country near the mouth of the Rogue River had been good for fishing and hunting. His people wanted to return. "What George had said is our heart." He wanted the president to know the truth about their situation. "This Tyee [J. Ross Browne] is writing our names on paper. We hope that paper will be sent back to us. We are afraid to have our names on it. If it should be lost we will all die."

The chiefs' speeches highlighted several themes. First, that Indians had fought courageously while at war, but had been overpowered by white firepower. Second, that they had sold some but not all of their land in making treaties. Third, that they had been promised they would be able to return to a restricted home territory, but had not been allowed to do so. Fourth, that despite some improvement in reservation conditions over the first year, people were still dying and wanted to return home. Finally, the chiefs gave assurances that they would not fight again.

The speeches put Joel Palmer in an unfavorable light. They suggested that he had lied to the Indians about whether they would be able to return to a remnant of their former territory. In their emphasis on deaths on the reservation, the chiefs undercut Palmer's basic premise that their lives would be safer on a reservation remote from their homeland. But the fact that the chiefs had believed in Palmer's promises shows the importance of his role in negotiations ending the war.

A more positive view of Palmer emerged from oral history told among descendants of the Kalapuya Indians of the Willamette Valley twenty years later. Peter Kenai was anthropologist Albert S. Gatschet's informant on the Grand Ronde Reservation in November-December 1877. He provided Gatschet with Kalapuya narratives that included one of conversations between Palmer and several Kalapuya leaders in 1855. I have condensed, paraphrased, quoted from, and reorganized the Gatschet material in Melville Jacobs' *Kalapuya Texts* (1945).[35] The narrative is written from Peter Kenai's point of view as a relative of Qayaqats and the person given control over his estate by the Indian agent.

> American troops arrived and promised that the Kalapuya people will receive everything they wanted, such as cattle, horses, wagons, and blankets. They were promised a trading house, an "iron house" or blacksmith shop, a "paper book" house or school, and twenty acres of land for each person. They were told they would become like an American.
>
> Qayaqats (a Tualatin chief) spoke to his people and advised them to "throw away" their land and take up the Grand Ronde Reservation land. He said that otherwise "The Americans will never leave us alone." Then Joel Palmer spoke, and told them to remain on their land three more years. At the end of that time he would take them to Grand Ronde, and there they would have everything they wanted.
>
> Qayaqats replied: "Very well. We will take your word. You are a good man, Palmer. Take care of us." Yetegawa, another chief, Palmer's translator, spoke. "I only translate your words," he said. But if the people were satisfied he was. He asked Palmer when they would receive food and horses. Palmer replied that they would get horses in two Sundays, one for each of the chiefs.
>
> Yetegawa and Qayaqats got into an argument over who was to receive which horse. Yetegawa threatened to kill Qayaqats. Later, two of Qayaqats's friends ambushed Yetegawa and wounded him. He fled to Palmer's house, where he remained two weeks. Then Palmer summoned Qayaqats and his people.
>
> They arrived at Palmer's place. Palmer asked why Qayaqats tried to kill Yetegawa. Qayaqats said he thought Yetegawa was

> going to kill him. Then the two men agreed to be at peace. Afterwards Palmer took all the people to Grand Ronde. Palmer said to the Indians at Grand Ronde (Athapaskan,Takelma, Molala, Clackamas, and various Kalapuya bands): "Tomorrow assemble, to make one big headman, the headman" of everybody. Palmer told them to vote, and that the one with a majority would be the headman. Qayaqats ran against Sam, the upper Rogue River Takelma chief, and Qayaqats became headman of all the Tualatins.

Joel Palmer is presented in a favorable light as a white chief who dealt fairly with the Indian principals. He is credited with having had a reputation as a good white man, one who successfully mediated a serious dispute between two Indian headmen. Even though the first part of the narrative points to exaggerated promises by army officers and by Palmer, the narrative does not contain criticism of reservation conditions, and, in general, shows an absence of resentment, anger, or sense of injustice.

These recorded interviews with Rogue River Indian chiefs after the war, and later oral histories, present important details of the removal process and early reservation experience. They also give different Indian perspectives on Joel Palmer's role as a cultural intermediary in the peace negotiation process. The oral histories comment on Palmer's effectiveness and integrity (or lack thereof) as a negotiator and official-in-charge of Indian removal. J. Ross Browne's interviews with the Indian chiefs show the emergence of intellectual and moral dialogue over issues of justice (in the abstract) and legality (in the practical execution of treaty terms). Together, these Indian perspectives on the Rogue River War and Indian removal represent aspects of a continuing middle-ground between Indians and whites.

THE PROCESS OF REMOVAL after the war was intended to permanently separate Indians from whites and to put an end to any interpersonal relations existing between them up to that time. But some Indian women resisted the removal process and kept these middle-ground relations alive by continuing to live with white men, even after relatives and friends had been taken away to the reservation. This occurred most prominently in the coastal zone north of the Rogue River, where (except for some upper Coquille Indians), Indians had stayed out of the war. Along the Rogue River, the war's destruction and the end of village life probably forced a number of young Indian women into relationships with white men. The deaths of Indian men in fighting white volunteers and regulars made survival extremely difficult for Indian women and children; the population of young Indian men available to young women was especially depleted.

U.S. Army doctor Rodney Glisan's diary notes on Indians during the war highlighted considerable intermixing between Indian women and white men. He also noted the attraction of Indian women to aspects of white culture, especially clothing. He observed that, like Indian men, Indian women dressed in odds and ends of white and Indian clothes, but he also noted that many "have learned to make dresses similar to those of whites."[36] Dr. Glisan's remarks suggest that even if Indian women were treated as trade items, or as a medium of exchange, in deals between Indian and white men, they also may have entered into unions with white men motivated by a practical purpose of their own.

But how common was it for Indian women and white men to live together on the southern Oregon coast, that part of southern Oregon where such relations had made such a strong impression on white officials during and at the end of the war? The Collector of Customs for Port Orford wrote to Superintendent Joel Palmer on March 23, 1856 that nearly every white man in his district lived with an Indian woman.[37] Was Dunbar exaggerating?

In 1915, sixty years after the Rogue River War ended, a case came before the Circuit Court of Coos County that highlighted the issue of unions between Indian women and white men in the pioneer period. Susan Waters, daughter of a pioneer union between a white man, James Martin ("Mart") Davis, and an Indian woman known as Jane, brought a civil suit (which she lost) challenging the settlement of the Buford Davis estate. She claimed to be the legitimate offspring of a valid marriage and therefore entitled to a half portion of the Davis estate (principally, a large farm worth $60,000-100,000) that had been left to Buford Davis (a son of Mart Davis by legal marriage to a white woman) and, following his death, left to his wife Sarah Davis. The point of the civil trial that followed was to determine whether the relationship between Susan Waters' mother Jane and Mart Davis had been a valid marriage under Oregon law at the time of their living together.

Fifteen witnesses appeared at the civil trial, and many testified as to the common occurrence of unions between Indian women and white men in the 1850s.[38] Susan Waters' suit asserted that Mart Davis came to Coos Bay in 1854, and that a year later he began to live with Jane "according to the laws of the times." They lived together several years, then separated, and shortly thereafter, Susan Waters was born. Some years later (February 24, 1864), Davis married a white woman, Mary Ann Hurst (Hirst), with whom he had children, among them, Buford Davis.[39] Jane herself married a white man named James T. Jordan on August 4, 1863. She and her husband raised a large family on Haynes Inlet of Coos Bay.

One of the pioneers who testified was J. A. Yoakam, who had come to Coos Bay the same year as Mart Davis. Yoakam was only five years old at the time, but he had a good memory of what he knew and heard later about the relationship between Mart Davis and Jane.[40] Yoakam was questioned about Indian relations between white men and Indian women in the 1850s. The defense wanted to show that there had never been a valid marriage between Mart Davis and Jane, and that theirs had been a "meretricious" relationship.

Q. Tell whether or not numerous white men, when you first came to Coos Bay, lived with Indian women.

A. Most all but about five of the single men out of two or three hundred lived openly at times with Indian women.

Q. Did they marry them?

A. They did not marry them until the soldiers undertook to take the women away the first time. Ephraim Catching was the first man to marry an Indian. His woman that he lived with had a little son by him, that they called Jim, and to keep them from going, he married her. That was the only one that was married the first time.

Q. When did the white men first start to marry the Indian women and why did they start to do this?

A. After the first taking of the Indians. A number of the men found that they could not keep them in any other way, and a number of the men married them—amongst them, Jim Jordan.

Q. After the soldiers or Indian agents came to Coos Bay, did any of the white men give up the Indian women and refuse to live with them further?

A. All but a few.
Q. Do you know whether or not numerous white men lived openly with Indian women?
A. Yes, I do.
Q. Tell fully about this matter.
A. I will say that all of the single men out of two hundred men, with the exception of less than ten, did live with them, and lived with them openly.
Q. Did John Davis live with an Indian woman?
A. He did, openly.
Q. State whether the relationship of these white men with these Indian women was or was not a meretricious relation.
A. The relations of a great many of them, especially of those married men, who had left their wives in the East, was meretricious but the single men lived with them openly, treated them as they would their wives, even though they were not married to them, and when they got ready to leave, simply left them behind, to either go back to their folks or for anybody who wanted them.

Despite his young age at the time, Yoakam remembered many details concerning Indian Jane. He testified that Jane was married to an Indian man called Snubby, but lived some of the time with Davis. He recalled that "Jane came often to my father's house, and talked to my sisters. She was a young girl, I should judge from fourteen to sixteen years old." Yoakam and his father were working on the Davis farm one day when Snubby came to get Jane and got into a fight with Davis. Snubby retreated with Jane to his canoe, but Davis grabbed a muzzleloader, rushed to the riverbank, and shot Snubby as he passed by in the canoe. Jane and Snubby's daughter by another woman paddled the canoe to Empire with his body. Yoakam, his father, and William H. Jackson, who had been working with them, pledged themselves to secrecy, and the facts about the murder only came out years later.

Jane's story (at least the one Yoakam tells about her) is one of the most detailed we have of Indian women who lived with white men on the Oregon south coast during this period. Stripped of Yoakam's moral judgements, his story fits what we know from other sources. Corporal Royal A. Bensell, Company D, Fourth California Infantry, on a trip to round up Indians on Coos Bay wrote in his diary for May 2, 1864:

"The lumbermen up these bayous and sloughs are the roughest of men. Nearly all are married to squaws or else have a written obligation that they will marry rather than allow the Indian Agt to deprive them of their concubines. They conceal the Indians, warn them, and otherwise enhance the difficulties of catching the red devils. There are yet some 60 Indians on North Bend Slough, Kitchen Slough, and Coquille River. We arrive after rough voyage across the bay at camp by midnight. The fact of the business is, this rowing after Siwash is no part of a soldiers duty."[41]

Second Lieutenant Louis Herzer described the same trip: "We captured in all thirty-one Indians, some of whom have never lived on the reservation and some others who have been absent from it two years or over ... A party of seventeen Indians who had left the reservation last summer, and who had encamped near Empire City [a band of Coos Indians headed by Chief Doloose or Jackson], on learning of our arrival returned immediately to the reservation, preferring coming back of their own accord to being brought back under escort."[42]

The Bensell and Herzer journal entries show that a number of Indians were living in the Coos Bay area eight years after the Rogue River War ended. In the first few years after the war, south coast Indians frequently left the reservation to return to their homeland. They were encouraged by local white men with attachments to Indian women and a desire for Indian workers of both sexes. Lucy Smith, a Euchre Creek Indian, told anthropologist John Harrington years later that she and her mother ran away from Siletz: "My mother ran away from Siletz & packt me on her back way to Rogue River, sleeping in the brush, hiding out all the way." The last time she and her mother escaped, Lucy was three or four. "The officers already had me & my mother, and we were being led away when she suddenly said: I have forgotten my sewing materials. As she said this I dove into the brush & my mother after me. They never got us. We remained at Gold Beach. And that was the last time that officials ever attempted to carry back Inds. to Siletz—they never came again."[43]

In a study of mixed-blood Coos Indian woman Annie Miner Peterson, ethnobiographer Lionel Youst points out that many of the original group of nineteen men who formed the Coos Bay Commercial Company and settled the Coos Bay area in 1853, had married Indian women. As a result: "As wives and mothers, Indian women very soon became an integral and influential part of the local scene, a role that was never available to the Indian men." The two earliest mills set up on Coos Bay in 1857 employed Indian men at the same time that most Coos Indians were being moved from the lower Umpqua River temporary reserve site farther north on the coast to Yachats.[44] The ease with which Indians could resist moving to the reservation paralleled in a more limited way the situation in Washington State described by historian Brad Asher, where "Indians routinely traveled beyond the boundaries of their reserves."[45]

Despite the official policy of trying to keep Indians on the reservations, "leaving the reservation," became, as historian E. A. Schwartz states, "an ordinary aspect of reservation life."[46] Cpl. Bensell's roundup on Coos Bay was probably in response to growing white concern about Indians being off the reservation. Two years earlier, in August, half the population was gone from the reservation, either with or without permits. Most were probably working for whites on farms in the Willamette Valley or along the coast. In October 1864, the Oregon State Legislature prohibited Indians and "half-breeds" from leaving the reservation without permission. It also became unlawful to help them escape from an agent's control.[47] But the practice of leaving the reservation to find work continued. Schwartz observes that attempts at self-sustaining agriculture on the reservation were inadequate, and Indians "had to rely on their earnings as migratory workers to feed and clothe themselves."[48]

White men living with Indian women on Coos Bay opposed their forced removal, but soldiers armed and ready to use force insisted on carrying out orders. When Charlie Metcalf, who had run off Indian Agent Harvey the previous year, protested removal to 2d Lt. Herzer, "after taking a reasonable amount of abuse [he] took a musket and give Mr. Metcalf one minute to leave in."[49] When four soldiers went to "South Bend Slough" (South Slough) two days later, Metcalf pleaded with them but offered no resistance. Ethnobiographer Youst remarks: "Evidently, a significant portion of the white population were appalled at the forcible removal of the Indians from Coos Bay [in 1864]."[50] Local Empire City hotel owner, R. W. Cussans, tried to get the Circuit Court to issue a writ of habeas corpus for the release and return of the captured Indians, but the judge refused.[51]

Coos County marriage certificate/license records show that there were a total of forty marriages in the county between June 18, 1854 and August 28, 1864.[52] Of these, thirteen were marriages of white men to Indian women. Indian-white marriages in this period cluster in the years 1857-58 and 1863, perhaps because of efforts at the time to remove all Indians to the reservation. Over the next four years (August 10, 1864 to April 6, 1868), there were forty more marriages, but only three, in 1864 and 1865, involved white men and Indian women. Despite an 1866 law prohibiting white-Indian intermarriage, at least two more Indian women married white men in 1872 and 1873. Marriage records identify most Indian women by the phrase "an Indian woman" and a first name only, but in the records for 1864, some Indian women appeared with a white surname. Several of these women had the same surname as the white man they were marrying, indicating that they were formalizing a pre-existing relationship.[53]

White pioneer settlers and gold miners were not the only ones to have sexual relations and living relationships with Indian women. As testimony in the Waters case indicated, army officers and enlisted men took advantage of their position as "guardians" of Indians on and off the reservation. Y. A. Yoakam's deposition highlighted the intermixing of officers and enlisted men with Indian women. But most of the references in pioneer reminiscences are to officers, perhaps because their rank teased the moral and racial prejudices of the pioneers. Two officers (Captain Andrew J. Smith, officer-in-charge of Fort Lane, and 2d Lt. Philip Sheridan of later Civil War and Indian-fighting fame), who were assigned to police control of the Grand Ronde reservation, figure prominently in stories of relations between white men and Indian women. Smith fathered a child at Fort Lane, while in command there, with an Indian woman later known as Betsy Smith.[54] A son named Andrew Smith was born to Betsy Smith in 1854; he and his mother went to the Grand Ronde Reservation in late 1855. Sheridan, while posted to Fort Hoskins on the northern reservation lands, lived with an Indian woman named Frances, a Rogue River Indian.[55] Sheridan later arranged a visit to Washington, D. C. for Frances, her brother, and two other Indians. Sheridan's biographer Paul Andrew Hutton wryly comments: "There was no chance, however, of Sheridan going native; he seemed to gain no appreciation or understanding of the Indian way of life from this liaison."[56] Sheridan also may have fathered a child with another Indian woman at Fort Hoskins.[57]

In the years following the Rogue River War, the number of and opportunities for interracial unions varied from one sub-region to another. On the Siuslaw and Umpqua rivers, the fur-trade era left behind mixed-blood families with French surnames.[58] In the Rogue River Valley, immediately after the Rogue River War, there were few local Indians left. Most had been removed to the Grand Ronde and Siletz reservations. But some Indian women remained behind or returned, their presence documented by newspaper stories, census reports, and court records. In 1858, three Hawaiian men (called Kanakas), married Indian women. A number of Indian women appeared in the 1880 Jackson County census as housekeepers. From time to time, fights were reported at Kanaka Flat, on the outskirts of Jacksonville, involving Indian women and Hawaiian and African-American men.[59]

At the end of the Rogue River War, Indians living in the Klamath Lakes area—Klamath, Modoc, and Paiute—still had not signed treaties or been placed on reservations. Ethnohistorian Theodore Stern writes: "About 1861, the Rogue River settlements were plagued by an influx of Klamath, Modoc, and Paiute, who were soon supporting themselves by trading with whites, by theft, and by prostitution of their women."[60] In 1869, a Rogue River Valley Indian agent "reported a total of 60 Indians, 28 of them Klamath or Modoc, comprising Indian women living in casual unions with whites, together with their children."

On the coast of southern Oregon, south of the Rogue River, most of the Indian holdouts after the Rogue River War were removed or killed by bounty hunters. But on the Rogue River, upstream from coastal settlements, a small community of mixed Indian-white families developed. Historian Kay Atwood, who has told the stories of these mixed-blood families, suggests one view of the Indian woman's situation: "The Indian woman discovered union with these men [white miners] was an alternative to exposure and starvation. Leaving villages and relatives behind was hard: scrounging for food and trying to clear disease-encrusted eyes was worse." Young marriageable girls and women caught up in the war had few choices. Charles Foster, a white volunteer and guide, gathered up thirteen girls at the end of the war to be wives for himself and other volunteers. He married one of the girls, with whom he had a daughter, Clementine. He later married Sunnah, a Karok woman, with whom he had two more children and lived on the Rogue River until he died.[61]

When Joel Palmer was Indian agent at the Siletz Reservation in the early 1870s, he showed concern about the marital status of Indian women living with white men. He wondered if it was legal for reservation officials to encourage such marriages in view of the Oregon law's prohibition against them. On a trip to the south coast in 1871, he observed many Indian women living with white men. "The Coose Bay and Rogue River districts have become notorious for that class of cases—and where there are no binding obligations, the women and children are often thrown upon the cold charities of a prejudiced people without any redress," he wrote. In November 1872, Palmer told a correspondent that 250 or more Indians lived off the reservation, either working at agricultural jobs or, in the case of Indian women, living with white men. He remarked that this made it difficult to take an accurate census of the reservation population.[62]

Coos Bay mixed-blood Indian woman Annie Miner Peterson illustrates many aspects of unions between Indian women and white men. In the 1930s, anthropologist Melville Jacobs interviewed her and later compiled two monographs of Coos myth stories and customs based on her information about pre-contact Hanis and Miluk Coos life. She also provided details of her own, as well as her mother's, life. Annie's father was a white man named Miner. Before her mother married Miner, she had marriages with two Indian men:

> *Long, long ago when they (whites) began to drive the people (onto reservations), my mother at that time had an Indian husband. She had had six children already (three by her first husband, a Hanis Coos). Her (second) husband (from Gardiner, on the Lower Umpqua) had a number of wives. That husband of hers shot her (using a shotgun)(because) the other wives had lied about her (being jealous of her greater favor with him). When she recovered she left her husband, because he had almost killed her for nothing. That is why she left. When she returned here (to Coos country) to her parents, a white man [Annie's father] came and wanted my mother.*

Army regulars, shortly after the war ended, took Annie and her mother to the southern end of the Siletz Reservation at Yachats. When her white father, who worked away from home all week, returned one weekend, his family was gone. Annie's mother then married a Lower Coquille Indian, with whom she had another child.[63]

Annie, in her talks with Jacobs, went on to tell her own life story. On reaching puberty, she was "bought in marriage" by a Hanis Indian,

Annie Miner Peterson, Coos Indian, with items from her basket, bead, and dentalium collection, at Empire, Coos Bay, 1914.

who beat her. She left him, leaving her baby behind (as was the Indian custom in divorce). She remarried an Alsea Indian, but he "began to consort with (other) women," so she left him, this time taking her second baby with her. She went to live with her mother's brother at the Siuslaw River, and then about 1880 returned to Empire, where "some of the (Coos) people (including my older sister [Fanny]) were living." Annie found that "the moving people (the whites) were bad, they bothered (annoyed the Indian girls)," so she became a live-in housekeeper with a respectable white family and "from that time on … did not live any more with the Indians." She began to learn English, lived at several different places on Coos Bay, and washed clothes for white families. After a terrible marriage to an alcoholic white man, she moved to Portland with Ida Wasson, a mixed-blood Klamath woman. There she met and married another white man, her last and best husband, Carl Peterson.

Annie's middle-ground experience illustrates the difficulties facing Indian women in the reservation and post-reservation era.[64] She lived in both white and Indian worlds, as did other women in her family. Her Indian heritage was strong, reflecting the way Indian mothers and grandmothers taught their daughters knowledge of food gathering, crafts, stories, and language itself (making her bilingual in Hanis and Miluk dialects). But in her twenties she also learned to speak English (making it possible for her to help Jacobs with translation of her native-language myths and ethnographic material), and she learned to live among white people. In her talks with Jacobs in the 1930s, Annie, at age seventy-three, became one of the last voices of pre-contact Hanis and Miluk people. The two volumes of texts Jacobs recorded from his interviews with her provide the most complete picture of Coos culture that we have. Annie's life illustrates the fact that removal did not bring the middle-ground experience to an end, even if it temporarily restricted opportunities for Indian-white interactions. Even those restrictions gradually disappeared in the face of Indian resistance and reservation officials' acquiescence to the employment of Indians off the reservation on farms, in mills, and in white homes. Through the experience of Indian women like Annie Miner Peterson, and despite the destructive aspects of the reservation era, the culture of southern Oregon Indians survived for future generations.

Conclusion

THE STORY OF INDIAN-WHITE RELATIONS in the United States is a tragic one, and the history of those relations in southern Oregon in the 1820s-1860s is a chapter in that larger story. But our sense of this tragic dimension is related to our consciousness of the Indians and whites who tried to achieve interracial accommodation. Despite the story of violent conflict associated with this history, there also is a story of middle-ground interactions and connections. Whatever we call it—whether middle ground, transcultural zone, cultural borderland, or something else—this social, economic, and moral space, where Indians and whites met, communicated, and entered into temporary or more lasting relationships, existed from the first Indian-white contacts. The middle ground reappeared time and again as naturally as its opposite—the killing ground of territorial aggression and defensiveness.

This study has focused on the development of a middle-ground in Indian-white relations in southern Oregon out of the uncertain encounters of the fur-trade and early settlement periods. In contrast to the positive response of coastal Indians from the Columbia River north to Vancouver Island, the Indians of southern Oregon resisted fur-trade overtures. Umpqua River and coastal Indians, living within a few days travel of the HBC's Fort Umpqua, did engage in fur trade from the 1820s until the early 1850s. But upper Rogue River Indians developed a reputation for hostility to whites that stood in the way of middle-ground relations until the 1850s. Coastal Indians south of the Coquille River probably participated minimally in the Fort Umpqua fur trade. The most obvious explanation for this resistance to middle-ground relations is the remote geographical location of the region south of the Umpqua and Coquille river drainages. But the limited experience of the region's Indians in trading with Indians outside of southern Oregon, as well as the HBC's treatment of southern Oregon as a transportation route to California, rather than as a focus of fur trapping and fur trade, also contributed to their resistance. The negative impact of early encounters on the upper Rogue River proved an obstacle to middle-ground relations until white migration and settlement forced Indians to negotiate with whites.

The limited middle-ground of the fur-trade era (1820s-1840s) expanded to include a wider range of interactions after the negotiations of Joseph Lane with upper Rogue River Indians in the early 1850s. Despite Lane's support of military action against hostile Indians, he initiated a limited middle-ground that lasted until the beginning of the Rogue River War in 1855. Most histories of southern Oregon in the early 1850s present a story of nearly continuous skirmishes and larger battles between Indians and white volunteer militiamen and U.S. Army regulars. But Indians and whites were involved in periods of uncertain peace between major outbreaks of fighting far more than in episodes of fighting. Indians and whites did business, ate, talked, gambled, and formed sexual unions with each other. Indians worked for whites, and white Indian agents and army officers worked with Indians to settle disputes between Indians and whites on and off the temporary Table Rock Reserve.

These everyday human interactions comprising the middle-ground in southern Oregon before the Rogue River War grew increasingly uncertain in the months leading up to the war. The division of Indian groups into war and peace factions intensified, and a loss of faith in efforts at accommodation increased among Indians as well as whites. The Takelma Indians under chiefs Joe (Apserkahar) and Sam (Toquahear), who made peace in 1853, remained at peace; but the Indian bands on the periphery of the Rogue River Valley—Shastas, Applegates, and Cow Creeks—because of their greater vulnerability to white attacks off the reserve, went to war. Local white politicians in southern Oregon used the Indian issue to win votes, playing on white fears of an Indian uprising. Preemptive action by white volunteers, committed to exterminating Indians, ended the uncertainties of middle-ground relations and turned white fears into reality. And Indian-white armed conflict in Washington Territory reinforced belief in a coordinated Indian uprising against whites in the Pacific Northwest as a whole, leading to the calling up of militia forces in both Oregon and Washington territories.

Superintendent of Indian Affairs Joel Palmer, who had been part of middle-ground peace negotiations in southern Oregon since 1853, redoubled his efforts to obtain federal approval of reservations remote from southern Oregon as new homes for the region's Indian population.

His belief that to avoid extermination of southern Oregon Indians they must be permanently separated from whites provided the primary federal objective in fighting the Rogue River War.

The Rogue River War collapsed the scope of middle-ground relations, narrowing it to a minority of southern Oregon Indians who resisted the removal process, either by escaping initial removal at the end of the war or later by ignoring reservation leave-permit rules. The objective of removal—separation of Indians and whites—proved limited and temporary. Total separation never occurred. Sickness and disease on the reservations took hundreds of lives so that the peace seemed as destructive as the Rogue River War had been; but many Indians survived, both on and off the reservations, and children born to Indian women insured the survival of an Indian population.

Survival rates for southern Oregon Indian groups seem to have varied dramatically, even though reservation censuses became increasingly misleading indicators as Indians moved off the reservations in the 1870s. The upper Rogue River Takelma Indians, who had made peace with whites the earliest, proved to be the least successful at survival. Indian groups from the Coquille River north to the Siuslaw River, who stayed out of the Rogue River War, and who had the most continuous middle-ground relations with whites, seem to have survived the best. Indian women who married white men were probably most successful in giving birth to children who survived and continued Indian culture in later years. Annie Miner Peterson was one of these mixed-blood children, a person who, long after her death, continued to play an exceptional role as a cultural intermediary and transmitter of southern Oregon Indian culture.

Interracial unions produced a new generation of people with mixed Indian and white identities. Personal choice and white prejudice led many of the children of these unions to think of themselves as more Indian than white. Both on and off the reservations, mixed-blood children lived between white and Indian worlds. But they held onto their culture despite the efforts of Indian agents and missionaries to discourage a sense of Indian identity. The permeable nature of reservation boundaries, eventually disappearing altogether, allowed the culture of southern Oregon Indians to move off the reservations. A middle-ground survived as much at the core of individual Indians' lives as in their relations with white society.

The history of Indian-white relations in southern Oregon from the 1820s to 1860s, when viewed from a middle-ground perspective, leads to the following conclusions. First, the HBC's fur-trade relations with southern Oregon Indians were unsuccessful in establishing more than a limited middle-ground in southern Oregon. Second, the reputation of Indians living along the Rogue River for being "rogues" was undeserved. Over a twenty-five-year period, Rogue River Indians showed as much restraint as white parties traveling through their territories. Third, despite annual skirmishing between whites and Indians in the early 1850s, after the gold rush and white settlement began, most individuals and groups on both sides tried to avoid hostilities and sought accommodation in a variety of ways. Fourth, when the Rogue River War began, the limited middle ground that had developed collapsed, except for the roles of cultural intermediary and peace negotiator played by Joel Palmer and military officers in the field, and relationships between Indian women and white men, primarily in the coastal zone. The interpersonal relationships between Indian women and white men became the basis for a continuing middle ground in the reservation era. Fifth, removal of southern Oregon Indians to the Grand Ronde and Siletz reservations, although intended to separate whites and Indians absolutely and permanently, failed to do so. Many Indians escaped removal, and others later disregarded reservation limits. Within a few years of removal, white reservation officials had to grant permission to Indians on the reservations to leave and find work in white communities. By the 1860s, a new middle-ground had developed that involved Indians and whites in many of the same relations as in the 1850s, but without fighting and threat of war. Finally, despite the destructive impact of reservation life for survivors of the Rogue River War, limited middle-ground relations of the prewar, wartime, and postwar periods helped make it possible for southern Oregon Indian remnant populations and cultures to survive.

Appendix 1

Estimates of Indian Populations and Mortality

POPULATION ESTIMATES have been important for this study in evaluating the impact of white gold mining, settlement, and warfare on Indian groups in southern Oregon. Federal Indian agents in the early 1850s took censuses of Indian groups in the region for the first time. I have made frequent use of the counts of Indian populations on the upper Rogue River and along the coast (so-called Port Orford District) from the Coquille River to the Chetco River undertaken in the period 1854-55 by agents Samuel H. Culver, George H. Ambrose, and Josiah L. Parrish. For the purpose of analyzing the destructive impact of encounters with whites in the 1850s, these population estimates seem to provide a fairly accurate picture of events, when adjusted for disparities as I have done in the last section of Chapter 6. The population counts taken on the Grand Ronde, Siletz, and Umpqua River reservations in 1856-57 provide a baseline from which to reconstruct a fairly accurate demographic picture for the years 1850-56. Reported deaths from diseases, massacres, and warfare for the period 1851-56, when added to an 1856-57 baseline figure of 3,108 suggest a southern Oregon Indian population of about 3,800 in 1850 (see Introduction note).

The question of how large the Indian populations of southern Oregon were prior to the early 1850s is, of course, related to the question of the impact of epidemic diseases over the previous seventy-five years of more limited contact with whites. The establishment of population baselines from which to measure the impact of epidemic diseases on Northwest coast Indians is one of several major achievements of Robert T. Boyd in *The Coming of the Spirit of Pestilence* (1999). I will consider only those parts of his study relating directly to coastal and inland-valley Indian groups of southern or southwest Oregon.

Boyd notes that for the Northwest coast as a whole "the earliest surviving population statistics date from the 1792 Vancouver expedition."[1] The Hudson's Bay Company reported population numbers for Indian groups near its posts. But Meriwether Lewis and William Clark compiled the earliest comprehensive population estimates for Indians north and south of the Columbia River while at Fort Clatsop in the winter of 1805-6, estimates which they revised on their return trip. Other individuals have made population estimates for Lower Columbia River and Willamette Valley Indian groups, but Lewis and Clark's estimates for Oregon coastal Indians were the only ones made prior to the 1850s.[2] As a baseline for "Takelma/Interior Athapascans" (upper Umpqua River and upper Rogue River groups), Boyd relies on Samuel Parker's 1836 report of his journey to Oregon. HBC officials informed Parker of 3,450 "Umbaqua" Indians (located between the Willamette Valley and Sacramento Valley).[3] This is the extent of estimates of Indian population to be found in historical documents prior to the 1850s. There are no estimates of village populations in the journals of Jedediah Smith and Harrison G. Rogers. At Coos Bay, Rogers wrote: "the Inds. Very numerous, they call themselves the Ka Koosh."[4] Similarly, Alexander McLeod wrote of an Indian village at the mouth of the Umpqua River: "Village pretty populous."[5]

Before turning to Lewis and Clark's estimates, I want to consider how they arrived at them. Boyd writes: "The explorers used a combination of methods, in particular house counts and informant testimony, to arrive at their numbers. Peoples encountered on the explorers' route along the banks of the Columbia were estimated twice, in the autumn 1805 descent and spring 1806 ascent of the river. Numbers for those away from the river were computed after discussions with knowledgeable informants, apparently through the limited vocabulary of the Chinook jargon."[6] But the double check of autumn and spring counts does not apply to their estimates of Indian population on the Oregon coast , and there are no house-count figures for Indian groups south of the Tillamook Indians.

In fact, Lewis and Clark's methodology probably was less rigorous than Boyd's statement implies. There is little in their journals to tell us how they arrived at their estimates. Clark saw the remains of an old, northern "Kil a mox Town" and observed other sites in the distance down the coast that were pointed out to him.[7] Beyond that observation, the captains depended on Indian informants for what lay beyond Nehalem Bay. Lewis at one point wrote: "I have lately learned that the natives whome I have heretofore named as distinct nations, living on the sea coast S. E. of the Killamucks, are only bands of that numerous nation, which continues to extend itself much further on that coast than I have enumerated them, but of the particular appellations of those distant bands I have not yet been enabled to inform myself."[8] There is only one other entry in the Lewis and Clark journals that is related to identifying and enumerating Oregon coast Indian groups. It was made on the day of departure from Fort Clatsop:

"The Indians repeated to us the names of eighteen distinct tribes residing on the S. E. coast who spoke the Killamucks language, and beyound those six others who spoke a different language which they did not comprehend."[9] In the "Estimate of Western Indians," Clark wrote, as part of the entry for the "Cook-koo-oose [Coos Indian] Nation": "I saw several prisones [prisoners?] from this nation with the Clatsops and Kilamox, they are much fairer than the common Indians of this quarter, and do not flatten their heads."[10] As we will see, the list of Oregon coast Indian names corresponds to known Indian groups. Prisoners, perhaps, from the south coast of Oregon, provided information to the northern Indians. But as far as house counts and numbers of Indians are concerned, Lewis and Clark would only have had first-hand information about the Clatsops. It is also worth noting that in preparing their "Estimate of the Eastern Indians," Lewis and Clark followed this guideline: "h. The probable Number of Souls of this Numbr. Deduct about 1/3 generally."[11] Entries usually show two numbers: what might be called a baseline estimate, and a second number that is one-third less. In the "Estimate of Western Indians," only one estimated number appeared. The guideline followed in the earlier estimate acknowledged a substantial margin of error in population estimates offered by Indian informants. Boyd notes that Lewis and Clark's estimates of interior Indians ("Multnomah Shoshones") probably were limited to the Kalapuya, leaving interior Indians south of the Willamette Valley out of their estimates.

James P. Ronda in *Lewis and Clark Among the Indians* (1984) points out that the expedition members were not particularly happy with their stay at Fort Clatsop and disliked the local Indians.[12] There was little visiting between the expedition and local Indians as there had been at Fort Mandan the previous winter. Lower Columbia River Indians were used to trading with whites, who came along the coast by ship; but the Lewis and Clark expedition had little to trade. Lewis and Clark never visited the largest Clatsop settlement at Point Adams. They did little to establish diplomatic relations with lower Columbia Indian tribes. Local Indian chiefs had to initiate visits to Fort Clatsop. Although Lewis and Clark prepared an "Estimate of the Western Indians," it lacked the comprehensiveness of their earlier "Estimate of the Eastern Indians."[13] As Boyd himself points out, the expedition was also hindered in its communication with local

Indians because no expedition member could speak the Chinook jargon or interpret for them (even though local Indians knew a few English words used in trading). How these factors affected the accuracy of population estimates Lewis and Clark recorded for the Oregon coast, it is impossible to know. But Ronda's analysis of the situation at Fort Clatsop suggests that access to information was more restricted there than it had been at Fort Mandan.

In "Estimate of the Western Indians," contained in Codex I to the Lewis and Clark *Journals*, Indians south along the Oregon coast are listed with their populations as follows (with editor Moulton's identification of modern names and spellings in parentheses):[14] There are no lodge/house entries for "Nations" south of the Kil-la-mucks. A later "Supplement" to the "Estimate of the Western Indians" in Clark's hand, made some time after leaving Fort Clatsop, contains the same listing of "Nations" on the Oregon coast; the "Probable No. of Souls" entries are also the same. It contains slight variations in the spelling of names, which I have bracketed.

Kil-la-mucks (Tillamooks), 50 h[ouses].	1000
Luck-ton (Salishans; perhaps Nestuccas)	200
Ka-hun-kle[e's] (Salishans)	400
Lick-â-wis [Lick-a-wis] (Yaquinas)	500
Youck-cone [Yorick-cone's] (Yaquinas)	700
Neck-ê-to[o's] (Alseas)	700
Ul-se-âh[h's] (Alseas)	150
You-itts[ilts] (Yahaches; Alseas)	150
Shi-â-stuck-kle [She-a-stuck-kle's] (Siuslaws)	900
Kil-la-wats (Lower Umpquas)	500
Cook-koo-oose (Coos)	1500
Shal-la-lah (Nasomahs; Coquilles?)	1200
Luck-kar-so (Tututnis)	1200
Han-na-kal-lal (Tututnis?)	600

Lewis and Clark's list of the names of Oregon coast Indian groups corresponds in part to names familiar to anthropologists who have studied coastal languages (especially, Kil-la-mucks, Youck-cone, Ul-se-âh, Kil-la-wats, and Cook-koo-oose).[15] The last three names on the list (Shal-la-lah, Luck-kar-so, Han-na-kal-lal) do not correspond to identifiable place or group names. However, the fact that the sequence of identifiable names from north to south is accurate suggests that the last three names refer to known populations at or adjacent to the Coquille River and Rogue River and serves to authenticate the information received by Lewis and Clark.

How accurate were Lewis and Clark's population estimates? The estimate for the Kil-la-mucks is actually less than an 1838 Hudson's Bay Company estimate of fifteen hundred (although William R. Seaburg and Jay Miller indicate that the HBC estimate "included some Alseans and Siuslawans").[16] There is no population estimate for the Alseas prior to the epidemics of the 1820s-30s other than the one by Lewis and Clark. Yaquina Bay on the Yaquina River and Alsea Bay on the Alsea River offered rich marine and riverine environments. But Lewis and Clark's estimates of twelve hundred Yaquinas and one thousand Alseas (eight hundred fifty on Alsea Bay) represent populations close to the estimate for Coos Bay, a larger estuary with greater food resources. By the 1850s, after epidemic diseases had drastically reduced lower Columbia, Willamette Valley, and northern coastal Indian groups, the largest coastal populations centered on Coos Bay-Coquille River and the lower Rogue River. Therefore Lewis and Clark's estimates for these sections of the Oregon coast seem probable as to relative size. Lewis and Clark's total for the south coast from the Coquille River to Rogue River and beyond was three thousand. Indian Agent Parrish counted 1,311 Indians in this same sub-region (the "Port Orford District") in 1854.

The accuracy of Lewis and Clark's estimate of Oregon south coast populations depends on the impact of epidemic diseases. Boyd's study of epidemic diseases among Northwest coast Indians is thorough and exhaustive. He used Lewis and Clark's estimates as his baseline for Oregon coast Indians, but he also assumed, as for other Northwest coast Indians, that the "aboriginal [or pre-contact] population" had been seriously affected by smallpox in the 1770s. Therefore, he adjusted the Lewis and Clark population estimates: "An across-the-board mortality of one-third is assumed for all peoples from the first smallpox epidemic."[17] This would assume an aboriginal population greater than the Lewis and Clark estimate: for the Coos the increase would be from 1,500 to 2,250 and for all Indian groups south of the Alseans from 5,900 to 8,939 (Boyd's estimate is slightly lower at 8,850).

Lewis and Clark probably did not include estimates for Indian groups south of the Willamette Valley Kalapuyans (although their use of the term "Sho-Sho-nes of the Multnomah" is ambiguous). As we have seen, the earliest estimate relevant to southern Oregon is Samuel Parker's 1836 estimate of 3,450 "Umbaqua" Indians from the Willamette Valley to the

Sacramento Valley.[18] Boyd uses Parker's estimate (minus four hundred fifty, or three thousand) as his baseline for hypothesizing an "aboriginal population" of forty-five hundred Takelma/Interior Athapascans prior to the assumed one-third reduction in population due to the 1770s smallpox epidemics.

By comparison with other methods and estimates, Boyd describes as "conservative" his method of estimating original populations "by working backward from the earliest reliable historical number [what he calls an anchor number] ... and compensating for preceding epidemic mortality."[19] Although his estimates are the most painstakingly researched we have for the Northwest coast as a whole, his estimate of an "aboriginal population" for the Indian groups in southern Oregon (coastal and interior valley) rests on less solid evidence. I believe that the region was more sheltered from epidemic diseases than the lower Columbia, Willamette Valley, and Washington-British Columbia coastline. It is true that English and American ships occasionally stopped and traded with Indians from Port Orford on north, but reported contacts were few and far between. Oregon coastal bays were small (except for Coos Bay) and difficult to enter (Coos Bay also). The Hudson's Bay Company annually sent fur brigades through southern Oregon's interior valleys from the late 1820s through the early 1840s, but except at Fort Umpqua and on the lower Umpqua River, their contacts with the native people were limited. The Indians south of the Umpqua River had a bad reputation for being "rogues," which kept whites and Indians separated from each other except for brief, tense encounters at the upper Rogue River crossing. Upper Umpqua River Indians attacked Fort Umpqua and threatened expeditions from 1838 to 1841 because of smallpox brought back from California in 1837. But the only other report of epidemic disease suffered by Indians in southern Oregon is one by Indian Agent Parrish in 1854. He observed physical signs that Tututni Indians of the lower Rogue River had suffered attacks of smallpox and measles eighteen (1836) and thirty years (1824) earlier (to use Boyd's correction of Parrish's sequencing).[20] Parrish reported that "many of their once populous villages are now left without a representative," indicating that he believed the earlier epidemics had seriously reduced either the number of villages or the populations of surviving villages. Neither Ogden nor McLeod in 1826-27 reported evidence that epidemic diseases had reached southern Oregon. Dr. John J. Milhau, who served as post physician at Fort Umpqua, wrote to ethnologist George Gibbs in 1856 that although "some years ago the smallpox killed off a great many of the indians north of Perpetua ...

south of that cape its ravages were very limited." Perhaps the outbreak whose evidence Parrish observed decades later had been limited to the lower Rogue River. Dr. Milhau, in any case, saw no evidence of earlier smallpox outbreaks among the Coos, Lower Umpqua, and Siuslaw Indians. He did bear witness, however, to local Indian reports of many deaths from consumption or tuberculosis over the previous twenty years (1830s-1850s).[21]

By comparison with the evidence of epidemic disease on the lower Columbia River and Willamette Valley, evidence that southern Oregon Indians (other than the Umpquas) suffered the same outbreaks of epidemic disease, or outbreaks of substantial magnitude, is quite limited. Boyd acknowledges that southern Oregon falls outside the range of evidence available on other regions: "The one area where neither epidemiological nor social analyses have yet identified a [epidemic] 'region' but where there may in fact have been one is southwest Oregon." His follow-up argument in support of considering it to be an epidemic region is that: "Epidemiologically, all southwest Oregon peoples experienced the 1836-37 smallpox epidemic (in its southern extension). Trade and movement between coastal and interior peoples on both the Umpqua and the Rogue Rivers, though not sufficiently documented, are likely. Future research should concentrate on this possibility."[22]

Documentary literature has been thoroughly sifted by historians and anthropologists, so perhaps archaeologists will have to turn up new information on the impact of epidemic diseases in southern Oregon to settle this question. In the absence of strong evidence for the impact of epidemic diseases in southern Oregon, I am inclined to construct an "aboriginal population" baseline on more conservative assumptions. There are two possible alternatives: one is to use Lewis and Clark's coastal population estimates without revision, and to add to them an estimate based on later 1850s enumerations of upper Rogue River Indians. Another alternative—which I prefer—is to work backward from a hypothetical baseline for the early 1850s. Lewis and Clark's estimate of coastal Indians from the Siuslaw River south to the Rogue River totals 5,900 people. This compares to Boyd's estimate for the same coastal region of 8,850. It compares to a postwar 1857 southern Oregon coastal population of about 2,000.

For the interior-valley population of the upper Rogue River, Lewis and Clark offer no assistance. Samuel Parker's estimate of 3,450 "Umbaqua" people likely includes northern California as well as southern Oregon

Indians. Indian Agent George H. Ambrose estimated the Rogue River Valley population of Takelma and Shasta Indians at 837 in 1855, but noted that 25 percent of the population on the Table Rock Reserve had died since the fall of 1853 (Palmer revised this estimate down to 20 percent). If one assumes that Indians living off the reserve suffered an equal number of deaths in this difficult period, the 1853 population might have been about 1,115. If that figure is adjusted for an assumed epidemic-disease impact of one-third over the previous three decades of Hudson's Bay Company and American passage through southern Oregon, then there might have been a population on the upper Rogue River of close to 1,700 in 1820. (I assume that the epidemics from the 1770s through first decade of the 1800s discussed by Boyd had little or no impact on Indians south of the Umpqua River drainage.)

Unfortunately, the only reference to population in the Rogue River Valley from the Hudson's Bay Company is one by Peter Skene Ogden, who identified the village of Dilomi, just west of lower Table Rock, as containing "six large Houses" sufficient for "100 Indians."[23] Dilomi has been identified as probably the largest village site in the Rogue River Valley area. By 1854 there were about fourteen large and small bands with permanent and semi-permanent village sites on the upper Rogue River. The largest of the village sites were home to about one hundred people; the average was about half that number. The population of the largest ones on the reserve could have numbered one hundred thirty or more a year earlier, before disease and sickness reduced the population by about 25 percent. It is possible that the village site of Dilomi might have numbered two hundred or more at its seasonal population peak during salmon harvesting. It is not difficult to imagine a dozen Indian bands on the upper Rogue River averaging one hundred to one hundred fifty people in the pre-epidemic period, which would have amounted to an overall population of twelve to eighteen hundred people. This range is close to my earlier hypothetical estimate based on corrections to Indian Agent Ambrose's 1855 census figure. It is considerably less than Boyd's estimate of a pre-epidemic population of forty-five hundred "Takelma/Interior Athapascans," which includes upper Umpqua River Indians as well as upper Rogue River Indians.

The first alternative to Boyd's "aboriginal [or pre-contact] population" model, that combines Lewis and Clark's coastal estimates with a corrected estimate for upper Rogue River Indians, leads to a hypothetical aboriginal population of about 7,600, compared to Boyd's 13,350. The second alternative, working back from my 1850 figure of 3,800, would lead, if corrected by an assumed epidemic disease impact of one-third in the period 1820s-1840s, to a hypothetical aboriginal population of about 5,758. I believe that either of the two alternative aboriginal population baselines are more consistent than Boyd's with the lack of evidence for a catastrophic decline in southern Oregon of the magnitude of about 10,000 people or 75 percent between the 1770s and 1856-57.

The only early estimate of Umpqua Indians, aside from Samuel Parker's all-inclusive one, is by Superintendent of Indian Affairs Anson Dart. In 1851 he estimated the number of Umpquas at 243 persons.[24] (Dart's estimate of 560 "Callapooyas" is the post-epidemic number used by Boyd, and probably is equally accurate for the Umpquas.) Again, it seems more likely than not that the Umpquas were spared from the 1770s epidemic. The 1830s "fever and ague" or malarial epidemic that left less than a tenth of the Kalapuya population appears to have had a major impact on the Umpqua Indian population as well, as demonstrated by attacks on Fort Umpqua. However, there is no estimate for the population of the Umpquas before the epidemics of the 1830s, as there is for the Kalapuya people. If half were stricken, the pre-epidemic population would have been about five hundred people; but if only 10 percent survived then the pre-epidemic population would have been about twenty-four hundred. But there is no way to know how severely the 1830s epidemic reduced the Umpquas' population. We can only hypothesize by extrapolating from the Kalapuya experience, as Boyd has done, or by assuming a lesser impact away from the Willamette Valley.

It is important to construct and consider alternative hypotheses with regard to the "aboriginal population" of southern Oregon. It matters if one wants to compare deaths from epidemic diseases with deaths from the impact of the Rogue River War and early reservation life; a higher estimate of the aboriginal population lessens the relative seriousness of later war and reservation impacts on the population. It also matters in many other ways related to efforts to reconstruct a picture of Indian life prior to the arrival of whites. For example, hypothetical estimates of aboriginal population have implications for assumptions about natural-resource usage as well as assumptions about interactions between Indian groups within a region. Robert Boyd's study of the impact of infectious diseases on Northwest coast Indian populations provides an excellent basis for further discussion and research on demographic questions.

Appendix 2

Statistical Tables

Table 1. Hostile Rogue River Indian Bands [1]

Bands (by band, chief, or place name)	*Men*	*Women*	*Boys*	*Girls*	*Total*
Scotans/Deer Creek	33	42	20	11	106
Galice Creek	23	26	18	10	77
Kiota Jim (of Leland Creek)	4	3	1	0	8
Grave Creeks	4	15	6	2	27
Jake (Bute Creek)	26	32	11	15	84
Old John (Applegates)	18	30	16	14	78
Bill	14	14	8	9	45
George & Limpy (Umpquas)	25	38	17	17	97
Cow Creeks (not enumerated)					
Total	147	200	97	78	522

Table 2. Indians Killed by Whites in Southern Oregon, 1851-56 [2]

		Number killed	*Source*
Warfare 1851-52		95	
1851:	Rogue River Valley	50	BE:52
	Port Orford	17	DOD:37
1852:	Rogue River Valley	13	W:203
	Coquille River	15	BE:67
Warfare 1853		60+	
Massacres 1854-58		66+	(See Table 4)
Warfare 1855-56		187-205	
		+ 10-20 (at Battle of Big Bend)	(See Table 4)
Total		418-446	

Table 3. Whites Killed by Indians in Southern Oregon 1851-56 [3]

Whites Killed/Time	*Number*	*Sources*
Civilians,* 1851-56	111	DR:3-8
Volunteers/regular force, 1851-52	3 (regulars)	BE:51
Volunteers/regular force, 1853	18 (volunteers only)	DR:14/FW
Volunteers/regular force, 1855	24 (18 volunteers; 6 regulars)	DR:35 (estimate of 35 for 1855-56)/ FW
Volunteers/regular force, 1856	26 (11 regulars; 15 volunteers)	S:140/H.Doc.1
Total	182	

* Drew's tally of whites killed by Indians in southern Oregon and northern California attributes a number of deaths to southern Oregon Indians that were committed by Modocs, Klamaths, Shastas, and Pitt Rivers. Only about 111 out of 237 deaths are clearly identifiable as having been committed by southern Oregon Indians in southern Oregon and not in northern California.

Table 4. Indian Fatalities (Massacres/Warfare) 1854-58[4]

	Place	*Indians Killed*	*Source*
Massacres			
January 28, 1854	Coquille River	16 (15 men/1 woman)	BE: 135; DOU: 107
February 15, 1854	Chetco River	12 men	BE: 136
October 8, 1855	Vicinity Fort Lane	23+ (8 men/15 women & children)	BE: 152; S. 85
May 28, 1858	Geisel homestead (north of Rogue River)	15-19 men	BE: 189; S: 150; DOD: 81
Warfare			
October 10, 1855	Wagoner's House	5 men	S. Doc. 113
October 31- November 1, 1855	Battle Hungry Hill (Grave Creek hills)	20 men (8-20?)	BE: 159; S: 98
November 17, 1855	Jump Off Joe Creek	8 (men & women?)	BA: 387
December 25, 1855	East of Table Rock	26-31 men	S 107; BE: 164; CCH: 1/9/56

continued on page 202

	Place	Indians Killed	Source
December 1855 -January 1856	Coquille River	4 men (1 hung)	BE: 172
March 17-19, 1856	Pistol River	12 men	V: 384-85
March 19, 1856	Junction Rogue River – Illinois River	5 men	BE: 181
March 23-24, 1856	Cow Creek/Illinois River/south of Camas Valley	18-20 men	H. Doc. 118
March 26, 1856	Below Skookum House Prairie (Rogue River)	8 men (3 drowned)	BE: 181
April 1, 1856	Coquille River	20 men (40 women & children captured)	BE: 182; S: 123
April 22, 1856	Lobster Creek (Rogue River)	12 (out of a party of 12 men & 3 women)	BE: 184
April 27, 1856	Little to Big Meadows (Rogue River)	20-30 (men, women & children)	BE: 183; S: 131
End of April 1856	Chetco River	"several" (3 to 5 men?)	BE: 184
May 27-28, 1856	Big Bend (Rogue River)	Indian losses unknown (largest battle of war; estimate 10-20 killed)	S: 137
May 28-29, 1856	Upstream from Big Bend (Rogue River)	3 (2 men & 1 woman)	S: 142
May 29, 1856	Pistol River	5 men	H. Doc. 1
June 5, 1856	Shasta Costa village (downstream of Big Bend)/Painted Rock/Lower Rogue River	18 men shot (and men, women & children drowned)	BE: 187-88; H. Doc. 1; S. Doc. 92
June 15-17, 1856	Pistol River/ Chetco River	3 men	S: 145

Table 5. Census of the To-To-Tin Indians, Port Orford District, Oregon Territory, 1854[5]

Band name	*Men*	*Women*	*Boys*	*Girls*	*Total*
Nasomah	18	20	10	11	59
Chocreleatan	30	40	18	17	105
Quahtomah	53	45	22	23	143
Cosuttheutun	9	9	6	3	27
Euquachee	24	41	18	19	102
Yahshute	39	45	24	12	120
Chetlessentun	16	15	11	9	51
Wishtenatin	18	26	12	10	66
Cheattee	117	83	22	19	241
Tototin	39	47	22	12	120
Mackanotin	32	58	17	17	124
Shistakoostee	53	61	23	16	153
Total	448	490	205	168	1311

Table 6: Selected Reservation Populations from Southern Oregon (Upper Rogue River and Coquille River South), 1857 [6]

	Men	*Women*	*Children*	*Total*
Siletz Reservation				
Upper Rogue River	118	202	234	554
Tututni	228	316	292	836
Chetco	61	86	89	236
Upper Coquille	82	104	127	313
Chasta Costa	32	43	33	108
Grand Ronde Reservation				
Upper Rogue River	58	100*	109*	267
Totals	579	851	884	2,314

*estimated

Table 7: Comparison of Censuses 1854 and 1857 for Selected Bands [7]

	Parrish 1854	*Siletz 1857*
Selected Bands		
Tututni	806	836
	(283 men)	(228 men)
	(286 women)	(316 women)
	(237 children)	(292 children)
Joshua/Yashute	120	179
Tototin	120	202
Mackanotin	177	129
Port Orford	272	242
Euquachee	102	84
Chasta Costa/Shistakoostee	100	108/110
Coquille	164	313
Chetco/Cheattee	241	215/236
	(117 men)	(61 men)
	(83 women)	(86 women)
	(41 children)	(89 children)
All bands	1,311	1,472-1,495

Notes

A full citation is given when a work first appears. A short citation (last name and short title) is used thereafter. Abbreviations: *OHQ=Oregon Historical Quarterly*; *WHQ=Western Historical Quarterly*; *CHQ=California Historical Quarterly;* OHS=Oregon Historical Society; CHS=California Historical Society; UO=University of Oregon; OSU=Oregon State University; OSUP=Oregon State University Press; UWP=University of Washington Press; UOP=University of Oklahoma Press; UNP=University of Nebraska Press; UBCP=University of British Columbia Press; UCP=University of California Press; JHUP=Johns Hopkins University Press; CUP=Cambridge University Press; UMP=University of Manitoba Press.]

Introduction

1. Richard White, *The Middle Ground: Indians, Empires, and Republics in the Great Lakes Region 1650-1815* (Cambridge and New York: CUP, 1991). For other examples, see Terry G. Jordan and Matti Kaups, *The American Backwoods Frontier: An Ethnic and Ecological Interpretation* (Baltimore: JHUP, 1992), 87-93; Colin G. Calloway, *New Worlds for All: Indians, Europeans, and the Remaking of Early America* (Baltimore and London: JHUP, 1997), 152-77. On survival of middle ground descendants, see Frank W. Porter III, "Nonrecognized American Indian Tribes in the Eastern United States: An Historical Overview," 1-42, and Marshall Becker, "The Okehocking Band of Lenape: Cultural Continuities and Accommodations in Southeastern Pennsylvania," 43-83, in Frank W. Porter III, ed. *Strategies for Survival: American Indians in the Eastern United States*, Contributions in Ethnic Studies, 15 (Westport, Conn.: Greenwood Press, 1986).
2. For a more restricted use of the "middle ground" concept, see Brad Asher, *Beyond the Reservation: Indians, Settlers, and the Law in Washington Territory, 1853-1889* (Norman: UOP, 1999) and Alexandra Harmon, *Indians in the Making: Ethnic Relations and Indian Identities around Puget Sound* (Berkeley: UCP, 1998). Asher and Harmon point out that in Washington Territory, Indians continued to live among whites and to interact with them in various ways outside the reservation setting, even after the period of treaty-making and warfare in the 1850s.
3. Louis Owens, *Mixedblood Messages: Literature, Film, Family, Place* (Norman: UOP, 1998), 40. Owens traces the treatment of the mixed-blood character in Native American novels as a "hybridized individual" and as a "cultural breaker"; his term for middle ground is "transcultural zone." Owens provides a remarkable look into the mixed-blood experience and consciousness.
4. Margaret Connell Szasz, ed. *Between Indian and White Worlds: The Cultural Broker* (Norman and London: UOP, 1994); Colin G. Calloway, "Neither White Nor Red: White Renegades on the American Indian Frontier," *WHQ* 17 (Jan. 1986), 43; also, Calloway, "Simon Girty: Interpreter and Intermediary," 38-58, in James A. Clifton, ed. *Being and Becoming Indian: Biographical Studies of North American Frontiers* (Chicago: Dorsey Press, 1989); Calloway, *New Worlds for All*, 162-64. See also, Jill Lepore, *The Name of War: King Philip's War and the Origins of American Identity* (New York: Knopf, 1998), 21-47, on John Sassamon, an Algonquian Indian, as an example of a cultural intermediary.

5. White, *The Middle Ground*, 323, 355-59.
6. For a discussion of Klamath Mountains, Coast Range, and Cascade Range, see Samuel N. Dicken and Emily F. Dicken, *The Making of Oregon: A Study in Historical Geography* (Portland: OHS, 1979), 19-28. The complexities of the Siskiyou Mountains and upper Rogue River drainage are discussed in Dennis J. Gray, *The Takelma and Their Athapascan Neighbors: A New Ethnographic Synthesis for the Upper Rogue River Area of Southwestern Oregon*, UO Anthropological Papers, No. 37, Eugene, 1987, 3-6.
7. On early occupation dates, see Kay Atwood and Dennis J. Gray, *People and the River: A History of the Human Occupation of the Middle Course of the Rogue River of Southwestern Oregon*, Vol. I, U.S. Department of Interior, Bureau of Land Management, 1996, 14-16, 19, 34-35, and C. Melvin Aikens, *Archaeology of Oregon* (Portland: U.S. Department of the Interior, Bureau of Land Management, 1993), 147.
8. Laurence C. Thompson and M. Dale Kinkade, "Languages," 30-51, in Wayne Suttles, ed. *Northwest Coast*, Vol. 7, *Handbook of North American Indians*, edited by William C. Sturtevant (Washington, D. C.: Smithsonian Institution, 1990).
9. For the clearest delineation of southern Oregon language divisions, see Jeff Zucker, Kay Hummel and Bob Høgfoss, *Oregon Indians Culture, History & Current Affairs* (Portland: Western Imprints/The Press of the OHS, 1983), 48-53.
10. Stephen Dow Beckham, *Requiem for a People: The Rogue Indians and the Frontiersmen* (Norman: UOP, 1971; reprint Corvallis: OSUP, 1996), p. 9, and E. A. Schwartz, *The Rogue River Indian War and Its Aftermath, 1850-1980* (Norman and London, UOP, 1997), p. 149, state that the Indian population in southern Oregon in 1851 numbered about 9,500. This conclusion is based on Alfred Kroeber's "Cultural and Natural Areas of Native North America," *University of California Publications in American Archaeology and Ethnology*, Vo. 38 (1939), 36. Kroeber relied on the calculations of James Mooney in *The Aboriginal Population of American North of Mexico*, Smithsonian Miscellaneous Collections 80 (7) (Washington, D.C., 1928). As Beckham notes: "Alfred Kroeber, using a reworking of population figures compiled by James Mooney, set 8,800 as a probable number for the Athapascans and 500 for the Takelmas" (p. 9). Beckham left out of his count Mooney's estimate of 2,000 "Kus," but he added 250 Shastas based on an 1854 Indian agent census.

   How did James Mooney arrive at his figures? Douglas H. Ubelaker, "The Sources and Methodology for Mooney's Estimates of North American Indian Populations," 243-88, in William M. Denevan, ed., *The Native Population of the Americas in 1492* (Madison: University of Wisconsin Press, 1976) points out that for the lower Columbia, Mooney used Meriwether Lewis and William Clark's estimates. He also may have used their estimates of "Sho-Sho-new on the Multnomah" as a basis for estimating the Athapascan population (Mooney links some but not all of his estimates to specific sources). For the Coos, Mooney increased Lewis and Clark's estimate by one-third. Ubelaker notes that Kroeber used Mooney's estimates except in the case of California, for which he used his own. But Mooney's estimates were of the "aboriginal" or pre-contact population, not the Indian populations as of the mid-nineteenth century. Mooney died in 1921, and his aboriginal population estimates were published posthumously. He did not complete his research on post-contact population decline. By using an aboriginal population count, Beckham and Schwartz have established a population baseline for 1851 from which the Indian population of southern Oregon (exclusive of the Coos, Lower Umpqua, and Siuslaw) declined from

9,500 to an estimated 1,943 (or my estimate of 2,314) by 1856-57, a "catastrophic loss" of about 7,557 people in the period 1851-57. Robert Boyd, *The Coming of the Spirit of Pestilence: Introduced Infectious Diseases and Population Decline among Northwest Coast Indians, 1774-1874* (Vancouver and Toronto: UBC Press and Seattle and London: UWP, 1999) has arrived at an even higher "aboriginal population" for southern Oregon than James Mooney. But my concern here is with the Indian population at the beginning of the 1850s, after fifty or more years of white contact. (I refer readers to my discussion of Boyd's "aboriginal population" estimates in Appendix 1.) In my opinion, white reports on Indians in the period 1850-53, an estimate of Table Rock Reserve deaths in 1853-54, and estimates of deaths from warfare 1850-56 do not support use of the Kroeber-Mooney aboriginal population figures as a basis for the Indian population in 1850-51.

My figure of approximately 3,800 has been reached in the following way. I have counted back from 3,108 people from southern Oregon (821 Shasta and upper Rogue River, 1,493 Coquille to Chetco, and 444 Coos, Lower Umpqua, and Siuslaw Indians) on the Siletz, Grand Ronde, and Umpqua River reservations in 1856-57, plus approximately 350 Indians still at large after the war (about 100 Cow Creeks and 250 coastal Indians). I have added 446 war deaths and massacres; 100 disease-related deaths on the Table Rock Reserve; and 124 possible deaths (a 10 percent correction) inflicted on the 1,239 women and children of the hostile bands (even though the postwar census showed more women and children than an 1855 prewar census). This totals 3,778 people. A reasonable estimate of the southern Oregon Indian population in 1850-51 is critical to accurately assessing the destructive impact of Indian-white encounters in the period 1850-56. The Indians of southern Oregon numbered about 3,108 in 1856-57 after removal of most Indians to the Siletz, Grand Ronde, and Umpqua River reservations. A population decline from 3,778 to 3,108 represents 608 lives, or a decline of about 18 percent, whereas a decline from 9,500 to 3,108 represents 6,392 lives, or a decline of about 67 percent.

11. Aikens, *Archaeology of Oregon*, 143-44.
12. See, generally, Gray, *The Takelma and Their Athapascan Neighbors.*
13. On food resources, see Jeff LaLande, *The Indians of Southwestern Oregon: An Ethnohistorical Review*, Anthropology Northwest: Number 6, Department of Anthropology, OSU, Corvallis, 1991, 15-24; Gray, *The Takelma and Their Athapascan Neighbors*, 30-32, 48-51, 65.
14. On Lewis and Clark's observations, see Gary E. Moulton, ed. *The Journals of the Lewis & Clark Expedition*, Vol. 6, November 2, 1805-March 22, 1806 (Lincoln and London: UNP, 1990), 187. See discussions of trade goods and trade in Gray, *The Takelma and Their Athapascan Neighbors*, 34-35; Atwood and Gray, *People and the River*, 58; and LaLande, *The Indians of Southwestern Oregon*, 37-38. On Ogden's visit to the Klamaths, see Jeff LaLande, "Through A Strange Country Covered with Lakes," *Journal of the Shaw Historical Library*, Vol. 8 (1994), 1-28; on Smith's report, see Nathan Douthit, *A Guide to Oregon South Coast History* (Corvallis: OSUP, 1999), 118-19.
15. For a detailed discussion of cultural traits, see LaLande, *The Indians of Southwestern Oregon*; see on slavery, p. 31. See also on slavery, Gray, *The Takelma and Their Athapascan Neighbors*, 34; Philip Drucker, *The Tolowa and Their Southwest Oregon Kin*, University of California Publications on American Archaeology and Ethnology 36, No. 4, 221-300 (Berkeley: UCP, 1937), 242, 250, 273; Stephen Dow Beckham, *The Indians of Western Oregon: This Land Was Theirs* (Coos Bay,

Ore.: Arago Books, 1977), 54, 77; Zucker et al., *Oregon Indians, Culture, History and Current Affairs*, 55.

16. T. C. Elliott, "Vancouver's Journal," *OHQ* 30 (Mar. 1929), 34-41.
17. James R. Gibson, *The Lifeline of the Oregon Country: The Fraser-Columbia Brigade System, 1811-47* (Vancouver: UBCP, 1997), 4-7.
18. On Fort Nez Percés see Theodore Stern, *Chiefs & Chief Traders: Indian Relations at Fort Nez Percés, 1818-1855*, Vol. 1 (Corvallis: OSUP, 1993).
19. Alexander Ross, *The Fur Hunters of the Far West* (Norman: UOP, 1956), 132-33. Stephen Dow Beckham, *Land of the Umpqua: A History of Douglas County, Oregon* (Roseburg: Douglas County Commissioners, 1986), 50; Gibson, *The Lifeline of the Oregon Country*, 121.
20. On the Hudson's Bay Company and its development under McLoughlin, see Dorothy Nafus Morrison, *Outpost: John McLoughlin and the Far Northwest* (Portland: OHS Press, 1999).

Chapter 1

1. See, for example, The Works of Hubert Howe Bancroft, Vol.XXLX, [Frances Fuller Victor], *History of Oregon*, Vol. I, 1834-1848 (San Francisco, 1886), 36; Gloria Griffen Cline, *Peter Skene Ogden and the Hudson's Bay Company* (Norman: UOP, 1974), 182; Beckham, *Land of the Umpqua*, 91-92; William G. Robbins, "The Indian Question in Western Oregon: The Making of A Colonial People," in G. Thomas Edwards and Carlos A. Schwantes, eds. *Experiences in a Promised Land: Essays in Pacific Northwest History* (Seattle and London: UWP, 1986), 51-67.
2. These conclusions agree with the study of HBC policy in John Phillip Reid, "Principles of Vengeance: Fur Trappers, Indians, and Retaliation for Homicide in Transboundary North American West," *WHQ* 24 (Feb. 1993), 21-43.
3. K.G. Davies, ed. *Peter Skene Ogden's Snake Country Journal 1826-27* (London: The Hudson's Bay Record Society, 1961), xxxii-xxxiii.
4. Jeff LaLande, *First Over the Siskiyous: Peter Skene Ogden's 1826-1827 Journey Through the Oregon-California Borderlands* (Portland: OHS Press, 1987). On Ogden's life, see Cline, *Peter Skene Ogden*, 15-19, 25-50.
5. Alice Bay Maloney, ed. *Fur Brigade to the Bonaventura: John Work's California Expedition 1832-1833 for the Hudson's Bay Company* (San Francisco: CHS, 1945), v.
6. Davies, ed. *Snake Country Journal, 1826-27*, 33-67. On Ogden's relations with the Klamath Indians, see Jeff LaLande, "Through A 'Strange Country.' "
7. Davies, ed. *Snake Country Journal, 1826-27*, 35.
8. Ibid., 54, 60-68. Throughout this paper I have used the corrected dates from Ogden's journal, that is one day earlier than the date Ogden entered, as corrected by Davies.
9. Davies, ed., *Snake Country Journal, 1826-27*, 76. See also, 208-9, for Alexander McLeod's reference to women and children.
10. John C. Jackson, *Children of the Fur Trade: Forgotten Métis of the Pacific Northwest* (Missoula: Mountain Press, 1995), 57; Cline, *Peter Skene Ogden*, 45, 47, 52; Gibson, *Lifeline of the Oregon Country*, 121.
11. Davies, ed., *Snake Country Journal, 1826-27*, 76. See also, 208-9, for Alexander McLeod's reference to women and children.
12. John A. Hussey, "The Women of Fort Vancouver," *OHQ* 92 (Fall 1991), 286. On slavery and, especially, the slaves of Indian women, see note 66, p. 304.
13. Davies, ed., *Snake Country Journal, 1826-27*, 69.
14. Ibid., 69-71. See Reid, "Principles of Vengeance," for more on fur trappers' attitudes.

15. Rogue River Indians can be divided geographically and linguistically into five major groups: lower Rogue River (Athapascan), upper Rogue River (Takelma), Applegate River (Athapascan), Siskiyou Mountain (Shasta), and Illinois Valley (Athapascan). See Stephen Dow Beckham, *Requiem for A People: The Rogue Indians and the Frontiersmen* (Norman: UOP, 1971), 7-9; Gray, *The Takelma and Their Athapascan Neighbors*, 16-26. Distinctions between the territories of different Indian bands can be found in *Treaties and Agreements of the Indian Tribes of the Pacific Northwest* (Institute for the Development of Indian Law, Washington, D.C., 1974), 1-9. On possible Shasta links to the Illinois Valley, see George Gibbs, "Journal of the Expedition of Colonel Redick M'Kee, United States Indian Agent, Through Northwestern California, Performed in the Summer and Fall of 1851," in Henry R. Schoolcraft, *Archives of Aboriginal Knowledge*, Vol. 2 (Philadelphia, 1860), 157; on Takelma links, see Shirley Silver, "Shastan Peoples," in Robert F. Heizer, ed., *California*, Vol. 8, *Handbook of North American Indians* (Washington, D. C.: Smithsonian Institution, 1978), 211.
16. Davies, ed. *Snake Country Journal, 1826-27*, 71.
17. Ibid., 74-77.
18. Davies, ed. *Snake Country Journal, 1826-27*, 78-79.
19. Ibid., 82.
20. Ibid., 86.
21. Edward Sapir, "Notes on the Takelma Indians of South-western Oregon," *American Anthropologist* 9 (Apr.-June 1907), 255.
22. Davies, ed. *Snake Country Journal, 1826-27*, 96. On slave raiding and slavery among Indians, see earlier Introduction.
23. Ibid., 97-103. LaLande, *First Over the Siskiyous*, 124, suggests that Ogden's mention of "'new Graves' in the Rogue-Umpqua drainages (March 28) may provide a clue to the speed at which Old World diseases had spread from the lower Columbia or coast to other regions." However, prior to Ogden's party the Indians of southern Oregon probably had not made contact with whites. Boyd, *The Coming of the Spirit of Pestilence*, has identified Oregon smallpox epidemics in 1824-25 and 1836-37, and a "fever and ague" (malaria) outbreak in 1830-35.
24. Schwartz, *The Rogue River Indian War*, 23-24. Ogden made no mention of seeing the effects of smallpox.
25. Fur traders' use of the word "starve" and "starving" is analyzed in Mary Black-Rogers, "Varieties of 'Starving': Semantics and Survival in the Subarctic Fur Trade, 1750-1850," *Ethnohistory* 33 (Fall 1986), 353-83. Elizabeth Vibert, *Traders' Tales: Narratives of Cultural Encounters in the Columbia Plateau, 1807-1846* (Norman: UOP, 1997), 150-51, found that fur traders often viewed the claim of "starving" as a form of "begging." See also, Boyd, *Spirit of Pestilence*, 279-85: "Starvation runs like a leitmotif through Northwest myth texts" (279).
26. For comparison, see Paul C. Thistle, *Indian-European Trade Relations in the Lower Saskatchewan River Region to 1840* (Winnepeg: UMP, 1986), 83-84.
27. Quoted in Gibson, *Lifeline of the Oregon Country*, 256 n. 89.
28. A. J. Ray, "Men of Property and the Exercise of Title," 302, in *Aboriginal Resource Use in Canada*, ed. K. Abel and J. Friesen (Manitoba: UMP, 1991), cited in Jo-Anne Fiske and Caroline Mufford, "Hard Times and Everything Like That: Carrier Women's Tales of Life on the Trapline," 17, 27 n.7, in Jo-Anne Fiske, et al. *New Faces of the Fur Trade: Selected Papers of the Seventh North American Fur Trade Conference, Halifax, Nova Scotia, 1995* (East Lansing: Michigan State University, 1998).
29. LaLande, "Through A 'Strange Country,' " 16.

30. On Indian lines of trade, see Theodore Stern, *Chiefs and Chief Traders*, 22-23. Stern indicates that lines of trade between the Columbia Plateau Region and southern Oregon involved only the Klamath Indians. However, he also points out that Tualatin Kalapuya Indians' trading may have extended to southern Oregon. On the Rogue River, Ogden's men met a chief who stated that "the Umpqua River is far from this [O]ur neighbors trade with them occasionally and it is from them we obtain Knives and Axes which we barter for Beaver and Hyequa's [dentalium shells]...." (Davies, ed. *Snake Country Journal, 1826-27*, 89). Upper Rogue River Indians also may have engaged in trading with northern California Indians along the Klamath River (see Lee Davis, "Tracking Jedediah Smith Through Hupa Territory," *American Indian Quarterly* 13 (Fall 1989), 382). On coming upon a large Indian village near Lower Table Rock on the Rogue River, Ogden remarked that his men discovered a "Sickle and two China Bowls" in the possession of two men and a woman who remained in the village: "the Sickle they make us of as a substitute for a Knife and the Bowls are preserved as ornaments [T]hey would not part with either appearing to lay considerable value on both" (Davies, ed., *Snake Country Journal, 1826-27*, 86).
31. Edward Sapir, *Takelma Texts*, University of Pennsylvania Anthropological Publications of the University Museum, Vol. II, No.1 (Philadelphia: University Museum, University of Pennsylvania, 1909). The word "wulx" meaning enemies was "used generally to refer to Shasta Indians"(Sapir, 24, also n. 3, 188-189). Upper Rogue River Indians (Upper Takelma or Latgawa) also raided lower river villages (Sapir, 189-193). Leslie Spier, *Klamath Ethnography* (Berkeley: UCP, 1930), 25-26, describes raiding parties between the Klamath Indians and Upper Rogue River or Takelma Indians. Also, see LaLande, "Through 'A Strange Country,' " 18, on conflict between the Klamaths and Shastas.
32. Norman Dennis Schlesser, *Fort Umpqua: Bastion of Empire* (Oakland, Ore.: Schlesser, 1973), 16-17.
33. Davies, ed., *Snake Country Journal 1826-27*, 180-215; on McLeod, see Doyce B. Nunis, Jr., "Alexander Roderick McLeod," in LeRoy R. Hafen, ed., *The Mountain Men and the Fur Trade of the Far West*, Vol. VI (Glendale, Calif.: Arthur H. Clark, 1968), 279-97.
34. Davies, ed., *Snake Country Journal 1826-27*, 182, 185, 190 n.1, 198, 209. On Douglas, see John Davies, *Douglas of the Forests: The North American Journals of David Douglas* (Seattle: UWP, 1980). On Laframboise, see Doyce B. Nunis, Jr., "Michel Laframboise," in LeRoy R. Hafen, ed., *The Mountain Men and the Fur Trade of the West*, Vol. V (Glendale.: Arthur H. Clark, 1968), 145-70.
35. Gibson, *The Lifeline of the Oregon Country*, 62-63.
36. On the Iroquois Indians in the fur trade, see Theodore J. Karamanski, "The Iroquois and the Fur Trade of the Far West," *The Beaver* 312 (Spring 1982), 4-13; also Trudy Nicks, "The Iroquois and the Fur Trade in Western Canada," in Carol M. Judd & Arthur J. Ray, eds. *Old Trails and New Directions: Papers of the Third American Fur Trade Conference* (Toronto: University of Toronto Press, 1980), 85-101.
37. Davies, ed., *Snake Country Journal 1826-27*, 190 n.1; also 184-85.
38. Ibid., xxxiii-xxxiv, lviii.
39. Ibid., 182-214, for this and subsequent quotes from McLeod's journal.
40. James Arneson, "Property Concepts of 19th Century Oregon Indians," *OHQ* 81 (Winter 1980), 391-422. For ethnographic data on coastal Indians of southern Oregon, see Philip Drucker, *The Tolowas and their Southwest Oregon Kin*, 221-300;

Cora A. DuBois, "Tolowa Notes," *American Anthropologist* 34 (Apr.-June 1932), 248-62; Vernon Nielson, "Indian Tribes of Curry County," *OHQ* 32 (Mar. 1931), 24-6. On linguistic topics, see Henry B. Zenk, "Siuslawans and Coosans," in Wayne Suttles, ed., *Northwest Coast*, Vol. 7, *Handbook of North American Indians* (Washington, D. C.: Smithsonian Institution, 1990), 580-88; Roberta L. Hall, *The Coquille Indians: Yesterday, Today and Tomorrow* (Lake Oswego: Smith, Smith and Smith, 1984), 129-44; Robert L. Hall, ed., *People of the Coquille Estuary: Native Use of Resources on the Oregon Coast* (Corvallis: Words & Pictures, 1995), 25-38.

41. Peter Cook, "Symbolic and Material Exchange in Intercultural Diplomacy: The French and Hodenosaunee in the Early Eighteenth Century," 85, in Fiske, et al. *New Faces of the Fur Trade*; Marcel Mauss, *The Gift: The Form and Reason for Exchange in Archaic Societies*, trans. W. D. Halls (London: Routledge, 1990).
42. John Frederick Schenk, "The Hudson's Bay Company in Oregon, 1821-1860," masters thesis, UO, Eugene, 1932, 25.
43. E. E. Rich, ed. *The Letters of John McLoughlin from Fort Vancouver to the Governor and Committee, First Series, 1825-38* (London: Hudson's Bay Record Society, 1941), 68.
44. Dale L. Morgan, *Jedediah Smith and the Opening of the West* (1953; reprint, Lincoln: UNP, 1964), 193-215; Andrew F. Rolle, ed., "Jedediah Strong Smith: New Documentation," *Mississippi Valley Historical Review* 40 (Sept. 1953), 305-308; George R. Brooks, *The Southwest Expedition of Jedediah S. Smith: His Personal Account of the Journey to California 1826-1827* (Glendale, Calif.: Arthur H. Clark, 1977), 35-100. Brooks' book consists of a transcript of Smith's original journals and notes relating to his first Southwest Expedition of 1826-27. It also contains Harrison G. Rogers Daybook I, relating to the 1826-27 expedition. Rogers was Smith's second-in-command on both the first and second expeditions. Maurice S. Sullivan, ed., *The Travels of Jedediah Smith: A Documentary Outline Including the Journal of the Great Pathfinder* (Santa Ana, Calif.: Fine Arts Press, 1934), picks up Smith's account on June 22, 1827 and carries it through his second trip to California and Oregon in 1827-28. In addition to Rogers' journal for Nov. 26-Dec. 20, 1826 and Jan. 1-27, 1827 contained in Brooks' book, his journal for May 10-July 13, 1828 can be found in Harrison Clifford Dale, ed. *The Ashley-Smith Explorations and the Discovery of A Central Route to the Pacific 1822-1829*, rev. ed. (Glendale, Calif.: Arthur H. Clark, 1941), 242-275.
45. Sullivan, *Travels of Jedediah Smith*, 29-30; Morgan, *Jedediah Smith*, 236-255, 339.
46. Sullivan, *Travels of Jedediah Smith*, 34-53. Morgan, *Jedediah Smith*, 257, states that twenty men "departed Mission San Jose." But a letter to Gen. William Clark from Smith, Jackson, and Sublette stated that Smith started from California with twenty-one men and that two soon deserted (ibid., 340). Apparently, there were nineteen men in the expedition by the time it reached the Coquille River, and added an Indian slave boy named Marion, who was counted among the fifteen killed at the Umpqua River. However, another expedition member, Reubasco or Reubascan, does not appear in the list of the dead (Morgan, *Jedediah Smith*, 341). The addition of Marion would have brought the number in the expedition up to twenty, counting Reubasco, at the time of the Umpqua massacre; but the reported dead and survivors after the massacre numbered nineteen men.
47. Sullivan, *Travels of Jedediah Smith*, 85-102.
48. Ibid., 81-82.
49. Davis, "Tracking Jedediah Smith Through Hupa Territory," 382; Sullivan, *Travels of Jedediah Smith*, 91-92; Dale, ed., *Ashley-Smith Explorations*, 245-251.

50. Dale, ed., *Ashley-Smith Explorations*, 250-256; Sullivan, *Travels of Jedediah Smith*, 96-97.
51. Dale, ed., *Ashley-Smith Explorations*, 259; Sullivan, *Travels of Jedediah Smith*, 99.
52. Sullivan, *Travels of Jedediah Smith*, 137.
53. Dale, ed., *Ashley-Smith Explorations*, 262-265.
54. Sullivan, *Travels of Jedediah Smith*, 103; Dale, ed., *Ashley-Smith Explorations*, 265-66.
55. Dale, ed., *Ashley-Smith Explorations*, 267.
56. Ibid., 270.
57. Ibid., 271-72.
58. George B. Wasson, Jr., "The Memory of A People: The Coquilles of the Southwest Coast," in Carolyn M. Baun and Richard Lewis, eds., *The First Oregonians: An Illustrated Collection of Essays on Traditional Lifeways, Federal Indian Relations, and the State's Native People Today* (Portland: Oregon Council for the Humanities, 1991), 83-87.
59. Dale, ed., *Ashley-Smith Explorations*, 272.
60 Alice B. Maloney, "Camp Sites of Jedediah Smith on the Oregon Coast," *OHQ* 41 (Sept. 1940), 317.
61. Dale, ed., *Ashley-Smith Explorations*, 273-75.
62. "Extracts from Governor George Simpson's Report to the Governor and Committee of the Hudson's Bay Company, London, dated 1st March, 1829," Sullivan, *Travels of Jedediah Smith*, 147; see also Rich, ed., *Letters of John McLoughlin...1825-38*, 68-70.
63. S. A. Clarke, *Pioneer Days of Oregon History*, Vol. I (Portland: J. K. Gill, 1905), 216-17.
64. Rich, ed., *Letters of John McLoughlin...1825-38*, 57. See Jonathan R. Dean, "The Hudson's Bay Company and Its Use of Force, 1828-1829," *OHQ* 98 (Fall 1997), 262-95, for a discussion of HBC policy in the Pacific Northwest as a whole.
65. Rich, ed., *Letters of John McLoughlin...1825-38*, 64-65. See Dean, "The Hudson's Bay Company and Its Use of Force, 1828-1829" for details of the expedition against the Clallam Indians.
66. Sullivan, *Travels of Jedediah Smith*, 112-35, contains McLeod's journal of the salvage mission.
67. Sullivan, *Travels of Jedediah Smith*, 110-11, letter of McLoughlin to McLeod, Sept. 12, 1828; see also 143-50, extracts from Gov. Simpson's report of Mar. 1, 1829.
68. Ibid., 116-17, 120-31.
69. Ibid., 148.
70. Clarke, *Pioneer Days of Oregon History*, I, 216.
71. Rich, ed., *Letters of John McLoughlin...1825-38*, 282.
72. Gustavas Hines, *Wildlife in Oregon* (New York: R. Worthington, 1881), 109-12; Orange Jacobs, "Annual Address," Oregon Pioneer Association *Transactions, 1889*, 23. See Beverly H. Ward, *White Moccasins* (Cottage Grove, Ore.: Ward, 1986) for a retelling of the Smith expedition story from an Indian perspective.

Chapter 2

1. Nunis, Jr., "Alexander Roderick McLeod," 288, 290-94.
2. Doyce B. Nunis, Jr., ed. *The Hudson's Bay Company's First Fur Brigade to the Sacramento Valley: Alexander McLeod's 1829 Hunt* (Fair Oaks, Calif.: Sacramento Book Collectors Club, 1968), 31-39; McLoughlin to the Governor....Vancouver,

Nov. 15, 1843, in E. E. Rich, ed., *The Letters of John McLoughlin From Fort Vancouver to the Governor and Committee, Second Series, 1839-44* (London: Hudson's Bay Record Society, 1943), 116.

3. Maloney, ed. *Fur Brigade to the Bonaventura*, 77-78; Lewis A. McArthur, *Oregon Geographic Names* (Portland: OHS Press, 1974), 627.
4. Nunis, Jr., "Michel Laframboise," 145-69.
5. Nunis, Jr., "Michel Laframboise," 153; "John Work's Journey from Fort Vancouver to Umpqua River, and Return, in 1834, Introduction and Comments by Leslie M. Scott," *OHQ* 24 (Sept. 1923), 255-59; Sullivan, *Travels of Jedediah Smith*, 179 n.179.
6. Schlesser, *Fort Umpqua*, 25, notes that "the annual reports of the trade at Fort Umpqua no longer exist." This makes it impossible to know how many furs were received from coastal and Umpqua River Indians. On his salvage trip to the coast following the Smith party massacre, McLeod picked up "72 Large Beavers and 16 Large Land Otters" at the "Verveau" outpost near Scottsburg. See Sullivan, *Travels of Jedediah Smith*, 132; Nunis, Jr., "Michel Laframboise," 158 n. 52.
7. Rich, ed. *Letters of John McLoughlin…1825-38*, 125-28.
8. Kenneth L. Holmes, *Ewing Young: Master Trapper* (Portland: Binfords & Mort, 1967), 94-101.
9. Ibid., 102-103; see also Clarke, *Pioneer Days of Oregon History*, Vol. I, 296-298; Bancroft [Victor], *History of Oregon, 1834-1848*, 90, mentions "a difficulty with Indians of the Rogue River" but offers no details.
10. Bancroft, *History of Oregon, 1834-1848*, 95-97 n. 29; John Kirk Townsend, *Narrative of a Journey Across the Rocky Mountains to the Columbia River* (Lincoln and London: UNP, [1839] 1978), 218-219; McLoughlin in a letter of November 15, 1843, in Rich, ed. *Letters of John McLoughlin...1839-44*, 116, summarizes Hudson's Bay Company and American violent encounters with the Indians of southern Oregon, but he mistakenly assigns the date of 1832 rather than 1835 to the Turner party incident. The 1835 date is also confirmed by Edwards, in *California in 1837: Diary of Col. Philip L. Edwards, Containing An Account of A Trip to the Pacific Coast* (Sacramento: A. J. Johnston, 1890), 47, who places the "defeat" of Turner two years before his 1837 trip.
11. Rich, ed. *Letters of John McLoughlin...1825-38*, 202-203.
12. Douglas to the Governor, Fort Vancouver, Oct. 18, 1838, ibid., 252.
13. Douglas to the Governor, Fort Vancouver, Mar. 18, 1838, ibid., 282.
14. Bancroft, *History of Oregon, 1834-1848*, 142 n. 6.
15. Edwards, *California in 1837*, 41-47, 150.
16. Hines, *Wildlife in Oregon*, 30-42, 89-90.
17. Ibid., 92-99.
18. Schlesser, *Fort Umpqua*, 16-17.
19. Cline, *Peter Skene Ogden*, 11, 79. The Southern Party's demise is reflected in the profit figures for the Columbia Department (which accounted for one-third of total HBC profits). In the period 1826 to 1847, beaver returns for the Columbia District (as compared to New Caledonia) declined from two-thirds to one-third of the total. Chief Factor Ogden commented that the 1840-41 return for the Columbia District "was scarcely worth the expense of an outlay for a party of trappers" (Quoted in Gibson, *Lifeline of the Oregon Country*, 202). By 1841, the price of beaver pelts on the London market had dropped from a high of $5.99 to $2.62 a pound.
20. Schlesser, *Fort Umpqua*, 23-25.

21. Hines, *Wildlife in Oregon*, 99; cf. James Douglas to the Governor...Mar. 18, 1838, in Rich, ed., *Letters of John McLoughlin...1825-38*, 292.
22. John Harrington Papers, Reel 24, Frame 936, quoted in Lionel Youst, *Above the Falls* (Coos Bay, Ore.: Youst, 1992), 47.
23. Lionel Youst, *She's Tricky Like Coyote: Annie Miner Peterson, An Oregon Coast Indian Woman* (Norman and London: UOP, 1997), quoted at 10.
24. Hines, *Wildlife in Oregon*, 100. See 100-17, for Hines description of his trip down the Umpqua River.
25. Emmons middle name is shown as "Falconer" in Henry R. Schoolcraft, *Archives of Aboriginal Knowledge*, Vol. III, 202. However, William Stanton, *The Great United States Exploring Expedition of 1838-1842* (Berkeley: UCP, 1975) gives "Foster" as the correct middle name.
26. Carl S. Dentzel, "Introduction," in *Diary of Titian Ramsay Peale, Oregon to California Overland Journey, September and October, 1841*, Edited by Clifford Merrill Drury (Los Angeles: Glen Dawson, 1957), 23.
27. Stanton, *Great United States Exploring Expedition*, 18, 22; Rich, ed. *Letters of John McLoughlin...1825-38*, 125-28.
28. George M. Colvocoresses, *Four Years in A Government Exploring Expedition* (New York: Cornish, Lamport, 1852), 283.
29. Charles Wilkes, *Narrative of the United States Exploring Expedition During the Years 1838, 1839, 1840, 1841,1842*, Vol. V (Philadelphia: Lea & Blanchard, 1845), 225.
30. George Falconer [Foster] Emmons, "Replies to Inquiries Respecting the Indian Tribes of Oregon," in Schoolcraft, *Archives of Aboriginal Knowledge*, Vol. III, 202.
31. Boyd, *Spirit of Pestilence*; also, Boyd's earlier article, "Another Look at the 'Fever and Ague' of Western Oregon," *Ethnohistory* 22 (Spring 1975), 135-54. For further discussion, see Appendix 1.
32. Quoted in Gibson, *Lifeline of the Oregon Country*, 146.
33. Boyd, *Spirit of Pestilence*, 238-244.
34. Parrish to Palmer, Sept. 11, 1854, 53d Cong., 1st Sess., Sen. Ex. Doc. No. 25, Serial 3144, 24-32.
35. Wilkes, *Narrative of the United States Exploring Expedition*, 225.
36. Ibid., 227.
37. Ibid., 231; also *Diary of Titian Ramsay Peale*, 34-35. On the use of fire by Oregon Indians, see Robert Boyd, ed. *Indians, Fire, and the Land in the Pacific Northwest* (Corvallis: OSUP, 1999).
38. *Diary of Titian Ramsay Peale*, 32.
39. Colvocoresses, *Four Years in A Government Exploring Expedition*, 288; *Diary of Titian Ramsay Peale*, 36-38; Wilkes, *Narrative of the United States Exploring Expedition*, 234.
40. Emmons, "Replies to Inquiries," in Schoolcraft, *Archives of Aboriginal Knowledge*, III, 213-15.
41. *Diary of Titian Ramsay Peale*, 40-42.
42. Bancroft [Victor], *History of Oregon, 1834-1848*, 370-81; 27 Cong., 2d Sess., H. Rep. 830, Serial 410, 56-64.
43. Bancroft [Victor], *History of Oregon, 1834-1848*, 373.
44. See coverage of debate on the bill in *Nile's National Register*, vols. 61-64 (Sept. 4, 1841-Aug. 20, 1843), University Microfilms, American Periodical Series, 1800-1850, Reel 265.
45. Rich, ed. *Letters of John McLoughlin...1839-44*, 14.
46. 25th Cong., 3d Sess., Reports of Committees, Vol. I, 1838-39, Rep. No. 101, App. N.

47. Rich, ed., *Letters of John McLoughlin…1839-44*, 14.
48. Nellie B. Pipes, "Indian Conditions in 1836-38," *OHQ* 32 (Dec. 1931), 332-42, contains the letter of Rev. Beaver, which mentions the killing of six Indians by a party of trappers and sailors somewhere between the Columbia River and California. His references are vague as to the time, place, number of Indians killed, and responsible persons.
49. 27 Cong., 2d Sess., H. Rep. 830, Serial 410, 59. On Spaulding's report, see Bancroft [Victor], *History of Oregon*, 1834-1848, 377, which links the appearance of the report to Sen. Linn's reopening of debate on the subject of Oregon on Jan. 8, 1841.
50. Lester Burrell Shippee, "The Federal Relations of Oregon-II," *OHQ* 19 (Sept. 1918), 143-48.
51. Rich, ed. *Letters of John McLoughlin...1839-44*, 111-19, 143-48d., 144.
52. See Dean, "The Hudson's Bay Company and Its Use of Force, 1828-1829," 262-95.
53. Rich, ed. *Letters of John McLoughlin...1839-44*, 17.
54. Ibid., 185.
55. Nunis, Jr., ed. *The Hudson's Bay Company's First Fur Brigade*, 32, 35, 39.
56. Nunis, Jr., "Michel Laframboise," 150.
57. "John Work's Journey from Fort Vancouver to Umpqua River, and Return, in 1834, Introduction and Comments by Leslie M. Scott," *OHQ* 24 (Sept. 1923), 255-56.
58. Edwards, *California in 1837*.
59. In the period 1826-43, the following white men were reported killed by Indians south of the Columbia River: two members of the McLeod expedition (one near the Umpqua River and one at Coos Bay); two HBC trappers, by Tillamook Indians; fifteen men of Jedediah Smith's expedition, killed by lower Umpqua (Kalawatset) Indians; two métis HBC trappers near Fort Umpqua; and four men (Americans?) from the Turner party. This is a total of twenty-five white men killed (nineteen Americans and six HBC personnel).
60. Lansford W. Hastings, *The Emigrants' Guide to Oregon and California* (Princeton: Princeton University Press, 1932), ix-xiv, 52-57.
61. Ibid., 64-65.
62. Beckham, *Requiem for A People*, 37-38; Hastings, *The Emigrants' Guide*, xiii-xiv.
63. Charles Camp, ed., *James Clyman, Frontiersman* (Portland: Champoeg Press, 1960), 156-62, 170.
64. Lindsay Applegate, "Notes and Reminiscences of Laying Out and Establishing the Old Emigrant Road into Southern Oregon in the Year 1846," *OHQ* 22 (Mar.1921), 12-45; Bancroft, *History of Oregon, 1834-1848*, 542-572; Devere Helfrich, "The Applegate Trail I," *Klamath Echoes* No.9 (1971), 1-106, and "Applegate Trail II: West of the Cascades," *Klamath Echoes* No.14 (1976), 1-102.
65. Applegate, "Notes and Reminiscences," 18-19; Helfrich, "Applegate Trail I," 3.
66. Letter of C.E. Pickett, Nov. 25, 1847, in *Oregon Spectator*, Feb. 24, 1848.
67. Applegate, "Notes and Reminiscences," 22.
68. Helfrich, "Applegate Trail I," 5, 8, 20, 23, 28-29; also Dale Morgan, ed., *Overland in 1846: Diaries and Letters of the California-Trail*, Vol. I (Georgetown, Calif.: Talisman Press, 1963), 116, 184.
69. Helfrich, "Applegate Trail I," 18-23; Morgan, *Overland in 1846*, I, 185; Tolbert Carter, "Pioneer Days," Oregon Pioneer Association *Transactions, 1906*, 73.
70. Carter, "Pioneer Days," 67-72: Oregon Spectator, Nov. 11, 1847.

71. Helfrich, "Applegate Trail II," 36-52; Kenneth L. Holmes, ed. *Covered Wagon Women: Diaries and Letters from the Western Trails 1840-1890*, Vol. I (Glendale, Calif.: Arthur H. Clark, 1983), 52-53.
72. Morgan, *Overland in 1846*, I, 186, 191, 194-95 and 397 n.4; Holmes, *Covered Wagon Women*, I, 55; Helfrich, "Applegate Trail II," 45.
73. Bancroft [Victor], *History of Oregon, 1834-1848*, 566-67; Helfrich, "Applegate Trail I," 8-9; John D. Unruh, Jr., *The Plains Across: The Overland Emigrants and the Trans-Mississippi West, 1840-60* (Urbana and London: University of Illinois Press, 1979), 349. In the *Oregon Spectator*, Oct. 14, 1847, Jesse Applegate reported in a letter of Oct. 2, 1847 that Levi Scott arrived in the Willamette Valley on Sept. 26 with a party of 25 wagons. *Oregon Spectator*, Nov. 11, 1847 reported that "two more companies of immigrants, one of eleven and the other of sixteen wagons" had arrived. *Oregon Spectator*, Nov. 25, 1847 reported that a "fourth" company of 20 wagons had arrived. This makes a total of 72 wagons in the 1846 emigration over the Southern Route.
74. Helfrich, "Applegate Trail I," 9-10.
75. Holmes, *Covered Wagon Women*, I, 215; Morgan, *Overland in 1846*, I, 164, 183. Ezra Meeker, *Ox-Team Days on the Oregon Trail* (Yonkers-on-Hudson: World Book, 1932): "A conservative estimate would be not less than six animals to the wagon, and surely there were three loose animals to each one in the teams" (p.50). In the *Oregon Spectator*, Oct. 29, 1846, Samuel K. Barlow reported that 145 wagons and 1,559 horses, mules, and horned cattle passed the tollgate in 1846, an average of 10.75 animals per wagon.

Chapter 3

1. *Oregon Spectator*, Aug. 6, 1846.
2. *Oregon Spectator*, July 9, 1846; Aug. 6, 1846.
3. Ibid., Mar. 19, 1846; Apr. 6, 1846; Dec. 10, 1846; Oct. 14, 1847; Dec. 23, 1847; Jan. 6, 1848.
4. Ibid., Nov. 26, 1846; Mar. 4, 1847; Apr. 29, 1847.
5. Ibid., Apr. 15, 1847.
6. Ibid., Apr. 29, 1847.
7. Ibid., May 27, 1847.
8. Prucha, *The Great Father*, 284.
9. Victor, *Early Indian Wars of Oregon*, 238-39.
10. *Oregon Spectator*, Sept. 2, 1847; Feb. 24, 1848, Pickett's letter of Nov. 25, 1847; Malcolm Clark, Jr., *Eden Seekers: The Settlement of Oregon, 1818-1862* (Boston: Houghton Mifflin Company, 1981), 189, 214.
11. *Oregon Spectator*, Oct. 14, 1847.
12. Victor, *Early Indian Wars*, 127-54.
13. Ibid., 153.
14. Ibid., 503-20.
15. Ibid., 195-200, 248.
16. Although told by a fictional narrator, Ronald B. Lansing's *Juggernaut: The Whitman Massacre Trail, 1850* (Pasadena, Calif.: Ninth Judicial Circuit Historical Society, 1993) is the most detailed study of the trial. However, readers need to compare the narrator's assertions with the footnotes, which identify the historical guesses. Victor, *Early Indian Wars*, 250-51.
17. Peter H. Burnett, *Recollections and Opinions of An Old Pioneer* (New York: D. Appleton, 1880), 254.

18. "Autobiography of Joseph Lane, Portland, 1878," MS P-A 43, Bancroft Library, University of California, Berkeley, 88-89; James E. Hendrickson, *Joe Lane of Oregon: Machine Politics and the Sectional Crisis, 1849-1861* (New Haven and London: Yale University Press, 1967), 20-23.
19. "Autobiography of Joseph Lane," 91-92.
20. Ibid., 94-95, 98-100; Walling, *History of Southern Oregon*, 191; *Treaties and Agreements of the Indian Tribes of the Pacific Northwest*, 1.
21. In northern California among the Shasta and Scott Valley Indians, A. M. Rosborough and Elijah Steele played a role similar to Lane's. See Alex J. Rosborough, "A. M. Rosborough, Special Indian Agent," *CHQ* 26 (Sept. 1947), 201-7; and Steele to Drew, Nov. 23, 1857, Oregon (Territory) *Laws and Journals*, 9th Sess. Leg. Assemb. (1857-58), Vol. 8, 41-52. Theodore Stern, "The Klamath Indians and the Treaty of 1864," *OHQ* 57 (Sept. 1956), 229-65, describes Steele's treaty-making activity among the Klamaths, Modocs, and Paiutes.
22. Hendrickson, *Joe Lane of Oregon*, 2, 7-20, 28-64, 222. On Lane's Mexican War experience, see Robert W. Johannsen, *To the Halls of Montezumas: The Mexican War in the American Imagination* (New York:, 1985), 36, 65, 89, 95, 123; Clark, Jr., *Eden Seekers*, 223-25.
23. Michael Paul Rogin, *Fathers and Children: Andrew Jackson and the Subjugation of the American Indian* (New York: Vintage Books, 1976); Hendrickson, *Joe Lane of Oregon*, 229-31; Prucha, *The Great Father*, 1289, index citations on "paternalism."
24. See Cheryll Ann Cody, "There Was No 'Absalom' on the Ball Plantations: Slave Naming Practices in the South Carolina Low Country, 1720-1865," *American Historical Review* 92 (June 1987), 563-96; James Axtell, *The Invasion Within: The Contest of Cultures in Colonial North America* (New York and Oxford: Oxford University Press, 1985), 167-169; 358 n.141; Sapir, "Notes on the Takelma Indians," 270; Theodore Stern, *The Klamath Tribe: A People and Their Reservation* (Seattle and London: UWP, 1966), 54; Catharine Holt, "Shasta Ethnography," *Anthropological Records* 3:4 (Berkeley and Los Angeles: UCP, 1946); Melville Jacobs, *The Content and Style of An Oral Literature: Clackamas Chinook Myths and Tales* (Chicago: University of Chicago Press, 1959), 45, 197-98.
25. James P. Ronda, *Lewis and Clark Among the Indians* (Lincoln and London: UNP, 1984), 254.
26. William M. Colvig, "Indian Wars of Southern Oregon," *OHQ* 4 (Sept. 1903), 229; quotes from Skinner to Dart, Nov. 25, 1851; July 26, 1852 (32d Cong., 2d Sess., H. Ex. Doc. 1, Serial 673, 451-55); Walling, *History of Southern Oregon*, 182. An amendment to the treaty of 1853 agreed to on Nov. 11, 1854 provides additional name information: Joe (Aps-er-ka-har) becomes "Aps-so-ka-hah, Horse-rider, or Jo"; Sam (To-qua-he-ar) becomes "Ko-ko-ha-wah, Wealthy, or Sam" (*Treaties and Agreements of the Indian Tribes of the Pacific Northwest*, 1, 3-4).
27. Skinner to Dart, July 26, 1852, 32d Cong, 2d Sess., H. Ex. Doc. 1, Serial 673, 455; Ambrose to Palmer, Oct. 20, 1855, 34th Cong., 1st Sess., H. Ex. Doc. 93, Serial 858, 88-90. From the 1853 and 1854 treaties, band leaders, number of bands, and locations may be summarized as follows. Rogue River-Leaders: Joe and Sam, Elijah, Tom, Henry, Jim, George, Sambo; 6-7 bands. Butte Creek-Leader: Jake; 1 band. Illinois Valley- Leader: Limpy; 1 band. Applegate Valley-Leaders: Old John, Applegate John, Bill; 3 bands. Siskiyou Mts., near Ashland-Leader: Tipsu (or Tipsey); 1 band. Cow Creek- 1 band. Grave Creek- 1 band. Lower Rogue River (to the great bend of the Rogue River)- 5 bands (Chasta 2, Scotons 3). Skinner to Dart, Aug. 6, 1852, 32d Cong, 2d Sess., H. Ex. Doc. 1, Serial 673, 453; for Ambrose's November count of 314 on the Table Rock

Reserve and 522 off the reserve, see letter, *Table Rock Sentinel*, Nov. 29, 1856[55], in Dowell MS 0063-4); a reserve figure of 303 appears in Ambrose to Palmer, Oct. 20, 1855, 34th Cong., 1st Sess., H. Ex. Doc. 93, Serial, 858, 88-90.

28. Ambrose to Palmer, Oct. 20, 1855, ibid.; George Gibbs, "Journal of the Expedition of Colonel Redick M'Kee, United States Indian Agent, Through Northwestern California, Performed in the Summer and Fall of 1851," 155, in Schoolcraft, *Archives of Aboriginal Knowledge*, Vol. 2. Elijah Steele, who was respected by the Indians of northern California and eventually became California's Indian superintendent, commented that as well as speaking the same language, the Rogue River and Shasta Indians also had at one time the same head chief, "the father of 'John' of Scotts Valley." After his death a rivalry ensued between his son John, Sam and Joe of Rogue River, and Scarface of Shasta Valley. Steele added: "The whites coming in among them, their difficulties ceased, and each chief took supreme control of his separate band" (Steele to Drew, Nov. 23, 1857, 41-52, in *Laws and Journals*). On Steele, see Bancroft [Victor], *History of Oregon, 1848-1888*, Vol. II, 239, 556-57. "Lafayette Grover's Statement: Interview with H. H. Bancroft, San Francisco, 1878," transcript. Oregon Collection, Special Collections, UO, Eugene, 33, partially supports Steele, noting that Chief Joe's daughter Mary told him that Joe "originated from a Northern California chief of Pit River Indians." See also the genealogy of Shasta Indians, that links the Shastas and Rogue River Indians, in Betty L. Hall, "Faces of the Shasta People: Who We Were and Who We Are The Shasta Nation," in *Living With the Land: The Indians of Southwest Oregon; The Proceedings of the 1989 Symposium on the Prehistory of Southwest Oregon*, edited by Nan Hannon and Richard K. Olmo (Medford: Southern Oregon Historical Society, 1990), 136-40.
29. James A. Cardwell, "Emigrant Company," MS P-A15, Bancroft Library, University of California, Berkeley, 2, 7.
30. Ibid., 9.
31. Steele to Drew, Nov. 23, 1857, in *Laws and Journals*, 41-52; Charles S. Drew, "An Account of the Origin and Early Prosecution of the Indian War in Oregon," 36th Cong., 1st Sess., Sen. Misc.Doc. No. 59 (reprint; Fairfield, Wash.: Ye Galleon Press, 1973), 3
32. Steele to Drew, Nov. 23, 1857, in *Laws and Journals*, 41-52; on Steele, see Bancroft [Victor], *History of Oregon, 1848-1888*, 239, 556-557.
33. George Gibbs to his mother, Oct. 23, 1851, in Vernon Carstensen, ed., "Pacific Northwest Letters of George Gibbs," *OHQ* 54 (Sept. 1953), 203.
34. Gibbs, "Journal of the Expedition of Colonel Redick M'Kee," 162.
35. Colvig, "Indian Wars of Southern Oregon," 229.
36. Bancroft [Victor], *History of Oregon, 1848-1888*, 225-26.
37. Kearney to Hooker, June 29, 1851, in Mark V. Weatherford, compiler, "Rogue River Indian War [Documents]," Knight Library, Oregon Collection, Special Collections, UO, Eugene, 18; Walling, *History of Southern Oregon*, 198.
38. Bancroft [Victor], *History of Oregon, 1848-1888*, 230-31; letter of Lane, *Oregon Statesman*, July 22, 1851; Victor, *Early Indian Wars of Oregon*, 279-80; Walling, *History of Southern Oregon*, 199.
39. Skinner to Anson Dart, Nov. 25 1851, 32d Cong., 2d Sess., H. Ex. Doc. 1, Serial 673, 452.
40. Colvig, "Indian Wars of Southern Oregon," 453; Victor, *Early Indian Wars of Oregon*, 280.
41. Walling, *History of Southern Oregon*, 200; *Oregon Spectator*, Jan. 6, 1852.

42. *Oregon Spectator*, Jan. 20, 1852.
43. Cardwell, "Emigrant Company," 15-21. Nan Hannon, "Tipsu Tyee: Last Chief of the Ashland Creek People," *Southern Oregon Heritage Today* 3 (Oct. 2001), 4-12. Hannon's article describes a significant middle-ground experience in the relationship between Tipsu and Thomas Smith, and it helps to explain Tipsu's hostility to whites. For Hannon's sources on Smith, see Thomas Smith, Pacific Mss. A-94, Bancroft Library, University of California, Berkeley, and Elwood Evans, *History of the Pacific Northwest—Oregon and Washington*, Vol. II (Portland: North Pacific History Company, 1889), 572-74.
44. Bancroft [Victor], *History of Oregon, 1848-1888*, 186; Walling, *History of Southern Oregon*, 337-40; Francis D. Haines, Jr., *Jacksonville: Biography of A Gold Camp* (n.p., 1967), 8.
45. Drew, "An Account of the Origin and Early Prosecution of the Indian War in Oregon." Although biased toward whites, Drew's report agrees closely with other white accounts. Reports of Indian deaths are scattered through other white accounts.
46. Steele to Drew, Nov. 23, 1857; see also Walling, *History of Southern Oregon*, 201.
47. Walling, *History of Southern Oregon*, 202, claims that this interpretation was mistaken; the daughter was too young to become a wife of Sam's son; the major issue was the payment of a beef. Skinner to Dart, July 26, 1852, 32nd Cong., 2d Sess., H. Ex. Doc. 1, Serial 673, 455-458.
48. Steele to Drew, Nov. 23, 1857, 49.
49. Ibid., 50.
50. Walling, *History of Southern Oregon*, 203.
51. Beckham, *Land of the Umpqua*, 93.
52. Steele to Drew, Nov. 23, 1857, 50.
53. Ashland *Tidings*, Sept. 13, 1878; see also Bancroft, *History of Oregon, 1848-1888*, 312. Taylor was hung June 1, 1853.
54. See Keith A. Murray, *The Modocs and Their War* (Norman: UOP, 1959), 22-27, for a detailed account of Modoc attacks and white counter-attacks; Drew, "An Account," 4; Victor, *Early Indian Wars of Oregon*, 299, estimated the number killed by the Modocs at 60-100.
55. Walling, *History of Southern Oregon*, 204.
56. Henry L. Wells, *History of Siskiyou County, California* (Oakland, Calif.: D. J. Stewart, 1881), 129; Frances Fuller Victor, "A Knight of the Frontier," *The Californian* 4 (Aug.1881), 152; *Oregon Statesman*, June 2, 1857.
57. On Joel Palmer's life see Terence O'Donnell, *An Arrow in the Earth: General Joel Palmer and the Indians of Oregon* (Portland: Oregon Historical Society Press, 1991); see reference to Palmer's second trip, 56-57; John [R.?] Wright to S. A. Clark[e], Mar.9, 1888, transcribed copy, Shaw Historical Library, Oregon Institute of Technology, Klamath Falls, on Wright's traveling with "Palmer's Train"; Palmer to Manypenney, Mar. 16, 1855, 53d Cong., 1st Sess., S. Ex. Doc. 25, Serial 3144, 32-33; Palmer to Wright, Sept. 4, 1854, ibid. On hearing of the death of Benjamin Wright, his father William Henry Wright wrote to Palmer asking him about any personal effects, real estate, or government claims, and requested him to give counsel to his other son William (Wright to Palmer, Apr. 14, 1856, Joel Palmer Papers, Letters, 1856, Apr.-June, Ax57/2/2, Knight Library, Oregon Collection, Special Collections, U O, Eugene). On Wright's service, see Victor, *Early Indian Wars of Oregon*, 520. Benjamin Wright is also listed as a person to whom expenses of $151.50 were certified by the Cayuse War Claims

Commissioner, Jan. 1851- Oct. 1851; see Cayuse Indian War Expense Claim Records 1848-1858, 89A-12, container 47 of 240, 1853 (47/18), Oregon State Archives, Salem, Ore.

58. Wells, *History of Siskiyou County*, 91, 92B; Francis Reinhart, *The Golden Frontier: The Recollections of Herman Francis Reinhart* 1851-1869, ed. by Doyce B. Nunis, Jr. (Austin: University of Texas Press, 1962), 32-33; Steele to Drew, Nov. 23, 1857, 45.
59. Wells, *History of Siskiyou County*, 123, 130, 133; O. W. Olney, *Morning Oregonian*, Nov. 22, 1885; Steele to Drew, Nov. 23, 1857, 46.
60. Wells, *History of Siskiyou County*, 123-26.
61. Ibid., 125-26.
62. Ibid., 130-31.
63. Ibid., 132-33. This is the best account by someone who was present. On Modoc revenge, see Richard Dillon, "Conflict Without Counterpoint: The 'Inevitable' Modoc War," *The Journal of the Shaw Historical Library* 3 (Fall 1988), 54-61.
64. Wells, *History of Siskiyou County*, 133; John E. Ross, "Narrative of an Indian Fighter, Jacksonville, 1878," MS P-A-63, 24, Bancroft Library, University of California, Berkeley.
65. Hitchcock to Cooper, Mar. 31, 1853, in 34th Cong., 3d Sess., H. Ex. Doc. 76, Serial 906, 78-79; Robert F. Heizer and Albert B. Elsasser, *The Natural World of the California Indians* (Berkeley and Los Angeles: Univesity of California Press, 1980), 5, 17-18, 30-37.
66. Hitchcock to Thomas, Aug. 15, 1853, 34th Cong., 3d Sess., H. Ex. Doc. 76, Serial 906, 79-80; Nathan Douthit, "Joseph Lane and the Rogue River Indians: Personal Relations Across A Cultural Divide," *OHQ* 95 (Winter 1994-95), 472-515; Thomas Jefferson Cram, "Topographical Memoir of the Department of the Pacific," 35th Cong., 2d Sess., H. Ex. Doc. 114 (reprint; Fairfield, Wash.: Ye Galleon Press, 1977), 40-41.
67. William T. Hagan, "Squaw Men on the Kiowa, Commanche, and Apache Reservation: Advance Agents of Civilization or Disturbers of the Peace," in *The Frontier Challenge: Responses to the Trans-Mississippi West*, edited by John G. Clark (Lawrence: University Press of Kansas, 1971), 171; *The Compact Edition of the Oxford English Dictionary*, Vol. II, P-Z (London: Oxford University Press, 1971), 736; Winfred Blevins, *Dictionary of the American West* (New York: Facts On File, 1993), 336-37. For a contemporary Indian perspective on use of "squaw" in the naming of land forms, see Owens, *Mixedblood Messages*, 212-13. He explains that it is viewed as "a word popularized by invaders who saw Indian women as objects to be used and abused like the land itself" (212).
68. William F. Strobridge, *Regulars in the Redwoods: The U.S. Army in Northern California 1852-1861* (Spokane: Arthur H. Clark, 1994), 89-90; Stern, *The Klamath Tribe*, 96-98; Palmer to Manypenny, July 3, 1856, 34th Cong., 3d Sess., Sen. Ex. Docs., No. 92, Serial 875, 763-71; Crook to Mackall, Dec. 25, 1857, in Robert F. Heizer, *The Destruction of California Indians* (Lincoln and London: UNP, Bison Edition, 1993), 94, 109-10, 303; Prucha, *The Great Father*, 219-20.
69. Steele to Steele, May 26, 1873, in Jeff C. Riddle, *The Indian History of the Modoc War* (Eugene, Ore.: Urion Press, [1914] 1974), 275. Descriptions of Indian-white cohabitation and intermarriage in northern California and southern Oregon, can be found in Jeff C. Riddle's book about his Indian mother and white father, esp. 201-223; Kay Atwood, *Illahe: The Story of Settlement in the Rogue River Canyon* (Ashland, Ore.: Atwood, 1978; reprinted Corvallis, Ore: OSUP, 2002); Beverly H. Ward, *White Moccasins* (Cottage Grove, Ore.: Ward, 1986).

70. Riddle, *The Indian History of the Modoc War*, 268-69.
71. Wells, *History of Siskiyou County*, 134.
72. Ibid., 136.
73. Albert L. Hurtado, *Indian Survival on the California Frontier* (New Haven and London: Yale University Press, 1988), 172-76.

Chapter 4

1. Palmer to Manypenny, June 23, 1853, 33d Cong., 1st Sess., S. Ex. Doc. 1, Serial 690, 447-451.
2. For biographical information, See O'Donnell, *An Arrow in the Earth*, esp. 11, 68, 72, 81, 120-21, 123, 137.
3. A physical description of Palmer appears at the beginning of the notes of Palmer's interview with Hubert Howe Bancroft, June 14, 1878, original in Bancroft Library, University of California, Berkeley. O'Donnell, *An Arrow in the Earth*, 294.
4. O'Donnell, *An Arrow in the Earth*, 130-31.
5. Ibid., 137-40; C.F. Coan, "The First Stage of the Federal Indian Policy in the Pacific Northwest, 1849-1852," *OHQ* 22 (Mar. 1921), 58.
6. O'Donnell, *An Arrow in the Earth*, 142.
7. Robert E. Bieder, *Science Encounters the Indian, 1820-1880: The Early Years of American Ethnology* (Norman and London: UOP, 1986), 33, 55-103; Alban W. Hoopes, *Indian Affairs and Their Administration with Special Reference to the Far West 1849-1860* (Philadelphia: University of Pennsylvania Press, 1932), 7-8; Prucha, *The Great Father*, 179-213.
8. See Prucha, *The Great Father*, 317, on support for this view by 1850.
9. 33d Cong., 1st Sess., S. Ex. Doc. 1, Serial 690, 449; Alban W. Hoopes, *Indian Affairs and Their Administration 1849-1860 with Special reference to the Far West 1849-1860* (Philadelphia: University of Pennsylvania Press, 1932), 43, 49, 53; Stevens to Manypenny, Sept. 16, 1854, 33d Cong., 2d Sess., H. Ex. Doc. 1, Serial 777, 455.
10. Walling, *History of Southern Oregon*, 21, 210.
11. Hannon, "Tipsu Tyee," 8.
12. J. W. Nesmith, "A Reminiscence of the Indian War of 1853," *Ashland Tidings*, May 16, 1879.
13. Walling, *History of Southern Oregon*, 212.
14. "The Last of Her Tribe," *Oregonian*, May 26, 1893.
15. "Mrs. Butler's 1853 Diary of Rogue River Valley," *OHQ* 41 (Dec. 1940), 337-366.
16. Ibid., 351, 353.
17. "Autobiography of Joseph Lane," 119-120; Walling, *History of Southern Oregon*, 213; Bancroft [Victor], *History of Oregon, 1848-1888*, 312, n.5. On the Taylor and Cow Creek incidents, see Beckham, *Land of the Umpqua*, 94-96.
18. Alden to Adjutant General of the Army, Oct. 18, 1853, 33d Cong., 1st Sess., H. Ex. Doc. 1, Serial 711, 41-42.
19. "Mrs. Butler's 1853 Diary," 352.
20. Dates vary; Alden says he turned over command to Lane on August 20, but Lane says he arrived August 21; Mrs. Butler's diary agrees with Lane. See Lane to Hitchcock, n.d., 33d Cong., 1st Sess., H. Ex. Docs., Vol. I, Pt. 2, 1853-54, 37; Alden to Adj. Gen., Oct. 18, 1853.
21. "Mrs. Butler's 1853 Diary," 353.

22. Walling, *History of Southern Oregon*, 214. Hannon, "Tipsu Tyee," 10-11, retells the story more favorably to Tipsu's band and with a chronology that differs from Walling's.
23. Lane to Hitchcock, n. d., 39-40.
24. Walling, *History of Southern Oregon*, 220; Thomas H. Smith, "An Ohioan's Role in Oregon History," *OHQ* 66 (Sept. 1965), 224.
25. Ibid., 225
26. "Mrs. Butler's 1853 Diary," 354-55.
27. Charles S. Drew, "An Account ...of the Indian War in Oregon," 13.
28. "Autobiography of Joseph Lane," 121.
29. Nesmith, "A Reminiscence of the Indian War of 1853."
30. "The Last of Her Tribe," *Oregonian*, May 26, 1893.
31. *Treaties and Agreements of the Indian Tribes of the Pacific Northwest*, 1-4; Culver to Palmer, July 20, 1854, 33d Cong, 2d Sess., H. Ex. Doc. 1, Serial 777, 502; for estimates of reserve area and land ceded, see O'Donnell, *An Arrow in the Earth*, 153 and Schwartz, *The Rogue River Indian War*, 59. Map measurement of treaty boundaries indicates a ceded land area of about forty by forty-eight lines-of-sight miles, or 1,920 square miles.
32. For a discussion of population estimates, see the last section of Chapter 6.
33. Walling, *History of Southern Oregon*, 227-29.
34. Lane to Nesmith, Apr. 28, 1879, in James W. Nesmith, "A Reminiscence of the Indian War, 1853," *OHQ* 7 (June 1906), 221.
35. Walling, *History of Southern Oregon*, 198; Steele to Drew, Nov. 23, 1857, in *Laws and Journals*, 49.
36. Bancroft [Victor], *History of Oregon, 1848-1888*, 312-320; Victor, *Early Indian Wars of Oregon*, 308-319; Walling, *History of Southern Oregon*, 213-217; "Mrs. Butler's Diary," 351-360; Drew, "An Account... of the Indian War in Oregon," 4-5.
37. S. H. Taylor stated in a letter dated Dec. 17, 1853 that 40 whites and 100 Indians died in the summer fighting. See "Documentary: Letters of S. H. Taylor to the Water town (Wisconsin) Chronicle," *OHQ* 22 (June 1921), 155.
38. "Benjamin Franklin Dowell Narrative, Jacksonville, Oregon, 1878," MS, P-A 26, Bancroft Library, University of California, Berkeley. See later in Chapter 17 on Dowell.
39. Matthew P. Deady, "Southern Oregon Names and Events," in Oregon Pioneer Association *Transactions, Salem, 1883*, 23-24; "Mrs. Butler's Diary," 354.
40. Lane to Nesmith, Apr. 28, 1879, *OHQ* 7 (June 1906), 220-221.
41. Deady, "Southern Oregon Names and Events," 25. Most historians have identified the site of the meeting simply as Table Rock, without distinguishing between Upper and Lower Table Rock. However, McArthur, *Oregon Geographic Names*, 712,, places the meeting on the slope of Upper Table Rock, as does Kay Atwood, "Asking as the World Goes On: The Table Rocks and the Takelma," *OHQ* 95 (Winter 1994-95), 525, relying on McArthur. Lower Table Rock, however, is the one recognized by pioneers as "Table Rock," because of its more spectacular features, which are highlighted in the descriptions of the meeting site by Matthew P. Deady and James W. Nesmith. Only Lower Table Rock is what Deady called "the noted bluff" about a "half mile" from the Rogue River; similarly, it fits Nesmith's description of "the huge perpindicular wall of the Table Rock" towering above the peacemakers. For photographs of Lower Table Rock that show its features see Sutton, *Indian Wars of the Rogue River*, 96-97, who correctly identifies it as the treaty-making site, and Atwood, 518-19.

42. Nesmith, "A Reminiscence of the Indian War, 1853," 217.
43. Deady, "Southern Oregon Names and Events," 25.
44. "Lafayette Grover's Statement: Interview with H. H. Bancroft, San Francisco, 1878," transcript, Oregon Collection, Special Collections, University of Oregon, Eugene.
45. *Treaties and Agreements of the Indian Tribes of the Pacific Northwest*, 3-4. J. C. Bonnycastle to John E. Wool, May 28, 1854, 35th Cong., 1st sess., H. Ex. Doc. 88, Serial 956, 77-83.
46. "Autobiography of Joseph Lane," 122-127.
47. Robert Carlton Clark, "Military History of Oregon, 1849-59," *OHQ* 36 (Mar. 1935), 31. By 1855, the command under Capt. Andrew J. Smith numbered about 120 men according to Rodney Glisan, *Journal of Army Life* (San Francisco: A. L. Bancroft, 1874), 263.
48. Welborn Beeson, Diary, Version 1, Vol. 1, 212 (66), typescript from the original, Knight Library,, Oregon Collection, Special Collections, UO, Eugene. The diary has been transcribed and contains diary page numbers in the left-hand margin (e.g. 212); typed page numbers have been renumbered (e.g. 66).
49. Ibid., 214-216 (67-68).
50. Ibid., 216 (68).
51. Ibid., 218 (68).
52. "Documentary: Letters of S. H. Taylor, 156. Cf. "Correspondence of Reverend Ezra Fisher," *OHQ* 19 (June 1918), 134-63, where Fisher states in a letter to Rev. Benjamin M. Hill, Feb. 3, 1853, that "2000 or 3000 souls have taken up their residence" in the Rogue River Valley (147). An 1853 census of whites living in the upper Bear Creek Valley (Eagle Mills to Mountain House) lists one hundred twenty persons (forty-eight of whom were under age twenty), and approximately forty households. See Kay Atwood, *Mill Creek Journal, Ashland Oregon 1850-1860* (Ashland: Atwood, 1987), 164-65, whose source is "the back of the Records of Marks and Brands, Southern Oregon Historical Society, Southern Oregon Archives, White City, Oregon."
53. *Genealogical Material in Oregon Donation Land Claims, Abstracted from applications filed in Roseburg, the Dalles and LaGrande Land Offices*, Vol.III (Portland: Genealogical Forum of Portland, Oregon, 1962); Walling, *History of Southern Oregon*, 339-40; Devere Helfrich, "The Applegate Trail I," *Klamath Echoes*, No. 9 (1971), 14; "Documentary: Letters of S. H. Taylor, 156-157.
54. "Mrs. Butler's 1853 Diary," 344, 353, 358-59.
55. Ibid., 359, 365.
56. "Documentary: Letters of S. H. Taylor," 152-53, 155, 158-59.
57. Anna B. Carter, "The Beeson Ancestry," *Our Family Through the Years*, unpublished family history compiled in 1955, cited in Ernest D. Zottola, "An Investigation into the Philsophy and the Subsequent Actions of John Beeson in Regards to the American Indians, unpublished student paper, Southern Oregon College, Ashland, May 1962.
58. Robert Winston Mardock, *The Reformers and the American Indian* (Columbia: University of Missouri Press, 1971), 10-14.
59. Beeson, Diary, Jan. 11, 1853, 47 (38).
60. Ibid., 223 (70), 225 (71)-235 (75).
61. Ibid., 221 (69).
62. *The Calumet*, I (Feb. 1860), 7, cited in Mardock, *The Reformers*, 10.
63. John Beeson, *A Plea for the Indians* (New York: John Beeson, 1858), 41.

64. Beeson, Diary, Vol. II, 5 (2)
65. Ibid., Vol. II, 8 (3).
66. Ibid., Vol. II, 5 (2), 8 (3), 10 (4), 13 (5). Other references to Indians, 22 (8), 32 (11).
67. Ibid., Vol. II, 14 (5)-18 (7), 26 (9)-30 (10).
68. Ibid., Vol. II, 56 (19)-81 (27).

Chapter 5

1. Palmer to Manypenny, June 23, 1853, 33rd Cong., 1st Sess., S. Doc. 1, Serial 690, 447-51.
2. Ibid., 449.
3. Palmer to Manypenny, Oct. 8, 1853, in C.F. Coan, "The Adoption of the Reservation Policy in Pacific Northwest, 1853-1855," *OHQ* 23 (Mar. 1922), 28-38.
4. Ibid., 31.
5. Coan, "The Adoption of the Reservation Policy in Pacific Northwest, 1853-1855," 33; O'Donnell, *An Arrow in the Earth*, 143. Pay was also contingency based. Agents used their own funds, then were reimbursed at a later date subject to audit approval.
6. O'Donnell, *An Arrow in the Earth*, 168-72.
7. Beckham, *Land of the Umpqua*, 72-75.
8. Albert Lyman, "The Journal of Captain Albert Lyman, 1850-51," transcript from microfilm of the original journal prepared by the Douglas County Museum Librarian, Douglas County Museum, Roseburg, Oregon.
9. Ibid., 9-10.
10. Ibid., 13.
11. Ibid., 14-15.
12. William Tichenor narrative in Orvil Dodge, *Pioneer History of Coos and Curry Counties, Or.* (Salem: Pioneer and Historical Association of Coos County, 1898), 22-24. For additional details, see J. M. Kirkpatrick, "The Hero of Battle Rock," in Dodge, *Pioneer History*, 33-50; and L. L. Williams, "First Settlements in Southwestern Oregon, 1878," MS. P-A77, Bancroft Library, University of California, Berkeley. Schwartz, *The Rogue River War*, 34-36, argues that whites started the fighting at Battle Rock.
13. Tichenor narrative, Dodge, *Pioneer History*, 31.
14. On the T'Vault expedition, see Beckham, *Requiem for A People*, 59-63. On Fort Orford, Robert W. Frazer, ed. *Mansfield on the Condition of the Western Forts 1853-54* (Norman: UOP, 1963), 118-19 and Sketch 26; Miller to Cross, June 8, 1852, 32d Cong., 2d Sess., H. Ex. Doc. 1, Serial, 659, 105-6.
15. Tichenor narrative, Dodge, *Pioneer History*, 29.
16. On the campaign against the Coquille Indians, see Beckham, *Requiem for A People*, 65-67.
17. See Henry H. Baldwin, "Wreck of the Captain Lincoln," and narrative of Philip Brack in Dodge, *Pioneer History*, 114-20, 122-25. The official report is in Miller to Cross, June 8, 1852.
18. Baldwin narrative in Dodge, *Pioneer History*, 120.
19. Youst, *She's Tricky Like Coyote*, 15-16.
20. Miller to Cross, June 8, 1852.

21. Agnes Ruth Sengstacken, *Destination West* (Portland: Binford & Mort, 1972), 129-30, 156-61.
22. Ibid., 156-61 on the Grosluis (lois) brothers.
23. Ibid., 129.
24. Ibid., 121.
25. Ibid., 121-27.
26. Ibid., 133.
27. R. C. Dement narrative, originally published serially in the *Myrtle Point Herald*, Aug. 6-Dec. 3, 1936, in Alice H. Wooldridge, compiler, *Pioneers and Incidents of the Upper Coquille Valley* (Myrtle Creek, Ore.: Wooldridge, 1971), 234.
28. Youst, *She's Tricky Like Coyote*, 17.
29. See Beckham, *Requiem for A People*, 172-73; Dodge, *Pioneer History*, 97-101; Youst, *She's Tricky Like Coyote*, 17.
30. Smith to Palmer, Feb. 5, 1854, 33rd Cong., 2d Sess., H. Ex. Doc. 1, Serial 777, 476-479.
31. Abbott to Smith, Jan. 28, 1854, ibid., 481.
32. Smith to Palmer, Feb. 5, 1854, ibid., 477.
33. Scott to O'Meally, Jan. 30, 1854, ibid., 484-85.
34. Smith to Palmer, Feb. 5, 1854, 33d Cong., 2d Ses., H. Ex. Doc. 1, Serial 777, 89, 476-79.
35. Palmer to Manypenny, Sept. 11, 1854, ibid., 465-67.
36. Ibid., 467.
37. Palmer to Manypenny, Mar. 11, 1854, ibid., 475.
38. Parrish to Palmer, July 10, 1854, ibid., 499.
39. Palmer to Wright, Sept. 4, 1854, 53d Cong., 1st Sess., S. Ex. Doc. 25, Serial 3144, 33.
40. Drew, "An Account…of the Indian War in Oregon," 38.
41. J. L. Parrish, June 15, 1878, Bancroft Interview, MS 0063-1, Bancroft Library, University of California, Berkeley. Hubert Howe Bancroft, *Literary Industries, The Works of Hubert Howe Bancroft*, Vol. 39 (San Francisco: The History Company, 1890), 541-51.
42. Richard Slotkin, *The Fatal Environment: The Myth of the Frontier in the Age of Industrialization 1800-1890* (New York: Atheneum, 1985), 62-63.
43. William V. Wells, "Wild Life in Oregon," *Harper's New Monthly Magazine* 13 (Oct. 1856), 595. This ends any further mention of Wright; Wells proceeds on to Flores(as) Creek.
44. Steele to Steele, May 26, 1873, in Riddle, *The Indian History of the Modoc War*, 273.
45. O'Donnell, *An Arrow in the Earth*, 68-81.
46. Joel Palmer Papers, Mss 114-3, Folder 5, Palmer to Manypenny, July 25, 1854, OHS Archives, Portland.
47. See O'Donnell, *An Arrow in the Earth*, 176-82.
48. Palmer to Wright, Sept. 4, 1854, ibid., 33. On causes of Indian sickness and death, see Robert T. Boyd, "Another Look at the 'Fever and Ague' of Western Oregon," *Ethnohistory* 22/2 (Spring 1975), 135-54.
49. Miller to Nesmith, July 20, 1857, 35th Cong., 1st Sess., S. Ex. Docs., No. 149, Serial 919, 651. See also Reginald R. Stuart and Grace D. Stuart, *Calvin B. West of the Umpqua, An Obscure Chapter in the History of Southern Oregon* (San Francisco: California History Foundation, 1961), 53-54, 59, 69 for more on white relations with Umpqua Indians.

50. 33d Cong., 2d Sess., H. Ex. Doc. 1, Serial 673, 403, 463, 467, 498; Glisan, *Journal of Army Life*, 250-51; see Drew to Palmer, Dec. 3, 1855, 34th Cong., 1st Sess., H. Ex. Doc. 93, Serial 858, 127, for a reference to employment of Indians on Coos Bay. It appears that Indians were employed much more as laborers in northern California than in southern Oregon. In 1848 an official report noted that half the labor force in the California gold fields was Indian. Oregonians arriving in northern California in 1849 protested competition from white-exploited Indian labor, but Indians continued to work in mining, agriculture, and domestic service through the next several decades (see James J. Rawls, *Indians of California: The Changing Image* (Norman: UOP, 1984), 109-26). On Indian labor in the Puget Sound region, see Harmon, *Indians in the Making*, 60-63 and Asher, *Beyond the Reservation*, 53-59.
51. Wright to Palmer, Sept. 17, 1854, 53d Cong., 1st Sess., S. Ex. Doc. 25, Serial 3144, 34.
52. Wright to Palmer, Nov. 19, 1854, ibid., 34-35. Schwartz, *The Rogue River Indian War*, 70-71, criticizes Wright's action for putting the Chetco Indians back into the hands of A. F. Miller, the man who attacked them in the first place. In general, Schwartz views Wright's peacekeeping efforts as self-serving and hypocritical, despite contemporary white observations to the contrary (see Glisan, *Journal of Army Life*, 269).
53. Joel Palmer Papers, MSS 114-3, Folder 6, Palmer to Wright, Apr. 14, 1855, OHS Archives, Portland.
54. O'Donnell, *An Arrow in the Earth*, 215-16; Schwartz, *Rogue River Indian War*, 81-82; Beckham, *Land of the Umpqua*, 98.
55. Glisan, *Journal of Army Life*, 239, 241.
56. Ibid., 246-47.
57. Ibid., 243-44.
58. See Hendrickson, *Joe Lane of Oregon*, n. 12, p.114, who argues that this was probably a false charge.
59. Beeson, *A Plea for the Indians*, 83.
60. Drew, "An Account...of the Indian War in Oregon," 6. Capt. A. J. Smith blamed a band of Shasta Indians.
61. See Capt. A. J. Smith's account, Smith to Townsend, Oct. 2, 1855, 53d Cong., 2d Sess., S. Ex. Doc. 113, Serial 3163, 2-3, and Fitzgerald to Sweitzer, Oct. 2, 1855, ibid.
62. Beeson, *A Plea for the Indians*, 23.
63. Ibid., 44-45.
64. Ibid., 46.
65. Ibid., 47.
66. Ibid., 48.
67. The book had three editions/printings in 1857 and 1858. For publishing history see Bert Webber's "Introduction" to the Ye Galleon Press reprint of the second edition. All quotes from the 3rd printing by Thomas Holman, Printer and Stereotyper, 1858.

Chapter 6

1. I want to acknowledge the invaluable assistance of Frank Walsh (author of *Indian Battles Along the Rogue River 1855-56* (Grants Pass, Ore.: Walsh, 1972), and long-time Rogue River War researcher), whose research notes on wartime casualties and knowledge of the Rogue River War contributed to this chapter.

2. Drew, "An Account of the Origin and Early Prosecution of the Indian War in Oregon," 27.
3. Ibid., 28-29. For variations on the story and massacre, see O'Donnell, *An Arrow in the Earth*, 216-19; Beckham, *Requiem for A People*, 151-52; Beeson, *A Plea for the Indians*, 47-49; Schwartz, *The Rogue River Indian War*, 78, 85-86.
4. Ambrose to Palmer, Oct. 9, 1855, 34th Cong., 1st Sess., H. Ex. Doc. 936, Serial 858, 65-67.
5. Drew, "An Account," 7.
6. Ambrose to Palmer, Oct. 28, 1855, 34th Cong., 1st Sess, H. Ex. Doc. 93, Serial 858, 90-92.
7. Ambrose to Palmer, Oct. 9, 1855.
8. Beeson, *A Plea for the Indians*, 64-66. Old John (Tecumtom or Tecumtum) is not the same person as Chief John (Tyee John) of Scott Valley, a confusion noted by Sutton, *Indian Wars of the Rogue River*, 48, and attributed by him to Victor, *Indian Wars of Oregon*, 292, 709. The confusion continues (see Nan Hannon, "Tipsu Tyee," 9), but military reports during the Rogue River War clearly locate the two chiefs separately in northern California and southern Oregon. See H. M. Judah to D. R. Jones, Mar. 8, 1856, 34th Cong., 1st & 2d Sess., S. Ex. Doc. 66, Serial 822, 52-53, which places Chief John of Scott Valley in northern California while Chief John/Old John (Tecumtom) was trying to evade capture on the Rogue River. Although official reports do not mention Old John and his band prior to 1853, references linking him to Klamath River-Shasta Valley Shastas suggest that he may have taken refuge in the Applegate River Valley prior to 1853 to escape white attacks against Indians on the Klamath River and in Shasta Valley. This also helps to explain close ties between Tipsu's and Old John's bands.
9. Chief Sam eventually took on even one more documented name. According to Frank Walsh, the St. Michael Parish Register shows that he was buried on May 8, 1861 at the Grand Ronde reservation under the name Augustine Sam.
10. I have used Ambrose's November count of 314 (see letter, *Table Rock Sentinel*, Nov. 29, 1856[55], in Dowell MS 0063-4), rather than the figure 303 that appears in Ambrose to Palmer, Oct. 20, 1855, 34th Cong., 1st Sess., H. Ex. Doc. 93, Serial, 858, 88-90. On Oct. 28, Ambrose reported 334 on the reserve, but 20 were from "hostile" bands (ibid., 90-92).
11. See Appendix 2, Table 1, "Hostile Rogue River Indian Bands."
12. Smith to E. D. Townsend, Oct. 14, 1855, 53rd Cong., 2d Sess., Sen. Ex. Doc. 113, Serial 3163, 3-4.
13. Ibid.
14. Palmer to Wool, Nov. 1, 1855, 34th Cong., 1st Sess., H. Ex. Doc. 93, Serial 858, 112.
15. *Oregon Statesman*, Sept. 15, 1855.
16. Galice Athabaskan text translations from Melville Jacobs' Galice Athabaskan field notebooks #126 and #127, ca. 1967, Melville Jacobs Collection Box 104-9, Manuscripts and University Archives, University of Washington Libraries, Seattle, Washington.
17. Smith to Townsend, Oct. 14, 1855.
18. Ambrose to Palmer, Oct. 20, 1855, 34th Cong., 1st Sess., H. Ex. Doc. 93, Serial 858, 88-90.
19. *Oregon Statesman*, Oct. 27, 1855. See Schwartz, *The Rogue River Indian War*, 74, 283 n. 23.

20. Dunbar to Palmer, Nov. 4, 1855, 53d Cong., 1st Sess., S. Ex. Doc. 25, Serial 3144, 42-43. Schwartz, *The Rogue River Indian War*, 95, questions Dunbar's praise of Wright, but finally admits: "Perhaps he did strive for peace...."(114). For an extended critique of O'Donnell's judgements on Wright's character, see Schwartz, 114, note 7.
21. In Victor, *Early Indian Wars of Oregon*, 552-53, 626-28, 638-40, the force is estimated at about 531. Frank Walsh's research in the *Oregon Statesman* indicates a force of about 415.
22. Smith to Townsend, Feb. 12, 1856, 53d Cong., 2d Sess., Sen. Ex. Doc. 113, Serial 3163, 5; Withers to Cooper, Nov. 12, 1855, 34th Cong., 1st Sess., H. Ex. Doc. 93, Serial 858, 14; Victor, *Early Indian Wars*, 626-28, 638-40; Letter of Ambrose to editors of the Jacksonville *Sentinel*, Nov. 29, 1856[55].
23. Spier, *Klamath Ethnography*, 31.
24. Sapir, "Notes on the Takelma Indians of Southwestern Oregon," 273.
25. Holt, *Shasta Ethnography*, 313-14.
26. *Oregon Statesman*, Oct. 18, 1853.
27. O'Donnell, *An Arrow in the Earth*, 228-29 corrects Mulkey's story with respect to her name, but misses the newspaper evidence for the earlier date. Schwartz, *The Rogue River Indian War*, 99, repeats Mulkey's story, but without correction.
28. Palmer to Wool, Nov. 1, 1855.
29. Paul Bourke and Donald DeBats, *Washington County: Politics and Community in Antebellum America* (Baltimore and London: JHUP, 1995), 160-165.
30. Schwartz, *The Rogue River Indian War*, 93-94, 101-3, 111-12, 116, and O'Donnell, *An An Arrow in the Earth*, 222-23.
31. Schwartz, *The Rogue River Indian War*, 75-90.
32. Quoted in O'Donnell, *An Arrow in the Earth*, 224.
33. 34th Cong., 1st Sess., H. Ex. Doc. 1, Serial 841, 83-87.
34. Robert M. Utley, *The Indian Frontier of the American West 1846-1890* (Albuquerque: University of New Mexico Press, 1984), 93-95; Richard N. Ellis, "The Humanitarian Generals," *WHQ* 3 (Apr. 1972), 169-78.
35. Harwood Perry Hinton, *The Military Career of John Ellis Wool, 1812-1863*, Ph.D. dissertation, University of Wisconsin, 1960, Mic 60-5750 University Microfilm, Inc., Ann Arbor, MI.
36. Ibid., 59.
37. Ibid., 81-135. On early federal Indian policy, see Prucha, *The Great Father*, 90-91, 112-14, 165-67, 183-213.
38. Hinton, *The Military Career of John Ellis Wool*, 133.
39. Ibid., 172-73.
40. Ibid., 239. See also, Unruh, Jr., *The Plains Across*, 205-6.
41. On Wool's Department of Pacific Service, see Hinton, *The Military Career of John Ellis Wool*, 383-74.
42. Wool to Davis, Jan. 7, 1854, 35th Cong., 1st Sess., H. Ex. Doc. 88, Serial 956, 3-5.
43. Geo. L. Curry, "By the Governor of the Territory of Oregon. A Proclamation," 34th Cong., 1st Sess., H. Ex. Doc. 1, Serial 841, 85-86.
44. Nesmith to Wool, Nov. 21, 1855 and Wool to Nesmith, Nov. 24, 1855, 34th Cong., 1st Sess., H. Ex. Doc. 93, Serial 858, 19-20.
45. Kent D. Richards, *Isaac I. Stevens: Young Man in a Hurry* (Pullman: Washington State University Press, 1993).
46. Beeson, *A Plea for the Indians*, 60-61.
47. Ibid., 71, 74.

48. Wool to Thomas, Jan. 19, 1856, 34th Cong., 1st Sess., H. Ex. Doc. 93, Serial 858, 32-34.
49. Hinton, *The Military Career of John Ellis Wool*, 351-53.
50. Franklyn Daniel Mahar, "Benjamin Franklin Dowell 1826-1897 Claims Attorney and Newspaper Publisher in Southern Oregon," masters thesis, UO, Eugene, June 1964; see chronology, pp. I-II.
51. Dowell Journal and Letters, Jacksonville, Oregon: 1850-56, MSS P-A 25, Bancroft Library, University of California, Berkeley. In 1853, Dowell was unsuccessful in trying to rescue an Indian boy from being hung by a white mob in Jacksonville (ibid., MSS P-A 26).
52. See also, T. J. Cram, "Topographical Memoir of the Department of the Pacific," 35 Cong., 2d Sess., H. Ex. Doc. 114, reprinted in Cram, *Topographical Memoir* (Fairfield, Wash.: Ye Galleon Press, 1977).
53. Hendrickson, *Joe Lane of Oregon*, 129.
54. "Trail of Tears: 1856 Diary of Indian Agent George Ambrose," edited with introduction by Stephen Dow Beckham, *Southern Oregon Heritage* 2 (Summer 1996), 16-21.
55. Glisan, *Journal of Army Life*, 270-71.
56. Ibid., 273-74.
57. Crescent City *Herald*, Feb. 13, 1856.
58. Ibid., 283-84.
59. Captain William Tichenor, "Among the Oregon Indians," MS P-A 84, 39, The Bancroft Library, University of California, Berkeley.
60. Ashland *Tidings*, Apr. 4, 1879, 1.
61. *Morning Oregonian*, Nov.22, 1885.
62. John Charles Frémont, *The Expeditions of John Charles Frémont*, Vol. 1, *Travels from 1838 to 1844*, edited by Donald Jackson and Mary Lee Spence (Urbana: University of Illinois Press, 1970), 426-28.
63. John C. Frémont, "A Report of the Exploring Expedition to Oregon and North California, in the years 1843-'44," in Frémont, *The Exploring Expedition to the Rocky Mountains* (Washington and London: Smithsonian Institution, [1845] 1988), 197.
64. Jackson, *Children of the Fur Trade*, 21-22, 57, n. 125.
65. Robert Ignatius Burns, *The Jesuits and the Indian Wars of the Northwest* (Moscow: University of Idaho Press, 1966), 50.
66. John A. Hussey, *Champoeg: Place of Transition, A Disputed History* (Portland: Oregon Historical Society Press, 1967) and Lou Ann Speulda, *Champoeg: A Frontier Community in Oregon, 1830-1861*, Anthropology Northwest, Number 3 (Corvallis: Dept. of Anthropology, Oregon State University, 1988), 54-55, 76; *Catholic Church Records of the Pacific Northwest: St. Paul, Oregon 1839-1898*, 3 vols., compiled by Harriet Duncan Munnick (Portland: Binford & Mort, 1979).
67. Herman Francis Reinhart, *The Golden Frontier: The Recollections of Herman Francis Reinhart 1851-1869*, edited by Doyce B. Nunis, Jr. (Austin: University of Texas Press, 1962), 80-81, 85 and n. 14.
68. Glisan, *Journal of Army Life*, 283; Victor, *Early Indian Wars of Oregon*, 379, 633; *Morning Oregonian*, Nov. 22, 1885; Ashland *Tidings*, Apr. 4, 1879; Dunbar to Palmer, Feb. 24, 1856, 34th Cong., 3d Sess., Sen. Ex. Docs., No. 81, Serial 875, 752-53; *Oregon Statesman*, Mar. 11, 1856.
69. Frances Fuller Victor, "A Knight of the Frontier," *The Californian* 4 (Aug. 1881), 161.
70. Ibid., 96-97; Dodge, *Pioneer History*, 73.

71. Victor, "A Knight of the Frontier," 161; Bancroft [Victor], *History of Oregon, 1848-1888*, 394, note 45; Voucher No. 18, U.S. Office of Indian Affairs: 1855, 4th quarter, Abstract of disbursements, Benjamin Wright, in Joel Palmer Papers, 1845-85, AX57/16/3, Knight Library, Oregon Collection, Special Collections, UO, Eugene; Bancroft Interview with Josiah L. Parrish, June 15, 1878, MS 0063-1, Bancroft Library, University of California, Berkeley.
72. Victor, *Early Indian Wars of Oregon*, 380.
73. Douthit, "Joseph Lane and the Rogue River Indians: Personal Relations Across A Cultural Divide," 503-4.
74. *Morning Oregonian*, Nov. 22, 1885.
75. My thanks to Lionel Youst for bringing Coquelle Thompson's narrative of the Rogue River War to my attention. Elizabeth D. Jacobs, Upper Coquille Linguistic and Ethnographic Notes, Folklore Texts (in English) from fieldwork with Coquille Thompson, Siletz, Oregon, 1935, Notebook 4 and 5, Melville Jacobs Collection, Manuscripts and University Archives, University of Washington Libraries. For more on Coquelle Thompson, see Lionel Youst and William R. Seaburg, *Coquelle Thompson, Athabaskan Witness: A Cultural Biography* (Norman: UOP, 2002).
76. "Soldiering in Oregon," *Harper's New Monthly Magazine* 13 (Sept. 1856), 525; Glisan, *Journal of Army Life*, 290.
77. Dodge, *Pioneer History*, 58.
78. F. A. Stewart in Dodge, *Pioneer History*, 76,78.
79. Ibid., 66, 68.
80. Glisan, *Journal of Army Life*, 291. My thanks to Frank K. Walsh for cross-checking names and dates related to the Rogue River War period.
81. *Report of the Adjutant General of the Territory of Oregon* (Salem: 1856), 7-9.
82. Glisan, *Journal of Army Life*, 293-94.
83. Buchanan to Jones, Apr. 23, 1856, in "Rogue River Indian War 1856: Miscellaneous Correspondence of Lt. Col. Robert C. Buchanan," MS 159, Maryland Historical Society, Baltimore, Maryland; *Ord's Diary in Curry County, Oregon, 1856*, transcribed by H. J. Newhouse from original manuscript in The Bancroft Library, University of California, Berkeley (Wedderburn, Ore.: Newhouse, 1970), see Apr. 20-May 4, 1856; Glisan, *Journal of Army Life*, 315.
84. Glisan, *Journal of Army Life*, 319. See also, Buchanan to Jones, May 1, 1856, in "Rogue River Indian War 1856."
85. Glisan, *Journal of Army Life*, 324-25, 329-30; *Ord's Diary*, May 16, 1856, p.13; Buchanan to Jones, May 22, 1856, in "Rogue River Indian War."
86. Buchanan to Jones, May 30, 1856, ibid.; Glisan, *Journal of Army Life*, 334-35. Estimates of persons killed and wounded vary; I have counted civilians as well as soldiers.
87. H. G. Gibson, "Old John of Rogue or Red River, Oregon," 22-27, in Oregon Pioneer Association *Transactions, 1927* (Portland, 1930); Walling, *History of Southern Oregon*, 280-81.
88. O'Donnell, *An Arrow in the Earth*, 268-72; William H. Wright to Palmer, Apr. 15, 1956, Joel Palmer Papers, 1845-85, AX57/2/2, Oregon Collection, Special Collections, UO, Eugene.
89. Pocket Diary of Joel Palmer for the Year 1856, Notes in back of book, 17, OHS Archives, Portland.
90. *The Table Rock Sentinel*, May 24, 1856.
91. Beeson became an Indian advocate and reformer. He returned briefly to the Rogue River Valley, probably in 1865 (his wife Ann died in 1866), and then

returned permanently in 1883 and remained until his death in 1889. See Bert Webber, "Introduction," to *A Plea for the Indian*, Ye Galleon Press edition. Robert Winston Mardock, *The Reformers and the American Indian* (Columbia: University of Missouri Press, 1971), 10-15, 208-9 on his career as an Indian reformer after 1856.

92. Buchanan to Jones, June 11, 1856, "Rogue River Indian War 1856"; Glisan, *Journal of Army Life*, 344-45.
93. Glisan, *Journal of Army Life*, 345-46.
94. See O'Donnell, *An Arrow in the Earth*, 254, 273 on concerns about "squaw men"; Dunbar to Palmer, Mar. 23, 1856, Joel Palmer Papers, AX57/2/1; also Dunbar to Lane, Feb. 15, 1856, cited in O'Donnell, 254.
95. Palmer to Manypenny, July 18, 1856, 34th Cong., 3d Sess., Sen. Ex. Docs., Serial 875, 772. This number included 183 men; 300 women; 72 boys; 71 girls; 103 boy and girl infants.
96. *Oregon Statesman*, July 8, 1856.
97. Although the Rogue River War receives only a two-sentence mention, Durwood Ball, *Army Regulars on the Western Frontier, 1848-1861* (Norman, UOP, 2001) does provide information on other military action west of the Mississippi River, especially in the Southwest and California in the 1840s-1850s.
98. Russell Thornton, *American Indian Holocaust and Survival: A Population History Since 1492* (Norman and London: UOP, 1987), 107.
99. Drew, "An Account," 8; Schwartz, *Rogue River Indian War*, 75-76, 158, on Drew.
100. My thanks, again, to Frank Walsh for help in developing this casualty summary.
101. Sources for military engagements: Beckham, *Requiem for A People*; Schwartz, *Rogue River Indian War*; U.S. Congress, Senate and House documents. See Appendix 2, Tables 2-4.
102. Nesmith to Denver, Sept. 1, 1857, 35th Cong., 1st Sess., S. Ex. Doc. 134, Serial 919, 603-13; Metcalfe to Nesmith, July 15, 1857, 35th Cong., 1st Sess., S. Ex. Docs., No. 147 Serial 919, 644-47; Stephen Dow Beckham, "History of Western Oregon Since 1846," in Wayne Suttles, ed. *Northwest Coast*, Vol. 7, of *Handbook of Northern American Indians*, edited by William C. Sturtevant (Washington, DC: Smithsonian Institution, 1990), 180-88. Table 3 (p. 184) summarizes the reservation population data for 1856-57. My Table 6, Appendix 2, is extracted and condensed from Beckham, Table 3, p. 184.
103. S. H. Culver to Joel Palmer, July 20, 1854, 33d Cong., 2d Sess., H. Ex. Doc. 1, Serial 777, 500-5.
104. Parrish to Palmer, July 10, 1854, 53d Cong., 1st Sess., S. Ex. Doc. 25, Serial 3144, 29. See Appendix 2, Table 5.
105. The 2,314 figure is based on R. B. Metcalfe's count at the Siletz Reservation plus John F. Miller's count of Rogue River and Shasta Indians remaining on the Grand Ronde Reservation. See Metcalfe to Nesmith, July 15, 1857, 35th Cong., 1st Sess., S. Ex. Docs., Nos. 147 and 149, Serial 919, 644-47, 649-56. Beckham, "History of Western Oregon Since 1846," Table 3, 184, summarizes reservation population data for 1856-57.
106. See Appendix 2, Table 7.
107. For similar extrapolations from existing population estimates to arrive at a hypothetical population base, see Daniel T. Reff, *Disease, Depopulation, and Culture Change in Northwestern New Spain, 1518-1764* (Salt Lake City: University of Utah Press, 1991), 209-30.

Chapter 7

1. O'Donnell, *An Arrow in the Earth*, 253.
2. Schwartz, *The Rogue River Indian War*, 168.
3. Boyd, *Spirit of Pestilence*, 82.
4. William Eugene Kent, *The Siletz Indian Reservation 1855-1900* (Newport, Ore: Lincoln County Historical Society, 1977),, 47, cites data from the Oregon Superintendent of Indian Affairs annual report for 1865; see Beckham, "History of Western Oregon Since 1846," 184, for 1856-57 figures; for 1877, see National Archives, RG 75, Records of the Bureau of Indian Affairs, Letters Received, 1824-80, Oregon, 1877. Youst, *She's Tricky Like Coyote*, 94-96, describes the choice many south coast Indians made in 1875 to return to their homeland rather than go onto the Siletz reservation when the Alsea Agency at Yachats closed in 1876.
5. Jack Norton, *When Our Worlds Cried: Genocide in Northwestern California* (San Francisco: Indian Historian Press, 1979); Carranco and Beard, *Genocide and Vendetta*; Thornton, *American Indian Holocaust and Survival.*
6. Walker to Palmer, Aug. 5, 1856, Joel Palmer Papers, 1845-85, AX57/2/2, Knight Library, Oregon Collection, Special Collections, UO, Eugene.
7. Joel Palmer Papers, MSS 114-3, Folder 30, Voucher No. 27, Abstract 3rd Qtr. 1856, Steamer *Enterprise* July 12, 1856, OHS Archives, Portland.
8. Dodge, *Pioneer History*, 101.
9. Palmer to Geo. W. Manypenny, July 3, 1856, 53d Cong., 1st Sess., S. Ex. Doc. 25, Serial 3144, 55.
10. Joel Palmer Papers, MSS 114-3, Folder 13, Palmer to Thompson, July 5, 1856, OHS Archives, Portland.
11. The 1857 war crime trial of the Nisqually Indian war leader Leschi by a territorial district court in Washington Territory raised the same issue. See Asher, *Beyond the Reservation*, 133-35; Richards, *Isaac I. Stevens*, 309-12; Harmon, *Indians in the Making*, 88-89, 92-94.
12. Joel Palmer Papers, MSS 114-3, Folder 13, Palmer to Walker, July 28, 1856, OHS Archives, Portland.
13. Full text of documents in Stephen Dow Beckham, "The Renegade Eneas (Enas)," *Curry County Echoes*, Mar. 1986, 2-4, "Charges & Specifications preferred against the half-breed Indian Eneas...Enclosure with F-17, Box 10, A1-Q1, RG393: Records of U.S. Army Continental Commands, 1829-1940, National Archives, Washington, D.C.
14. Lansing, *Juggernaut.*
15. Cf. Harmon, *Indians in the Making*, 57-58; Asher, *Beyond the Reservation*, 126. The first Oregon territorial court of the southern district opened in September 1853 with Matthew P. Deady serving as the presiding judge. See Caroline P. Stoel, "Oregon's First Federal Courts 1849-1859," in Carolyn M. Buan, ed. *The First Duty: A History of the U.S. District Court for Oregon* (Portland: U.S. District Court of Oregon Historical Society, 1993), 21; Mrs. Matthew P. Deady, "Crossing the Plains to Oregon in 1846," Oregon Pioneer Association *Transactions, 1928* (Portland, 1933), 63.
16. Wells, *History of Siskiyou County*, 129; Elijah Steele to C. S. Drew, Nov. 23, 1857, in *Laws & Journals*, 39-52; *Oregon Statesman*, June 2, 1855.
17. Asher, *Beyond the Reservation*, 136-137; see also 203-213 for a listing and disposition of cases.

18. Colonel George Wright and other military commanders ordered the hanging of about a dozen Indians during the fighting in eastern Washington in 1858. See Carl P. Schlicke, *General George Wright: Guardian of the Pacific Coast* (Norman: UOP, 1988), 180-83; Asher, *Beyond the Reservation*, 132; and Burns, *The Jesuits and the Indian Wars*, 156, 260-61. Military officers often opposed the hanging of Indians by civilians; and even Colonel Wright opposed the hanging of Nisqually Indian war leader, Leschi (see Richards, *Isaac I. Stevens*, 310).
19. *Commissioners Journal 1, Curry County*, April Session 1857, 28.
20. *Oregon Statesman*, May 12, 1857; my thanks to Frank K. Walsh for locating this article. See also Reinhart, *The Golden Frontier*, 94, n. 2, on the Enos hanging. In addition to previous citations, my count of hangings is based on Beckham, *Requiem for A People*, 115-16, 136.
21. Dodge, *Pioneer History*, 366-67; *Commissioners Journal 1, Curry County*, July Session 1857, 32.
22. *Commissioners Journal 1, Curry County*, December Session 1857, 56.
23. Dodge, *Pioneer History*, 367.
24. *Oregon Statesman*, May 12, 1857.
25. Dunbar to Palmer, Oct. 21, 1856, Joel Palmer Papers, 1845-85, AX57/2/2, Oregon Collection, Special Collections, UO, Eugene.
26. William Tichenor, "Among the Oregon Indians, 1883," MS P-A 84, Bancroft Library, University of California, Berkeley; see also *Report of the Commissioner of Indian Affairs, The Annual Report of the Secretary of the Interior for the Year 1858* (Washington, D. C.: 1858), 254-59.
27. In a recent tabulation of the Western Oregon Reservation Population, 1856-57, Beckham lists 234 Coos, 125 Lower Umpqua, and 85 Siuslaw Indians. See Beckham, "History of Western Oregon Since 1846," 184.
28. Beckham, *Land of the Umpqua*, 104-5.
29. Ibid., 106-8; Shannon Applegate, *Skookum: An Oregon Pioneer Family's History and Lore* (New York: Beech Tree Books/William Morrow, 1988), 331-33.
30. My thanks to William R. Seaburg and Lionel Youst for bringing this narrative by Hoxie Simmons and a later one by Coquelle Thompson to my attention. Galice Athabaskan text translations from Melville Jacobs' Galice Athabaskan field notebooks #126 and #127, ca. 1967, Melville Jacobs Collection Box 104-9, Manuscripts and University Archives, University of Washington Libraries, Seattle, Washington. For more on Melville Jacobs' career and interpretations of "oral traditional text," see William R. Seaburg and Pamela T. Amoss, eds., *Badger and Coyote Were Neighbors: Melville Jacobs on Northwest Indian Myths and Tales* (Corvallis: OSUP, 2000).
31. Elizabeth D. Jacobs, Upper Coquille Linguistic and Ethnographic Notes, Folklore Texts (in English) from fieldwork with Coquille Thompson, Siletz, Oregon, 1935, original field notebooks in the Melville Jacobs Collection, Manuscripts and University Archives, University of Washington Libraries, Seattle, Washington. Text condensed and paraphrased from an edited version by Elizabeth Jacobs (ca. 1972) in William R. Seaburg's possession; published in William R. Seaburg, *Collecting Culture: The Practice and Ideology of Salvage Ethnography in Western Oregon, 1877-1942* (Ph.D. diss., University of Washington, 1994), 206-11. For a biography of Thompson, see Youst and Seaburg, *Coquelle Thompson, Athabaskan Witness.*
32. O'Donnell, *An Arrow in the Earth*, 274.
33. Richard H. Dillon, *J. Ross Browne: Confidential Agent in Old California* (Norman: UOP, 1965).

34. J. Ross Browne, "Indian Affairs in the Territories of Oregon and Washington," 35th Cong., 1st Sess., H. Ex. Doc. 39, Serial 955, 44-46.
35. Melville Jacobs, *Kalapuya Texts*, University of Washington Publications in Anthropology, Vol. 11, June 1945 (Seattle: University of Washington, 1945), 167-71.
36. Glisan, *Journal of Army Life*, 247.
37. R. W. Dunbar to Palmer, Mar. 23, 1856, Joel Palmer Papers, AX57/2/1, Knight Library, Oregon Collection, Special Collections, University of Oregon, Eugene.
38. Coos Bay *Harbor*, Nov. 23, 1914.
39. See "Cost Bill," in Case #4055, Circuit Court of the State of Oregon, Coos County, Susan Waters, Plaintiff vs. R. A. Church, Sarah Davis Substituted. Judgement rendered May 18, 1915; Docketed May 18, 1915; Complaint Filed Nov. 20, 1914. Coos Bay *Harbor*, Nov. 23, 1914; Coos Bay *Times*, Apr. 20, 1915.
40. Newsclipping, July 4, 1915(?), Benjamin S. Fisher Scrapbook, Coos County Historical Society Museum, North Bend, Oregon, n. p.
41. Gunther Barth, ed., *All Quiet on the Yamhill: The Civil War in Oregon* (Eugene: UO Books, 1959), 146.
42. Ibid., 151, n. 43.
43. From John Harrington's field notes, Harrington Papers, National Archives Microfilm, C-153, Reel 027, 0568-69.
44. Youst, *She's Tricky Like Coyote*, 17, 29.
45. Asher, *Beyond the Reservation*, 5.
46. Schwartz, *The Rogue River Indian War*, 171.
47. *The Organic and Other General Laws of Oregon Together with the National Constitution, and Other Public Acts and Statutes of the United States, 1843-1872*, compiled and annotated by Matthew P. Deady and Lafayette Lane (Salem: Eugene Semple, State Printer, 1874), 619.
48. Schwartz, *Rogue River Indian War*, 181.
49. Bensell quote in Barth, *All Quiet on the Yamhill*, 145-46.
50. Youst, *She's Tricky Like Coyote*, 52.
51. Barth, *All Quiet on the Yamhill*, 147, n. 41; Youst, *She's Tricky Like Coyote*, 52-53.
52. Original marriage certificates/licenses archived at the Coos County Historical Society Museum, North Bend, Oregon.
53. Coos County marriage certificates, nos. 12-13, 15-18, 32-36, 38-40, 42-45 (6/18/1854-7/3/1865).
54. Fred Lockley, "Andrew Smith Rogue River Indian, Portland, Oregon," Oregon Journal, n.d., 77-80, in *The Lockley Files: Conversations with Bullwhackers, Muleskinners, Pioneers, Prospectors, '49ers, Indian Fighters, Trappers, Ex-Barkeepers, Authors, Preachers, Poets & Near Poets & All Sorts & Conditions of Men*, Vol. 2, compiled and edited by Mike Helm (Eugene, Ore.: Rainy Day Press, 1981).
55. Fred Lockley, "Reminiscences of Mrs. Frank Collins, Nee Martha Elizabeth Gilliam," *OHQ* 17 (Dec. 1916), 358-72.
56. Paul Andrew Hutton, *Phil Sheridan and His Army* (Lincoln: UNP, 1985), 10; see also Sherry L. Smith, *The View from Officers' Row: Army Perceptions of Western Indians* (Tucson: University of Arizona Press, 1990), 89, on Sheridan.
57. Barbara Hegne, *Settling the Rogue Valley: The Tough Times—The Forgotten People* (Eagle Point, Ore.: Hegne, 1995), 51.
58. Beckham, *Land of the Umpqua*, 92; Schlesser, *Fort Umpqua*, 32-33.
59. Hegne, *Settling the Rogue Valley*, 51-57.
60. Stern, *The Klamath Tribe*, 35.

61. Atwood, *Illahe*, 19, 29-30, 53-54. An excellent contemporary discussion of the mixed-blood experience will be found in Louis Owens, *Mixedblood Messages*, especially Chapter 10, "Blood Trails: Missing Grandmothers and Making Worlds," 135-66: "It is as human beings who loved one another while crossing borders and erasing boundaries and, despite immeasurable odds, *surviving* that they deserve our recognition and utmost respect" (148).
62. Joel Palmer Papers, MSS 114-3, Folder 22, Palmer to Meacham, Dec. 26, 1871, and Folder 24, Palmer to Thomas[?], Nov. 23, 1872, OHS Archives, Portland.
63. Melville Jacobs, *Coos Narrative and Ethnologic Texts*, University of Washington Publications in Anthropology, Vol. 8, No. 1, April 1939 (Seattle: University of Washington, 1939), 104-5. For a biography of Annie Miner Peterson, see Youst, *She's Tricky Like Coyote*.
64. See Schwartz, *The Rogue River Indian War*, 161-213 on the reservation era.

Appendix 1

1. Boyd, *Spirit of Pestilence*, 233.
2. See, ibid., Chap. 9, "Lower Columbia Population History, 1775-1855," 231-61.
3. Ibid., 265, note k to Table 3.
4. Dale, *Ashley-Smith Explorations*, 272.
5. Sullivan, *Travels of Jedediah Smith*, 128.
6. Boyd, *Spirit of Pestilence*, 234.
7. All references are to the edition of the journals edited by Gary E. Moulton. *The Journals of the Lewis and Clark Expedition*, Vol. 6, *November 2, 1805-March 22, 1806* (Lincoln: UNP, 1990), 182-83.
8. Ibid., 236.
9. Ibid., 430.
10. Ibid., 476.
11. *The Journals of the Lewis & Clark Expedition*, Vol. 3, *August 25, 1804-April 6, 1805* (1987), 388.
12. See Ronda, *Lewis and Clark Among the Indians*, Chap. 8, "The Clatsop Winter," 181-213.
13. Compare *Journals*, Vol. 3, 386-450, with Vol. 6, 473-92.
14. *Journals*, Vol. 6, 473-92.
15. See William R. Seaburg and Jay Miller, "Tillamook," 560-67; Henry B. Zenk, "Alseans," 568-71, "Siuslawans and Coosans," 572-70; Jay Miller and William R. Seaburg, "Athapaskans of Southwestern Oregon," 580-88, in Suttles, ed. *Handbook of North American Indians*, Vol. 7, *Northwest Coast*.
16. Seaburg and Miller, "Tillamook," 561.
17. Boyd, *Spirit of Pestilence*, Table 3, 264-65, note b.
18. Ibid., 265, notes c, k.
19. Ibid., 262-63.
20. Ibid., 133.
21. John J. Milhau to George Gibbs, Oct. 13, 1856, MS. 191A, Southwest Oregon Research Project: A Collection ... from the National Anthropological and National Archives in Washington, D.C.,, Knight Library, Oregon Collection, Special Collections, UO, Eugene. See also Boyd, *Spirit of Pestilence*, 78-81.
22. Ibid., 268.
23. LaLande, *The Indians of Southwestern Oregon*, 27.
24. 32d Cong., 1st Sess., S. Doc. 1, Serial 613, 477.

Appendix 2

1. This 1854 census of hostile bands appears in Ambrose's letter to Palmer, Oct. 20, 1855, as well as in a letter from Ambrose published in the *Table Rock Sentinel* on Nov. 19, 1855. The count of Grave Creek males differs in the two tables (4 in one, 24 in the other). I have used the lower number because it agrees with the totals that appear in both sources.
2. For 1853, see Bancroft [Victor], *History of Oregon, 1848-1888*, 312-20; Victor, *Early Indian Wars of Oregon*, 308-19; Walling, *History of Southern Oregon*, 213-17; and "Mrs. Butler's 1853 Diary," 351-60. For source abbreviations, see note 3.
3. Source abbreviations: BA=(Bancroft [Victor], *History of Oregon*, II); BE=(Beckham, *Requiem*); CCH=(Crescent City *Herald*, Jan. 9, 1856); DOU=(Douthit, *A Guide*); S=(Schwartz, *Rogue River Indian War*); DOD=(Dodge, *Pioneer History*); DR=(Drew, "An Account"); FW=(Frank Walsh, unpublished research notes); V=(Victor, *Early Indian Wars)*; W = (Walling, *History of Southern Oregon*); S. Doc. 113=(53 Cong., 2d Sess., S. Ex. Doc. 113, Serial 3163, 3); H. Doc. 118=(34 Cong., 1st Sess., H. Ex. Doc. 118, Serial 859, 24-25); H. Doc. 1=(34 Cong., 3d Sess., H. Ex. Doc. 1, Serial 894, 149); S. Doc. 92=(34 Cong., 3d Sess., S. Ex. Docs., No. 92, Serial 375, 767).
4. Source abbreviations: Same as Table 2, 3.
5. Parrish to Palmer, July 10, 1854, 33d Cong., 2d Sess., H. Ex. Doc. 1, Serial 777, 495. The same July 10, 1854 document is in 53d Cong., 1st Sess., S. Ex. Doc. 25, Serial 3144, 29, but it differs slightly in number of men for Mackanotin and Shistakoostee; however, totals are the same in both published sources. The table has been changed from the original to show totals and eliminating some data. Band names have been presented in non-syllabic format.
6. Nesmith to Denver, Sept. 1, 1857, 35th Cong., 1st Sess., S. Ex. Doc. 134, Serial 919, 603-13; Metcalfe to Nesmith, July 15, 1857, 35th Cong., 1st Sess., S. Ex. Docs., No. 147 Serial 919, 644-47; Beckham, "History of Western Oregon Since 1846," 180-88. Table 6 is extracted and condensed from Beckham, Table 3, p. 184.
7. The Parrish census is in Parrish to Palmer, July 10, 1854, 53d Cong., 1st Sess., S. Ex. Doc. 25, Serial 3144, 29. Beckham, "History of Western Oregon Since 1846," Table 3, 184 summarizes the reservation population data for 1856-57. However, for specific subgroups of the "Tututni," see Metcalfe to Nesmith, July 15, 1857, 35th Cong., 1st Sess., S. Ex. Docs., Nos. 147 and 149, Serial 919, 644-47, 649-56, for Rogue River and Shasta Indians still on the Grand Ronde Reservation.

Select Bibliography

The items in this bibliography consist of published books and articles. Manuscripts, government documents, newspapers, and most published diaries, letters, and reminiscences that have been used as reference sources appear in the Notes (with full citation at the first appearance, and short form used thereafter).

Asher, Brad. *Beyond the Reservation: Indians, Settlers, and the Law in Washington Territory, 1853-1889*. Norman: University of Oklahoma Press, 1999.

Atwood, Kay, and Dennis J. Gray. *People and the River: A History of the Human Occupation of the Middle Course of the Rogue River of Southwestern Oregon*, Vol. 1. Prepared for USDI—Bureau of Land Management, Grants Pass Resource Area. Medford, Oregon, 1995.

Atwood, Kay. *Illahe: The Story of Settlement in the Rogue River Canyon*. Ashland, Ore.: Atwood, 1978. Reprint: Corvallis: Oregon State University Press, 2002.

Bancroft, Hubert Howe [by Frances Fuller Victor]. *History of Oregon, 1834-1848*. Vol. I. *The Works of Hubert Howe Bancroft*, Vol. 29. San Francisco: The History Company, 1886.

———. *History of Oregon, 1848-1888*. Vol. II. *The Works of Hubert Howe Bancroft*, Vol. 30. San Francisco: The History Company, 1888.

Baun, Carolyn M., and Richard Lewis, eds. *The First Oregonians: An Illustrated Collection of Essays on Traditional Lifeways, Federal Indian Relations, and the State's Native People Today*. Portland: Oregon Council for the Humanities, 1991.

Beckham, Stephen Dow. "Lonely Outpost: The Army's Fort Umpqua," *Oregon Historical Quarterly* 70 (Sept. 1969), 233-37.

———. *Requiem for A People: The Rogue Indians and the Frontiersmen*. Norman: University of Oklahoma Press, 1971. Reprint: Corvallis: Oregon State University Press, 1996.

———. *The Indians of Western Oregon: This Land Was Theirs*. Coos Bay, Ore.: Arago Books, 1977.

———*Land of the Umpqua: A History of Douglas County, Oregon*. Roseburg, Ore.: Douglas County Commissioners, 1986.

———. "The Renegade Eneas (Enas)," *Curry County Echoes* (Mar. 1986), 2-4.

Beeson, John. *A Plea for the Indians*. New York: John Beeson, 1858. Reprint, 2d ed., Fairfield, Wash.: Ye Galleon Press, 1982.

Boyd, Robert. *The Coming of the Spirit of Pestilence: Introduced Infectious Diseases and Population Decline among Northwest Coast Indians, 1774-1874*. Vancouver and Toronto: UBC Press, and Seattle and London: University of Washington Press, 1999.

Burns, Robert Ignatius. *The Jesuits and the Indian Wars of the Northwest*. Moscow: University of Idaho Press, 1966.

Butler, America Rollins. "Mrs. Butler's Diary of Rogue River Valley," *Oregon Historical Quarterly* 41 (Dec. 1940), 337-66.

Carranco, Lynwood, and Estle Beard. *Genocide and Vendetta: The Round Valley Wars of Northern California*. Norman: University of Oklahoma Press, 1981.

Clark, Malcolm, Jr. *Eden Seekers: The Settlement of Oregon, 1818-1862*. Boston: Houghton Mifflin, 1981.

Clark, Robert Carlton. "Military History of Oregon, 1849-59," *Oregon Historical Quarterly* 36 (Mar. 1935), 14-59.

Cline, Gloria Griffen. *Peter Skene Ogden and the Hudson's Bay Company*. Norman: University of Oklahoma Press, 1974.

Coan, C. F. "The First Stage of the Federal Indian Policy in the Pacific Northwest, 1849-1852," *Oregon Historical Quarterly* 22 (Mar. 1921), 46-77.

———. "The Adoption of the Reservation Policy in Pacific Northwest, 1853-1855," *Oregon Historical Quarterly* 23 (Mar. 1922), 1-38.

Cram, Thomas Jefferson. "Topographical Memoir of the Department of the Pacific," 35 Cong., 2d Sess., H. Ex. Doc. 114. Reprinted in Cram, *Topographical Memoir* (Fairfield, Wash.: Ye Galleon Press, 1977).

Dale, Harrison Clifford, ed. *The Ashley-Smith Explorations and the Discovery of A Central Route to the Pacific 1822-1829*. Rev. ed. Glendale, Calif.: Arthur H. Clark, 1941.

Davies, K. G., ed. *Peter Skene Ogden's Snake Country Journal 1826-27*. London: The Hudson's Bay Record Society, 1961.

Dean, Jonathan R. "The Hudson's Bay Company and Its Use of Force, 1828-1829," *Oregon Historical Quarterly* 98 (Fall 1997), 262-95.

Dodge, Orvil. *Pioneer History of Coos and Curry Counties, Or.* Salem: Pioneer and Historical Association of Coos County, 1898.

Douthit, Nathan. "The Hudson's Bay Company and the Indians of Southern Oregon," *Oregon Historical Quarterly* 93 (Spring 1992), 25-64.

———. "Joseph Lane and the Rogue River Indians: Personal Relations Across A Cultural Divide," *Oregon Historical Quarterly* 95 (Winter 1994-95), 472-515.

———. "Between Indian and White Worlds on the Oregon-California Border, 1851-1857: Benjamin Wright and Enos," *Oregon Historical Quarterly* 100 (Winter 1999), 402-33.

———. *A Guide to Oregon South Coast History, Traveling the Jedediah Smith Trail*. Corvallis: Oregon State University Press, 1999.

Drew, Charles S. "An Account of the Origin and Early Prosecution of the Indian War in Oregon." 36th Cong., 1st Sess., Sen. Misc. Doc. No. 59. Reprinted in Drew, *An Account*.... (Fairfield, Wash.: Ye Galleon Press, 1973.)

Drucker, Philip. *The Tolowas and their Southwest Oregon Kin*, University of California Publications on American Archeology and Ethnology 36, No. 4 , 221-300. Berkeley: University of California Press, 1937.

Gibson, James R. *Otter Skins, Boston Ships, and China Goods: The Maritime Fur Trade of the Northwest Coast, 1785-1841*. Montreal: McGill-Queens University Press, 1992.

———. *The Lifeline of the Oregon Country: The Fraser-Columbia Brigade System, 1811-47*. Vancouver: University of British Columbia Press, 1997.

Glisan, Rodney. *Journal of Army Life*. San Francisco: A. L. Bancroft, 1874.

Gray, Dennis J. *The Takelmas and Their Athapascan Neighbors: A New Ethnographic Synthesis for the Upper Rogue River Area of Southwestern Oregon*, University of Oregon Anthropological Papers, No. 37. Eugene: Dept. of Anthropology, University of Oregon, 1987.

Hall, Roberta L. *The Coquille Indians: Yesterday, Today and Tomorrow*. Lake Oswego, Ore.: Smith, Smith and Smith, 1984.

Hannon, Nan, and Richard K. Olmo, eds. *Living With the Land: The Indians of Southwest Oregon; The Proceedings of the 1989 Symposium on the Prehistory of Southwest Oregon*. Medford: Southern Oregon Historical Society, 1990.

Harmon, Alexandra. *Indians in the Making: Ethnic Relations and Indian Identities around Puget Sound*. Berkeley: University of California Press, 1998.

Hegne, Barbara. *Settling the Rogue Valley: The Tough Times—The Forgotten People*. Eagle Point, Ore.: Hegne, 1995.

Helfrich, Devere. "The Applegate Trail I," *Klamath Echoes* No. 9 (1971), 1-106.

———. "Applegate Trail II: West of the Cascades," *Klamath Echoes* No. 14 (1976), 1-102.

Hendrickson, James E. *Joe Lane of Oregon: Machine Politics and the Sectional Crisis, 1849-1861*. New Haven and London: Yale University Press, 1967.

Hines, Gustavas. *Wildlife in Oregon*. New York: R. Worthington, 1881.

Hinton, Harwood Perry. "The Military Career of John Ellis Wool, 1812-1863." University of Wisconsin, Ph.D. dissertation, 1960. Mic 60-5750, University Microfilm, Inc., Ann Arbor, Michigan.

Holt, Catharine. "Shasta Ethnography," *Anthropological Records* 3:4. Berkeley and Los Angeles: University of California Press, 1946.

Hurtado, Albert L. *Indian Survival on the California Frontier*. New Haven and London: Yale University Press, 1988.

Jackson, John C. *Children of the Fur Trade: Forgotten Métis of the Pacific Northwest*. Missoula, Mont.: Mountain Press, 1995.

Jacobs, Melville. *Coos Myth Texts*. University of Washington Publications in Anthropology, Vol. 8, No. 2. Seattle: University of Washington, 1940.

Kent, William Eugene. *The Siletz Reservation 1855-1900*. Masters Thesis, Portland State University, 1973. Newport, Ore.: Lincoln County Historical Society, 1977.

LaLande, Jeff. *First Over the Siskiyous: Peter Skene Ogden's 1826-1827 Journey Through the Oregon-California Borderlands*. Portland: Oregon Historical Society Press, 1987.

———. *The Indians of Southwestern Oregon: An Ethnohistorical Review*, Anthropology Northwest: Number 6. Corvallis: Department of Anthropology, Oregon State University, 1991.

———. "Through A Strange Country With Lakes: Peter Skene Ogden and the Hudson's Bay Company in the Klamath Basin." *Journal of the Shaw Historical Library* 8 (1994), 1-28.

Lansing, Ronald B. *Juggernaut: The Whitman Massacre Trail, 1850*. Pasadena, Calif.: Ninth Judicial Circuit Historical Society, 1993.

Mackie, Richard Somerset. *Trading Beyond the Mountains: The British Fur Trade on the Pacific, 1793-1843*. Vancouver: UBC Press, 1997.

Maloney, Alice Bay "Camp Sites of Jedediah Smith on the Oregon Coast," *Oregon Historical Quarterly* 41 (Sept. 1940), 304-23.

———., ed. *Fur Brigade to the Bonaventura: John Work's California Expedition 1832-1833 For the Hudson's Bay Company*. San Francisco: California Historical Society, 1945.

McArthur, Lewis A. *Oregon Geographic Names*, 4th ed. Portland: Oregon Historical Society Press, 1974.

Morgan, Dale L. *Jedediah Smith and the Opening of the West*. 1953. Lincoln: University of Nebraska Press, Bison Book, 1964.

———, ed. *Overland in 1846: Diaries and Letters of the California-Trail*, Vol. I. Georgetown, Calif.: Talisman Press, 1963).

Morrison, Dorothy Nafus. *Outpost: John McLoughlin and the Far Northwest*. Portland: Oregon Historical Society Press, 1999.

Murray, Keith A. *The Modocs and Their War*. Norman: University of Oklahoma Press, 1959.

Nunis, Doyce B., Jr. "Alexander Roderick McLeod." In *The Mountain Men and the Fur Trade of the Far West*, Vol. 6, edited by LeRoy R. Hafen, 279-97. Glendale, Calif.: Arthur H. Clark, 1968.

———. *The Hudson's Bay Company's First Fur Brigade to the Sacramento Valley: Alexander McLeod's 1829 Hunt*. Fair Oaks, Calif.: Sacramento Book Collectors Club, 1968.

———. "Michel Laframboise." In *The Mountain Men and the Fur Trade of the West*, Vol.5, edited by LeRoy R. Hafen, 145-70. Glendale, Calif.: Arthur H. Clark, 1968.

O'Donnell, Terence. *An Arrow in the Earth: General Joel Palmer and the Indians of Oregon*. Portland: Oregon Historical Society Press, 1991.

Owens, Louis. *Mixedblood Messages: Literature, Film, Family, Place*. Norman: University of Oklahoma Press, 1998.

Peterson, Jacqueline, and Jennifer S.H. Brown, eds. *The New Peoples: Being and Becoming Métis in North America*. Winnipeg: University of Manitoba Press, 1985.

Prucha, Francis Paul. *American Indian Policy in Crisis: Christian Reformers and the Indian, 1865-1900*. Norman: University of Oklahoma Press, 1976.

———. *The Great Father: The United States Government and the American Indians*. 1984, 1986. 2 vols. in 1. Lincoln and London: University of Nebraska Press, Bison Book, 1995.

Rawls, James J. *Indians of California: The Changing Image*. Norman: University of Oklahoma Press, 1984.

Reid, John Philip. "Principles of Vengeance: Fur Trappers, Indians, and Retaliation for Homicide in Transboundary North American West," *Western Historical Quarterly* 24 (Feb. 1993), 21-43..

Reinhart, Herman Francis. *The Golden Frontier: The Recollections of Herman Francis Reinhart 1851-1869*. Edited by Doyce B. Nunis, Jr. Austin: University of Texas Press, 1962.

Rich, E. E., ed. *The Letters of John McLoughlin from Fort Vancouver to the Governor and Committee, First Series, 1825-38*. London: Hudson's Bay Record Society, 1941.

———. *The Letters of John McLoughlin From Fort Vancouver to the Governor And Committee*, Second Series, 1839-44. London: Hudson's Bay Record Society, 1943.

Riddle, Jeff C. *The Indian History of the Modoc War*. Eugene, Ore.: Urion Press, [1914] 1974.

Sapir, Edward. "Notes on the Takelma Indians of Southwestern Oregon," *American Anthropologist* 9 (Apr.-June 1907), 251-75.

Schlesser, Norman Dennis. *Fort Umpqua: Bastion of Empire*. Oakland, Ore.: Schlesser, 1973.

Schwartz, E. A. *The Rogue River Indian War and Its Aftermath, 1850-1980*. Norman and London: University of Oklahoma Press, 1997.

———. "Sick Hearts: Indian Removal on the Oregon Coast, 1875-1881," *Oregon Historical Quarterly* 92 (Fall 1991), 229-64.

Scott, Leslie M., ed. "John Work's Journey from Fort Vancouver to Umpqua River, and Return, in 1834," *Oregon Historical Quarterly* 24 (Sept. 1923), 238-68.

Seaburg, William R., and Pamela T. Amoss, eds. *Badger and Coyote Were Neighbors: Melville Jacobs on Northwest Indian Myths and Tales.* Corvallis: Oregon State University Press, 2000.

Stern, Theodore. *The Klamath Tribe: A People and Their Reservation*. Seattle and London: University of Washington Press, 1966.

Stoel, Caroline P. "Oregon's First Federal Courts 1849-1859." In *The First Duty: A History of the U. S. District Court for Oregon*, edited by Carolyn M. Buan, 1-61. Portland: U. S. District Court of Oregon Historical Society, 1993

Strobridge, William F. *Regulars in the Redwoods: The U. S. Army in Northern California 1852-1861*. Spokane: Arthur H. Clark, 1994.

Sullivan, Maurice S. *The Travels of Jedediah Smith: A Documentary Outline Including the Journal of the Great Pathfinder.* Santa Ana, Calif.: Fine Arts Press, 1934.

Suttles, Wayne, ed. *Northwest Coast*, Vol. 7, *Handbook of North American Indians*, edited by William C. Sturtevant. Washington, D. C.: Smithsonian Institution, 1990.

Sutton, Dorothy and Jack. *Indian Wars of the Rogue River*. Grants Pass, Ore.: Josephine County Historical Society, 1969.

Szasz, Margaret Connell, ed. *Between Indian and White Worlds: The Cultural Broker*. Norman and London: University of Oklahoma Press, 1994.

Thornton, Russell. *American Indian Holocaust and Survival: A Population History Since 1492*. Norman: University of Oklahoma Press, 1987.

Unruh, John D., Jr. *The Plains Across: The Overland Emigrants and the Trans-Mississippi West, 1840-60*. Urbana and London: University of Illinois Press, 1979.

Victor, Frances Fuller. *The Early Indian Wars of Oregon*. Salem: F. C. Baker, State Printer, 1894.

———. "A Knight of the Frontier," *The Californian* 4 (Aug. 1881), 152-62.

Walling, A[lbert]. G. *History of Southern Oregon*. Portland: Walling, 1884.

Walsh, Frank K. *Indian Battles Along the Rogue River 1855-56*. Grants Pass, Ore.: Walsh, 1972.

Ward, Beverly H. *White Moccasins*. Cottage Grove, Ore.: Ward, 1986.

Wells, Harry L. *History of Siskiyou County, California*. Oakland, Calif.: D. J. Stewart, 1881.

White, Richard. *The Middle Ground: Indians, Empires, and Republics in the Great Lakes Region 1650-1815*. Cambridge and New York: Cambridge University Press. 1991.

Youst, Lionel. *She's Tricky Like Coyote: Annie Miner Peterson, An Oregon Coast Indian Woman*. Norman and London: University of Oklahoma Press, 1997.

Youst, Lionel, and William R. Seaburg. *Coquelle Thompson, Athabascan Witness: A Cultural Biography*. Norman: University of Oklahoma Press, 2002.

Zucker, Jeff, Kay Hummel, and Bob Høgfoss. *Oregon Indians, Culture, History, and Current Affairs: An Atlas and Introduction*. Portland: Western Imprints, The Press of the Oregon Historical Society, 1983.

Index